Dr. Mudd
and the
Lincoln
Assassination

Dr. Mudd
and the
Lincoln Assassination
THE CASE REOPENED

Edited by

John Paul Jones

COMBINED BOOKS
Pennsylvania

PUBLISHER'S NOTE

Combined Books, Inc., is dedicated to publishing books of distinction in history and military history. We are proud of the quality of writing and the quantity of information found in our books. Our books are manufactured with style and durability and are printed on acid-free paper. We like to think of our books as soldiers: not infantry grunts, but well dressed and well equipped avant garde. Our logo reflects our commitment to the modern and yet historic art of bookmaking.

We would like to hear from our readers and invite you to write to us at our offices in Pennsylvania with your reactions, queries, comments, even complaints.

We encourage all of our readers to purchase our books from their local booksellers, and we hope that you let us know of booksellers in your area that might be interested in carrying our books. If you are unable to find a book in your area, please write to us.

For information, address:
COMBINED BOOKS, INC.
151 East 10th Avenue
Conshohocken, PA 19428

Library of Congress Cataloging-in-Publication Data
Dr. Mudd and the Lincoln assassination: the case reopened / edited by John Paul
    Jones.
        p.   cm.
    Includes bibliographical references and index.
    ISBN 0-938289-50-0
    1. Mudd, Samuel Alexander, 1833-1883.   2. Lincoln, Abraham,
    1809-1865- -Assassination.   I. Jones, John Paul, 1947-   .
    E457.5.D7   1995
    364.1'31'092--dc20   95-9720
                                                               CIP

Combined Books Edition 1 2 3 4 5
Published in the U.S.A. in 1995 by Combined Books and distributed in North America by Stackpole Books, Inc., 5067 Ritter Road, Mechanicsburg, PA 17055. Distributed internationally by Greenhill Books, Lionel Leventhal, Ltd., Park House, 1 Russell Gradens, London NW11 9NN.

Printed in the United States of America.

Table of Contents

Introduction

On June 30, 1865, Samuel A. Mudd was convicted of conspiring with John Wilkes Booth and others to assassinate President Lincoln and other leaders of the Union. The Maryland planter and physician was also found guilty of aiding and abetting the assassins in the execution of their plot. Dr. Mudd's conviction, and a sentence to prison for the remainder of his life, issued from a type of military court known as a commission. Seven senior officers of the Union army comprised the commission that tried Dr. Mudd. Its most senior member, Major General David Hunter, acted as its president; history has given it his name.

As Commander in Chief, President Johnson had convened the Hunter Commission and referred to it Mudd's case, and those of seven others said to comprise Booth's gang. Samuel Mudd fared better than most; after a trial of eighteen days, the commission found all eight defendants guilty, and sentenced four, David Herold, George Atzerodt, Lewis Payne, and Mary Surratt, to death. The commission spared from the gallows Mudd and three others, Michael O'Laughlin, Edward Spangler, and Samuel Arnold, sentencing them instead to prison. President Johnson reviewed and approved the sentences. He ordered that Mudd serve his life sentence at Fort Jefferson, an island penitentiary off the coast of Florida. Mudd's lawyers then tried for a writ of habeas corpus, but to no avail. In the United States District Court for the Southern District of Florida, Judge Thomas J. Boynton refused to hold that the Hunter

Commission lacked authority to try a civilian like Mudd for the crimes in question. Judge Boynton's opinion represents the only formal assessment of Mudd's case by a federal judge to date. Never officially published, it appears in this book as Appendix A.

As it happened, Mudd served less than four years before the same President pardoned him. There is no hint in that pardon that the President acted to correct a miscarriage of justice by the doctor's earlier conviction; indeed, the President took the opportunity to reaffirm his satisfaction that the evidence proved Mudd had aided and abetted Booth and Herold in their escape. Instead, the President based his decision to pardon Mudd on the doctor's humanitarian efforts in combatting a yellow fever epidemic at Fort Jefferson. In 1869, the President, therefore, merely freed Samuel Mudd; he did not absolve him. Mudd returned to Maryland where, notwithstanding prison's toll on his health, he lived another fourteen years, siring fourteen children. For the rest of his life, he would publicly insist on his innocence of any complicity with Booth. After Mudd's death, his family and friends would continue to agitate on his behalf, seeking some definitive statement that the United States had convicted and punished an innocent man.

For the most part, that campaign focused on the likelihood of prejudice in a jury of Union officers, some of them personally acquainted with the murdered President, on the manner in which the trial was conducted, and on the evidence that was offered by the government. The United States has never admitted error, but the resultant and enduring controversy has made the doctor a *cause célèbre*, an American Dreyfus.

In early 1992, lawyers representing Dr. Mudd's family obtained a hearing before the Army Board for the Correction of Military Records, a tribunal of civil servants hearing claims that particular military records are in error. Typically, the board hears cases from aggrieved soldiers and veterans who claim they were wrongfully denied an award or promotion, insufficiently compensated, or refused disability benefits. The board acts somewhat like a court, taking evidence and making findings of fact and conclusions of law. Unlike a court, however, the board lacks the power to decide; it can only recommend that military records be altered in the interests of justice. Its findings and conclusions serve only to inform the final decision maker, the Secretary of the Army, or his designated subordinate. In Dr. Mudd's case, the family argued, and the board found, that, since the conviction existed in the record of a military court, the board could hear the family's claim of error, and, if it agreed, recommend that the record be expunged. The board heard arguments and evidence offered by the family, the most important of which was the opinion of an expert, Colonel Jan Horbaly, that no basis existed in 1865 for assertion by the military of jurisdiction over crimes by civilians in the circumstances of Lincoln's assassination. The board looked only at the question of whether the law permitted a military commission to try a civilian like Dr. Mudd; it carefully avoided weighing the evidence on which Dr. Mudd's conviction must have been based.

The board's hearings are not adversarial; an Examiner, trained in law and acting for the board, presents the salient facts and relevant law in the case. The board may put questions to its Examiner; it may direct him or her to conduct additional investigation of the facts or research in the law and report back. Otherwise, the board may conclude on what is placed before it. Thus, in the hearing on Dr. Mudd's conviction, it was not out of the ordinary that nobody appeared to defend President Johnson's convening order and its execution by the Hunter Commission. The board subsequently adopted its Examiner's recommendation that relief be granted Samuel Mudd and his family, and referred the case to the Secretary for final action. The board's report appears in this book as Appendix B.

On behalf of the Secretary of the Army, the Acting Assistant Secretary then reviewed the board's findings, but rejected its recommendation. Secretary Clark refused to act in Dr. Mudd's case because he found it improper for the board to reconsider historical controversies so long after legal authorities had rendered their best judgments. His letter communicating this decision to the board appears in this book as Appendix C.

After the board had submitted its assessment of the Mudd family's case, but before Secretary Clark could issue his opinion, the University of Richmond School of Law approached the family's tireless spokesman, Richard Mudd of Saginaw, Michigan. The law school proposed a full, adversarial, and expert hearing for the family's claims, in a moot staged in its courtroom. For more than three hundred years, students of the law have considered hypothetical cases and difficult legal issues in moots, simulated hearings before mock judicial panels. The practice originated in the English Inns of Court, where barristers had trained since the fifteenth century, and experienced a revival in American law schools in the nineteenth century. Nowadays, several moots occur each academic year in most law schools. The University of Richmond proposed an appellate hearing before experienced jurists trained in military law, a hearing in which not only the commission's jurisdiction might be considered, but also the fairness of the way in which Dr. Mudd's trial was conducted, as well as the persuasiveness of the evidence originally offered against him. In accordance with a fundamental principle of judicial review, the moot court's judges and advocates would be asked to limit themselves to addressing the commission's 1865 decision, and therefore only those facts and legal rules available to the commission at the time.

For the family, Richard Mudd accepted with enthusiasm.

The novelty of the questions and the drama in the facts enabled the school to enlist exceptionally experienced courtroom lawyers to present Dr. Mudd's case for expungement and the United States government's defense of its commission. F. Lee Bailey appeared for the petitioner with Candida Ewing Steel, the great great granddaughter of Union Army Brigadier Thomas Ewing, Jr., who had so ably represented Samuel Mudd at trial. Rear Admiral John S. Jenkins, former Judge Advocate General of the Navy and Special Counsel to the Secretary of the Navy, joined Colonel John Jay Douglass, former Commandant of the Judge Advocate General's School and Dean of the National College of District Attorneys, in defending the decision and workings of the Hunter Commission. For each side, the law school recruited a staff of student researchers and brief writers. Furnished with copies of the commission's actual records, and the contents of the ten best military law collections in American libraries, the two teams labored for more than three months drafting the appellate briefs for each side.

To constitute a court for the hearing of Dr. Mudd's case, the law school had no choice but to indulge in a legal fiction. In fact, no judicial organ existed in 1867 to consider the decisions of either courts martial or military commissions. Except when the sentence was death, the judgment of any military court after trial was final, subject only to action by the military commander who had convened it and thus could set aside its findings or reduce the sentence it recommended. In those cases in which a death penalty was approved by the convening authority, the Commander in Chief had also to concur. Not until 1920 would Congress at last establish a board of judge advocates, and thus, for the first time, guarantee for military convictions review by professionals trained in the discipline. Not until 1950, would Congress at last appoint civilian judges to a genuine court reviewing military cases. If Mudd's case were to receive contemporaneous review by a true appellate court, history would have to be altered, at least a little. This was accomplished by simply inventing the three-judge Special Court of Military Appeal, and the 1865 Act of Congress that created it.

During their preparations, the team representing Dr. Mudd learned that, at the time of Dr. Mudd's trial, the government had possessed a diary written by John Wilkes Booth. The prosecution had not offered the diary in evidence at the trial, nor had it informed the defense of its existence, although mention of it had appeared in the New York Times and other newspapers almost two weeks before the trial began. On behalf of Dr. Mudd, his legal team argued strenuously in 1992 that the Special Court ought to order the government to either share the document or else deny its possession. With equal vigor, the government argued that, even if the diary were produced, it would be inadmissible as evidence because it would constitute hearsay, i.e., a statement made out of the court's presence offered as proof of what it says. Without reaching either petitioner's argument that the prosecution had concealed potentially exculpatory evidence, or the government's argument that the diary was inadmissible anyway, the court refused to permit the diary to be added to the record before it. In the court's view, newspaper stories about the diary before trial put defense counsel on notice then, and counsel's failure to raise the matter at trial could not be excused sufficiently to warrant action so long afterward. Skirmishing complete, preparation continued.

To hear the case as the Special Court of Military Appeal, the law school recruited three eminent jurists well-versed not only in the military law of the United States, but in the international law of armed conflict (for the government was sure to argue that jurisdiction rested on *jus belli*, the law of war). The Honorable Robinson O. Everett, former Chief Judge of the United States Court of Military Appeals (and now Senior Judge of its successor, the United States Court of Appeals for the Armed Forces) accepted an invitation with enthusiasm. The Honorable Edward D. Re, Chief Judge Emeritus and Senior Judge (ret.) of the United States Court of International Trade and Judge Walter Thompson Cox III of the then Court of Military Appeals (now Court of Appeals for the Armed Forces) promptly joined Judge Everett to form the three-judge panel.

The hearing took place at the law school, in a packed courtroom on February 12, 1993. Despite a severe winter storm, other spectators crowded three adjacent classrooms and watched on closed-circuit television. For ninety minutes, the two sides presented their positions orally and fielded questions from the bench. When they were done, the court adjourned to consider what it had heard, returning within the hour to render judgment and share the considerations that produced it. Each judge offered his own opinion. All agreed that the judgment of the Hunter Commission had been in error and should be set aside.

Part One of this book presents the arguments for Dr. Mudd and the government, a verbatim record of the oral argument, and the final versions of the judgment and opinions of the court. Part One concerns itself with a question narrow in scope: whether the Hunter Commission made a legal blunder that ought to have been corrected. As the Acting Deputy Assistant Secretary of the Army correctly noted last year, the commission's judgment should not be impeached by resort to modern legal standards foreign to the era in which the trial occurred. Similarly, the commission's judgment should not be impeached by reference to facts of which it had no inkling at the time. Part One, therefore, answers only the question of whether Mudd was wronged by the commission, not whether he was wronged by history.

Part Two offers the comments of several legal and historical experts familiar with the law and facts relevant to the case. Part Two concerns itself with the broader and remaining question: whether the light of history reveals that Samuel Mudd was wrongly condemned. The essayists in Part Two have been left free to use facts unknown to the commission, some emergent only long after the trial. Their work taps the full measure of history's preoccupation with this particular case, among the thousands tried by Union military commissions during the Civil War. Part Two, therefore, judges not the commission but the accused.

Final judgment remains to be pronounced. It has not come from this moot court, and it will not come from the Secretary of the Army, who has yet to rule on Mrs. Steel's appeal on behalf of the family. Samuel Mudd has become history's chattel, and history shall judge him again and again. To its record, this book is submitted by the authors.

A number of people contributed generously in various ways to the moot court and to this book. The encouragement and support of Joe Harbaugh, Dean of the University of Richmond School of Law, were vital to the success of the former and the realization of the latter. Nancy O'Brien, my secretary and right arm, managed innumerable tasks and delicate situations throughout. David Madden, Director of the U.S. Civil War Center at Louisiana State University, kindly furnished advice essential to the book's publication. The law firm of Hunton & Williams, Virginia's largest, generously supported its editing. Sean Everhart, Janet Jenness, Janet Munro, and Adele Nighman, outstanding members of the Class of 1995, exhibited exceptional initiative, rare savvy, and formidable endurance in preparing the manuscripts for print. Shelley Jones stood by with patience, love, and a sharp eye. For all the pleasure I took from this sojourn in scholarship, I am, to them all, very grateful.

John Paul Jones
Richmond, 1994

Part One

The Appeal

Brief on Behalf of Samuel A. Mudd

Catherine Stuart Greer,* W. Scott Magargee,**
and John Thurston Pendleton[†]

INTRODUCTION

On the night of April 14, 1865, John Wilkes Booth apparently assassinated Abraham Lincoln, the President of the United States, in Washington, D.C. Somehow, the assassin injured his leg after shooting the President. Accompanied by David E. Herold, Booth sought medical attention early the next morning at the Charles County, Maryland residence of Dr. Samuel A. Mudd. Several days later, Federal troops killed Booth near Fredericksburg, Virginia as he resisted apprehension. Thus, the person said to be the President's murderer was never brought to book; eight other persons, however, including Dr. Mudd, were subsequently arrested by Federal authorities and tried in connection with the assassination.

All the defendants were civilians. Even though ordinary courts were open and functioning regularly in both the District of Columbia and Maryland, President Johnson ordered Dr. Mudd and the others tried by a military commission of the new President's choosing. On June 30, 1865, that tribunal found the defendants guilty, sentencing four to death and Dr. Mudd to imprisonment at hard labor for life. On July 5,

* J.D., 1993, University of Richmond; B.A., 1988, University of Virginia.
** J.D., 1993, University of Richmond; A.B., 1988, Princeton University.
[†] J.D., 1993, University of Richmond; B.A., 1989, Trinity College.

President Johnson approved the sentences. It is from this conviction that Dr. Mudd appeals to this Special Court of Military Appeal.

For three reasons, Dr. Mudd's conviction was unlawful: first, it came at the hands of a tribunal that lacked authority to try him; second, it resulted from a process contrary to the United States Constitution and to the law of the United States governing military trials; and third, it came after the prosecution had failed to carry its burden of proof. Each of these errors will be set forth in greater detail in what follows.

PART ONE: JURISDICTION

The Special Court of Military Appeal must find the commission's judgment in Dr. Mudd's case invalid and set it aside because the commission lacked jurisdiction, the power to decide. The first section of Article III of the United States Constitution vests the judicial power of the United States "in one Supreme Court and in such inferior courts as the Congress may, from time to time, ordain and establish." Congress did not vest the military commission that tried Dr. Mudd with judicial power. Thus, the proceedings of this commission must be declared a nullity unless the Constitution could otherwise authorize its jurisdiction.

Heretofore, as the Attorney General admitted in his opinion for President Johnson on the Constitutional power of a military commission to try this case, such a tribunal has had jurisdiction to try civilians in the United States only for crimes committed during a period of martial law or for violations of the law of war.[1] Martial law derives from the laws and usages of war, as well as from reason. Like martial law, the laws of war are based in reason and exist, according to the Supreme Court, to "mitigate the cruelties and misery produced by the scourge of war."[2]

Neither martial law, nor the laws of war, authorized a military commission to try Dr. Mudd in June 1865 in Washington, D.C. The case against him involved neither public necessity nor an offense peculiar to the laws of war, so there was no reason for substituting an extraordinary military tribunal for the ordinary civil courts in the trial of a civilian resident of a loyal state. Without such justification, a military commission lacked jurisdiction over this case and this defendant.

Pursuant to traditional concepts of martial law, a military commission may try crimes only in cases of public necessity. As a New York court noted recently in *Matter of Egan*,[3] a state of such necessity must be proved definitively by the one claiming it. Absent such proof, the doctrine of necessity does not justify the exercise of martial law when the civil laws can be exercised.

In *Luther v. Borden*[4], the United States Supreme Court admitted that a real crisis in government may lead to martial law, but cautioned that this does not mean martial law can serve as a pretext for oppression. Even where martial law exists, the Constitution remains superior to martial law as the guardian of the private citizen who is neither a government enemy nor a hostile foe. Such was the position taken recently by the Supreme Court of Kentucky in *Corbin v. Marsh*.[5]

That martial law may exist only by necessity is beyond dispute. Blackstone and Hale, for example, agree that this restriction forms part of the common law.[6] As Blackstone put it, "The necessity of order and discipline in an army is the only thing which can give it countenance; and therefore, it ought not to be permitted in time of peace, when the king's courts are open to all persons to receive justice according to the laws of the land." The despotism made possible by martial law and enforceable by a military commission ought not prevail when the regularly established civil courts are capable of routinely administering justice.

The United States Supreme Court has recently and completely settled this issue, finding martial law an inadequate excuse for the exercise of military jurisdiction over a civilian resident of a loyal state. In *Ex parte Milligan*,[7] the Court reviewed the conviction by military commission of a civilian residing in Indiana. Among the numerous charges against Milligan were those that he had afforded aid to rebels, incited insurrection, engaged in disloyal practices, and violated the laws of war. Before the Supreme Court, the government argued that loyal states were placed within military districts and that martial law existed because Indiana properly constituted a "theater of military operations." The Court could find, however, no condition of necessity that would have warranted martial law in Indiana at the time of Milligan's arrest and trial. The mere existence of strife in one part of the country does not sanction the suspension of laws pursuant to martial law in other, loyal parts of the country where the Constitution and other laws are capable of enforcement by ordinary means. According to the Court, martial law permits trial by military authority only if the necessity that creates martial law is real and existing. As the Court saw it, armies were present in Indiana only to be located to another district where hostilities were actually occurring. In Indiana, "There was no hostile foot; if once invaded, that invasion was at an end and with it all pretext for martial law."

The Court went on to reject the argument that martial law could exist in response to a "threatened invasion," observing that, "the necessity must be actual and present; the invasion real, such as effectually closes the courts and deposes the civil administration." Martial law is properly limited to the "locality of actual war" and in time by the necessity creating its existence. "It is," wrote Justice Davis for the Court, "the birthright of every American citizen when charged with a crime, to be tried and punished according to law."

The government also contended in *Milligan* that a military commission could have jurisdiction to try a civilian under the "laws and usages of war." The Supreme Court rejected this contention as well, stating that, "It can serve no useful purpose to inquire what the laws and usages are, ... they can never be applied to citizens in states which have upheld the authority of the government, and where the courts are open and their process unobstructed." Because the civil courts in Indiana were open and operating regularly, a military commission could not try a civilian residing in Indiana. The ancient and fundamental right of trial by jury found in the Bill of Rights "cannot be frittered away on any plea of state or political necessity."

The President's suspension of the writ of habeas corpus does not warrant a different conclusion in this case. The power to suspend the Great Writ set forth in Article I, Section 9 should not be read as inferring a condition in addition to those expressly limiting the grant of judicial power in Article III, Section 1. Indeed, the Court in *Milligan* found that the Constitution "does not say after a writ of habeas corpus is denied a citizen, that he shall be tried otherwise than by the course of the common law; if it had intended this result, it was easy by the use of direct words to have accomplished it."

If the Constitution does not authorize jurisdiction over a civilian by a military commission, the commission's proceedings against Dr. Mudd must be a nullity. The Supreme Court noted in *Milligan* that the Constitution lays down the law in war as well as in peace, finding that, "No doctrine, involving more pernicious consequences, was ever invented by the wit of man than any of its provisions can be suspended during any of the great exigencies of government." The Court's holding in *Ex parte Milligan* is simple and clear: even in time of civil war, the Constitution does not permit military jurisdiction over a civilian resident in a loyal state when the civil courts are open and operating.

The law enunciated by the Supreme Court binds this court. "The practical effect of a judicial precedent of the Supreme Court is to settle a rule of construction for all inferior courts."[8] If, despite the circumstance of martial law, military jurisdiction over Mr. Milligan could not lie in the State of Indiana in 1864, it surely could not lie over Dr. Mudd in the State of Maryland or in the District of Columbia a year later.

In this case, the government has not even attempted to meet its burden of proving that the courts of the District of Columbia and the State of Maryland were not open and operating at the time of appellant's arrest and trial. Indeed, such an attempt would have been futile, as the published decisions of those courts in numerous cases decided at that time make abundantly clear. Attorney General Speed, in his opinion for the President, admitted that, notwithstanding the declaration of martial law in the District of Columbia, "The civil courts were open and held their regular sessions, and transacted business as in times of peace."[9] The same could as easily have been said of the civil courts of Maryland. It follows, therefore, that this court must find that, like the military commission convened at Indianapolis to try Mr. Milligan, the military commission convened at Washington to try Dr. Mudd was without authority under the Constitution.

Nor can it be said that the law of nations permits what the Constitution does not. Even if it were assumed for the moment that the law of nations implicitly limits the United States Constitution respecting both the judicial power and the Bill of Rights, international law would not warrant jurisdiction over

Dr. Mudd in this case. That aspect of the law of nations known as *jus belli*, the law of war, operates only between belligerents.

The law of war applies only in a state of war. War arises from acts of sovereignty, creating rights of belligerency, making enemies of opposing factions. At best, the Confederacy represented states in insurrection or rebellion as declared by Congress in the Act of July 13, 1861. Indeed, the United States never declared war because, as Wheaton puts it, "there was no body-politic against which to declare it, the very existence of the Confederate government being treason ... ."[10] An insurrection does not warrant application of the law of war unless the rebels assume the legal status of belligerents. According to the War Department's own General Orders No. 100, issued April 24, 1863, an insurrection may lead to rebellion that can rise to civil war, but there remains a distinction between insurgency and belligerency. A civil war remains an insurgency until the government recognizes its adversary as a belligerent. In the words of Chancellor Kent,

> But though a solemn declaration, or previous notice to the enemy, be now laid aside, it is essential that some formal act, proceeding directly from the competent source, should announce to the people at home their new relations and duties growing out of a state of war, and which should equally apprize neutral nations of the fact, to enable them to conform their conduct to the rights belonging to the new state of things.[11]

Without some formal act from the "competent source," notifying that the opposing factions would act as belligerents, the laws of war cannot govern.

No formal act of this nature respecting the Confederacy and its armies ever occurred. According to the eighth section of Article I of the United States Constitution, the Congress is the organ of government authorized to make such a notification, that is, to declare war. But the Congress did not declare war during the recent rebellion. By the Act of July 13, 1861, the Congress did permit the President to declare a state of insurrection, and, by the Act of July 29, 1861, it did authorize him to call forth the militia to suppress the rebellion in states opposing the United States laws, but it never declared war. A civil war *de facto*, perhaps, the rebellion nevertheless remained an insurrection *de jure* and never attained the legal status that would afford the rebels rights or liabilities derived by the law of nations from belligerency. There was simply never any acknowledgment by the United States that the seceding states had formed an independent nation.

That, from a civil war, may sometimes emerge a government enjoying international recognition and belligerency status does not mean that the Confederacy must. The recent experience of the United States is readily distinguishable from that of Great Britain during its civil war. At all times during the late insurrection, the United and Confederate States remained one nation, albeit one in which raged a rebellion. From April 1861 until its demise in 1865, the Confederacy never constituted even a de facto government engaged in war with the United States. Unlike Cromwell, the leaders of the Confederacy never succeeded in ousting the public officials of the Federal Government from this country, never formed treaties, and never gained recognition for the Confederacy as an independent power from the United States or a foreign nation. Cromwell's government was viewed by other nations as having the authority to make laws and contracts and to form treaties; Jefferson Davis's organization was not.

Rights of a belligerent can exist only during war. However, as the War Department has noted in General Orders No. 100, belligerent *status* is not conferred upon the mere treatment and exchange of prisoners of war, the acceptance of flags symbolizing truce, the proclamation of martial law in rebel territory, or other agreements to moderate war. Although the United States may have treated the rebels in some respect as it would treat belligerents, this, according to Wheaton:

> was not a recognition of belligerent rights in the rebels, or a recognition of a legal *status* in them as belligerents. It was a course of policy from day to day, and from place to place, held under political discretion all the while ... .[12]

Certain practices by the United States government may have mitigated the harshness of the late hostilities, but, without the

intention that they do so, they cannot be not taken as acknowledgment of belligerency status.

What the Union did not intend, foreign sovereigns could
not otherwise accomplish. Recognition by the Queen of
England on May 13, 1861, of hostilities between the United
and the Confederate States was not sufficient to confer the
legal status of belligerency. So noted a Federal court in the
1862 case, *United States v. One Hundred Barrels of Cement*:

> The position of foreign nations with respect to this
> insurrection, it must be remembered, does not
> determine its status in American courts. The latter
> follow exclusively the decision of the political
> department of the United States government on that
> question. Even if other nations had recognized the so-
> called Confederate government as an independent
> power, their recognition would bind themselves and
> their subjects alone — not the United States ... . All
> American courts are bound to treat the insurrectionary
> states as integral parts of the Union, and subject to its
> constitution and laws.[13]

As the Supreme Court has said in the *Prize Cases*, proclamation by a foreign sovereign of hostilities between two nations
can preclude the sovereign's own people from denying the
existence of war, but only the government of the United
States, in exercise of the sovereignty of the United States, can
confer the legal status of belligerency upon opposing rebels.
The government made no such conferral in the late rebellion.

It might be argued that the exercise of a belligerent right
by the United States, in establishing a blockade of the Confederate states, had the consequence of conferring belligerent
status on those states and their armed forces. Even if this
exercise of a belligerent right by the United States during the
rebellion could be taken as the basis for conferring belligerency status on the rebels under the law of war, such status
would not have lasted as late as the time of appellant's arrest
and trial.

Blockade is a belligerent right under the law of nations. In
the *Prize Cases*, the Court held that the President's "proclamation of blockade [was] itself official conclusive evidence to the

Court that a state of war existed which demanded and authorized a recourse to such a measure ... ." The Supreme Court
deferred to the President's discretion in establishing the blockade, finding him the appropriate person to make this proclamation in his role as Commander in Chief. This court need not
in Dr. Mudd's case consider the separate question of whether
this act was sufficient to bestow belligerency rights upon the
Confederacy. Even if it were assumed that the President's
proclamation had such an unintended result, the fact remains
that a subsequent proclamation ended the blockade. By
proclamation on April 29, 1865, President Johnson declared:

> [t]hat all restrictions upon internal, domestic, and
> coastwise commercial intercourse be discontinued in
> such parts of the [southern] States ... [and] ... military
> and naval orders in any manner restricting internal,
> domestic, and coastwise commercial intercourse and
> trade with or in the localities above named be, and the
> same are hereby, revoked ... .

Even if this court were disposed to recognizing belligerency
status as a consequence of the blockade, it ought to defer with
grace equal to that of the Supreme Court in the *Prize Cases* and
find that a necessary consequence of President Johnson's
proclamation lifting the blockade was the termination of
whatever belligerency status President Lincoln's proclamation might have unintentionally conferred.

Absent belligerency, the law of war has no sway, and the
jurisdiction of a military commission to try a civilian resident
of a loyal state cannot survive the extinguishment of belligerency status. In this case, it follows therefore that trial by a
commission not even created until two days after the block-
ade-ending proclamation is unwarranted by the law of war.
By May 9, 1865, when Dr. Mudd's trial began, the war *de facto*
was over, and war *de jure* had never been declared. Lee had
surrendered his forces at Appomattox on April 9, and the
President had ordered the removal of all trade restrictions on
April 29. No formal surrender on behalf of the Confederacy
itself could be demanded or obtained because, as Wheaton
observed, the United States did not recognize any authority
competent to make such a surrender. The Presidents' procla-

mations in 1861 and 1865 thus represent the best evidence of both the beginning and the end of the war. On this evidence, Dr. Mudd was tried too late for the law of war to sanction trial by a military commission.

PART TWO: PROCEDURE

Samuel Mudd's conviction should also be overturned because his trial by a military commission in Washington, D.C. violated his rights under the United States Constitution's third article and its Fifth and Sixth Amendments.

As the Supreme Court declared in *Marbury v. Madison*,[14] the Constitution represents "the fundamental and paramount law of the nation." Indeed, the Attorney General advised the President that the military commission that convicted Samuel Mudd had a "duty" to try him in "obedience to the Constitution and the law." The Constitution protects persons within the United States during peace or war. As the court noted in *Corbin v. Marsh*, military power, even in the conduct of war, cannot authorize that which the Constitution prohibits, nor deny that which the Constitution guarantees.

The last sentence of the second section of Article III of the Constitution requires that the "Trial of all Crimes, except in Cases of Impeachment; shall be by Jury; and such Trial shall be held in the State where the said Crimes shall have been committed; but when not committed within any State, the Trial shall be at such Place or Places as the Congress may by Law have directed." Implicit in this specification of a particular procedure — trial by jury and venue in the state in which the crime is said to have been committed — is a Constitutional right on the part of the accused to trial as specified. In the Sixth Amendment, a similar specification of procedure and venue appears: "In all criminal prosecutions, the accused shall enjoy the right to a speedy and public trial, by an impartial jury of the State and district wherein the crime shall have been committed; which district shall have been previously ascertained by law ... ." Thus, both the basic document and its contemporaneous amendment by the Bill of Rights guarantee an accused trial by jury in the place in which his offense is said to have occurred. Dr. Mudd was accused of conspiring with Booth during the actor's visit to Charles County, Maryland, and of aiding and abetting Booth and his accomplice by sheltering them in his Charles County home, yet he was denied a trial in a Maryland court and a jury of the men of Charles County.

It is no defense of these Constitutional deprivations to note the existence of a rebellion in 1865. Even if the dying embers of that rebellion elsewhere could justify suspension of the writ of habeas corpus in loyal Maryland at that time, the rights to jury and venue, unlike the right to the Great Writ, are set out in absolute, not conditional terms. Every man's right to a writ of habeas corpus may be suspended in time of rebellion only because that exception is set forth explicitly where the Great Writ is mentioned in Article I. To the contrary, no man's rights to a jury and to proper venue can be suspended precisely because no exception appears in either Article III or the Sixth Amendment. Courts should not infer exceptions to Constitutional rights set down without exception by the Framers.

That the absolute terms of the jury and venue rights in Article III and the Sixth Amendment were not oversights by the Framers is reinforced by the text of the Fifth Amendment, which in pertinent part promises that, "No person shall be held to answer for a capital, or otherwise infamous crime, unless on a presentment or indictment of a Grand Jury, except in cases arising in the land or naval forces, or in the Militia, when in actual service in time of War or public danger." As this clause illustrates, where the Framers intended a different criminal process for military courts, the Framers took care to say so explicitly. The jury and venue rights of the Third Article and the Sixth Amendment ought to be read free of exceptions for military justice precisely because the Fifth Amendment contains such an exception. Speaking of the jury right, the Supreme Court recently said in *Ex parte Milligan*, a case on all fours with that of Dr. Mudd, that, "This privilege is a vital principle, underlying the whole administration of criminal justice; it is not held by sufferance, and cannot be frittered away on any plea of state or political necessity."[15] Dr. Mudd therefore correctly challenges his conviction as void for want of a jury and for want of a Maryland venue.

Dr. Mudd also attacks his conviction for want of prior Grand Jury action. By the express words of the Fifth Amendment, no person can be held to account for crimes of the sort of which Dr. Mudd was convicted unless on the presentment or indictment of a Grand Jury, except in cases arising in the land or naval forces. According to the Supreme Court in *Ex parte Milligan*, the Constitution preserves this right to every one accused of crime who is not attached to the army, the navy, or the militia in actual service. It is uncontested that Samuel Mudd was a civilian resident of a free state, and that he was unconnected with the military. His trial by a military commission in the District of Columbia therefore violated his Constitutional right to a Grand Jury as well as his Constitutional rights to a petit jury and to a Maryland trial. As the Supreme Court observed in the *Milligan* case:

> If it was dangerous, in the distracted condition of affairs, to leave Milligan unrestrained of his liberty, because he 'conspired against the government, afforded aid and comfort to rebels, ... ,' the law said arrest him, confine him closely, render him powerless to do further mischief; and then present his case to the grand jury of the district, with proofs of his guilt, and, if indicted, try him according to the course of the common law. If this had been done, the Constitution would have been vindicated, ... and the securities for personal liberty preserved and defended.[16]

Although the nation may have been "distracted" over the President's death, the civil courts in Maryland were capable of trying Dr. Mudd. His trial by military commission was improper under the Constitution, and his conviction should be set aside.

The government charged Dr. Mudd in such vague terms as to violate his Constitutional right to due process. The Fifth Amendment ensures that criminal charges will be set out with particularity sufficient to permit the accused to make an adequate defense. In this case, the charge and specification were deficient in three ways: first, they failed to advise the accused according to what law or code the commission would proceed; second, they failed to make clear for what crime previously recognized at law he would be tried; and third, the charge contained a series of separate and distinct accusations that were not set out in separate and distinct counts.

The military commission that tried Dr. Mudd failed to inform him of the law by which he would be tried. The government proceeded by reference to the custom or common law of war, but the charge and specifications are devoid of any reference to such a source. There is no body of law recognized as a common law of war. Instead, as Captain De Hart has observed, "The custom of war is rather sought for, as explanatory of some doubtful question in which, without its aid, a decision might be uncertain, than as a source of authority by itself."[17]

Even if Dr. Mudd had been notified by the charges and specifications that a common law of war formed the basis of his culpability, Dr. Mudd could not defend himself against a body of law that did not exist. The commission refused to say what precedents would be considered controlling under the common law of war leaving Dr. Mudd severely handicapped in the preparation of his defense. When invited to specify whether this "common law of war" referred to English common law, military common law, or the law of nations, the commission remained silent. Accordingly, Dr. Mudd was forced to construct his defense based on tentative assumptions regarding what law would both inform and bind the commission's rulings, hardly the opportunity envisioned by those who framed the Fifth Amendment.

Not only was Dr. Mudd denied adequate reference to the body of law according by which he was tried, he was also denied an adequate statement of the offense or offenses of which he stood accused. According to Major General Macomb, the Constitution, the Articles of War, and the common law agree that an accused is entitled to know and face the charges made against him. Specifically, the charge

> must set forth the crime or offense in a manner sufficiently specific, to enable the person accused to know to what he is to answer ... . The facts ought also to be distinctly specified or alleged, in such a manner, that neither the prisoner nor the Court can have any difficulty in knowing what is the precise object of the trial. The same minuteness and precision ought to be observed in specifying the time and place, when and where, the facts charged were committed.[18]

The correctness of General Macomb's statement of the applicable standard is borne out by *United States v. Sharp*.[19] In that case, the court refused to refer to a jury the charge of making a revolt, a capital offense "insufficiently defined by [the statute] or by any other standard, to which reference could safely be made ... . If we resort to definitions given by philologists," wrote Justice Washington, "they are so multifarious, and so different, that I cannot avoid feeling a natural repugnance, to selecting from this mass of definitions, one, which may fix a crime upon these men."

In *United States v. MacKenzie*, it was held that federal

> courts can take no cognizance of any matter not specifically declared to be a crime or offense by Act of Congress, and accordingly cannot inquire into violations of the common law, or law of nations, ... [unless] the act is prohibited and punished by express statutory provisions.[20]

What federal courts cannot do, federal military commissions cannot do. Even what the common law might permit, however, the law of war does not.

A military commission cannot make law as it goes along, that is, make definite by its own statement what the law of war does not. The customary law of war ought not to be confused with the common law. The former, part of the law of nations, cannot trace its development in the accretion of case decisions, as does the latter. Thus, military tribunals cannot make the law of war as courts embodying Anglo-Saxon tradition make common law. According to Whiting, a military commission can only hear cases that are "established by evidence, in conformity with known punishments in like cases in some one of the States of the United States of America."[21] Here, Whiting has simply refined, in the particular context of military law, a principle operating generally in federal law. Federal courts are not common law courts; the Constitution withholds from them the common law power to pronounce adjudicative law. In *United States v. Hudson*,[22] the Supreme Court held that a federal court could not entertain an indictment for libel on the President because the crime existed, if at all, only at common law and not by Federal statute. Because

Article III courts lack jurisdiction to hear cases involving common law crimes, they necessarily lack the power to add crimes to the common law's collection. A lawmaking power that the Supreme Court has denied Article III tribunals surely ought not be ascribed by this court to a tribunal empowered only by an inference from Article II. Without that power, the commission that tried Dr. Mudd could not have repaired the fatally imprecise charge and specification with which it was presented.

The single charge against Dr. Mudd and seven co-defendants improperly commingled facts and crimes. The military law of the United States incorporates the same pleading standard which Federal law has inherited from the common law.[23] In the words of General Macomb, "Facts distinct in their nature, are not to be included in one and the same charge, or specification of a charge, but must be the subject of a distinct charge or specification."[24] According to Captain De Hart, "The facts ought also to be distinctly specified or alleged, in such a manner, that neither the prisoner nor the court can have any difficulty in knowing what is the precise object of the trial."[25] Dr. Mudd was denied his right to a charge in conformity with this standard. The single count accusing Dr. Mudd and the others could be taken to refer to at least four crimes: conspiring in aid of the existing armed rebellion to murder the President and others; murdering the President in pursuance of this conspiracy, assaulting with intent to murder the Secretary of State; and lying in wait with intent to kill the Vice President and General Grant. Such a charge prevented Dr. Mudd from determining with which of the four crimes he himself was charged, and from thereby marshalling a responsive defense. The lack of specificity made it impossible for Dr. Mudd to know what evidence he needed to refute or establish in order to verify his innocence.

On this ground alone, Dr. Mudd's conviction ought to be overturned. As General Macomb put it, "The total want of specification in the charge, may be urged ... as a ground for acquitting the prisoner, and that such a defect would render the proceedings nugatory."[26]

The charge against Dr. Mudd stated that he "did, at Washington City, ... on or before the 6th day of March, A.D. 1865, and on divers other days and times between that day and the 20th day of April, A.D. 1865, advise, encourage, receive, entertain, harbor, and conceal, aid and assist" the conspiracy. Dr. Mudd could not construct an effective defense against such a general charge. No specific act was alleged, nor was a specific date or time set forth. The charge left the defendant to account for the entire period between the 6th day of March and the 20th day of April. Therefore, he was unable to rebut effectively the evidence submitted against him by the prosecution. According to General Macomb:

> The facts ought also to be distinctly specified or alleged, in such a manner, that neither the prisoner nor the Court can have any difficulty in knowing what is the precise object of the trial. The same minuteness and precision ought to be observed in specifying the time and place, when and where, the facts charged were committed, for such specification may be essentially necessary to the prisoner's defense.[27]

Before the military commission in Washington, therefore, Dr. Mudd was denied adequate notice of both the procedure according to which his trial would be staged and the specific offense to which he had to mount a defense. Either inadequacy constitutes reversible error in the form of a violation of the Fifth Amendment's guarantee of due process. Consequently, this court ought to reverse Dr. Mudd's conviction.

Even if it were admitted that the charge and specification against Dr. Mudd was not so vague and indiscriminate as to lack sufficient meaning for the Fifth Amendment, its most discernible meaning would be that Dr. Mudd was accused of treason. The only charge against Dr. Mudd opens by describing him as "maliciously, unlawfully, *and traitorously, and in aid of the armed rebellion against the United States* ... combining, confederating and conspiring." It follows by referring to the conspiracy as "malicious, unlawful, *and traitorous*." It reports that Dr. Mudd and others went about murder of the President, assault on the Secretary of State, and attempts to ambush the Vice President and General Grant "maliciously, unlawfully, *and traitorously*." Moreover, the only specification directed at Dr. Mudd describes him as acting in aid of the conspiracy by advising, concealing, aiding and assisting others "with knowledge of the murderous *and traitorous* conspiracy." Any ambiguity in the criminal charge and specification ought to be read against the drafter; here, the government. In this case, such a reading would lead naturally to the conclusion that the government's repeated use of the words "traitorous" and "traitorously" in the charge and specification shows that the government intended to try Dr. Mudd for treason. Such an interpretation would mean his conviction was unconstitutional.

If Dr. Mudd was tried for treason, he was convicted in violation of the Constitution. The third section of Article III defines treason as "levying war against the [United States], or in adhering to their enemies, giving them aid and comfort," and conditions conviction for treason on either the testimony of two witnesses to the same overt act or else the defendant's confession in open court. Thus, Dr. Mudd could not have been convicted of treason according to the Constitution unless the record of the military commission contained the requisite testimony of two witnesses or his confession. The record contains no such evidence. His conviction ought therefore be overturned for failure of compliance with the procedural prerequisites found in the third section of Article III.

The Constitution's Sixth Amendment guarantees every accused the assistance of counsel for his defense. Captain Benet noted recently that the right pertains equally in prosecutions at military law.[28] Twenty-five years ago, General Macomb wrote that a prisoner was not "precluded the advantage of [counsel's] presence."[29] Captain De Hart seconded this view when he wrote in 1846 that, "Courts-martial always admit counsel for the prisoner; and all military writers admit it to the custom to allow prisoners to have counsel."[30] Held incommunicado before trial, Dr. Mudd was arraigned without counsel, on charges unclear even to those trained in the law. He was only permitted counsel after his plea to the charge had been taken. He was then given but one night to collaborate with his counsel in preparation of a defense. Denying Dr. Mudd access to counsel during the pleading process is action by the commission contrary to the established military law of criminal procedure.

The commission also denied Dr. Mudd due process by

improperly limiting the admission of defense testimony to the
scope of the prosecution's case, contrary to accepted practice
in military courts. Military law permits a defendant to present
evidence not touched on in the prosecution's case or to im-
peach prosecution evidence by introducing new evidence of
his own. As General Macomb put it: "The utmost liberty
consistent with the interest of parties not before the court and
with the respect due to the court itself, should, at all times, be
allowed a prisoner .... The Court is bound to hear whatever
address, in his defense, the accused may think fit to offer, not
being in itself contemptuous or disrespectful."[31] Here again,
military law only reflects in its particular context a rule of law
generally recognized in the courts of the United States. See,
for example, *United States v. Craig*,[32] in which the court noted
that "the declarations of the prisoner may be admitted to
account for his silence when that silence would operate against
him," and *Sessions v. Little*,[33] where the court observed that
"whenever the conduct of a person at a given time becomes
the subject of inquiry, his expressions, as constituting a part of
his conduct and indicating his intention, can not be rejected as
irrelevant, but are admissible as part of the *res gestae*."

The commission refused on more than one occasion to
admit material evidence offered by Dr. Mudd in his defense.
For instance, the record shows that the commission refused to
hear a defense witness, Bennet Gwynn, tell his version of an
episode in 1863 or 1864 in which Dr. Mudd was said to have
concealed persons in Confederate service from Federal authorities. The prosecution had earlier introduced this episode
as tending to prove Dr. Mudd's inclination toward treason.
Dr. Mudd offered Gwynn's testimony to prove not only that
the episode had occurred years earlier than the prosecution
suggested, but also that the persons involved, while fugitive,
were not in Confederate service. The commission sustained
the Assistant Judge Advocate's objection that this line of
questioning went beyond the Government's case. Similar
objections by the Assistant Judge Advocate were sustained
when Dr. Mudd sought to question Dr. George Mudd and
Benjamin Gardiner. The defense had sought their accounts of
a meeting with Dr. Mudd on Sunday morning, April 16,
during which he was said to have expressed his intent to
inform federal authorities of the presence at his farm of two

suspicious persons. Such testimony went to the heart of the matter, that is, to whether Dr. Mudd knowingly or willingly concealed the escaping assassin and his henchman. Its exclusion, on the sole ground that it exceeded the scope of the government's case, is contrary to prevailing standards of military law and manifestly prejudicial to Dr. Mudd.

The commission also denied Dr. Mudd due process by improperly refusing severance of his trial from that of his co-defendants.

The compound charge against Dr. Mudd accused him and his co-defendants of conspiring to murder the President and other government officials. Compelling Dr. Mudd to accept trial jointly with his alleged co-conspirators denied Dr. Mudd the chance to exonerate himself through the testimony of the others, for a defendant cannot testify. In the aforementioned case of *United States v. Sharp*, the court granted a motion for severance of the trials of several sailors charged in one indictment with the same offense, endeavoring to make a revolt. In *Sharp*, as in Dr. Mudd's case, several co-defendants faced the same charge, a charge that required the government to prove concert of action. In *Sharp*, it was endeavoring to make a revolt; in Dr. Mudd's case, it was conspiring to murder the President. In both cases, joint trial would have denied an accused the opportunity to elicit exculpatory testimony from other defendants. The military commission denied Dr. Mudd his Fifth Amendment right to present his defense; otherwise, at the very least, it abused its discretion when it refused severance.

The 1827 case of *United States v. Marchant*[34] does not persuade an opposite conclusion. In that case, the Supreme Court declined to recognize co-defendants' rights to separate trials derived from co-defendants' common law rights to accept or oppose individual jurors for their jury panel. The Supreme Court properly limited its decision in *Marchant & Colby* to that question, and that case ought to be regarded as inapposite here, where no jury at all was involved.

At military law, a joint trial presents the same impediment for an accused, for, as Captain De Hart observes, "Persons collectively arraigned are incompetent for each other."[35] On the other hand, accomplices separately indicted for the same offense may be called to testify for each other. In their treatises, Captains De Hart and Benet agree that a prisoner who desires to avail himself of the testimony of others charged with the same offense, ought to petition the convening authority for a separate trial.[36] In the event that the convening authority declines, military law recognizes the military prisoner's right to judicial relief. In this case, by overruling Dr. Mudd's application for severance, the commission denied him the opportunity to elicit from his co-defendants testimony that he was no part of the alleged conspiracy. Contrary to notions of due process embodied in both the Constitution and military law of the United States, this decision warrants reversal of Dr. Mudd's subsequent conviction.

The commission also denied Dr. Mudd due process by refusing to admit the testimony of Mrs. Mudd. While it is generally true that the law does not permit a spouse to testify, military law sometimes recognizes an exception. According to Greenleaf, the other spouse may testify when the act with which the accused spouse is charged is so private that the other is the only one who can prove or disprove the charge.[37] Now that Booth is dead, the charge of treason against Dr. Mudd cannot stand without the testimony of Mrs. Mudd, for treason must be proved by the testimony of *two* witnesses, and only Herold and Mrs. Mudd were there when Dr. Mudd received the injured actor in his home on April 15, 1865. As Captain De Hart notes, the competence or incompetence of a spouse to testify does not depend on whether she testifies for or against the interests of her husband. Because Mrs. Mudd's testimony would be necessary to convict Dr. Mudd of treason, her testimony that he was not a traitor ought to have been admitted. The commission's failure to admit her testimony thus denied Dr. Mudd due process and warrants reversal of the conviction that followed.

PART THREE: PROOF

Even if the commission had jurisdiction to try Dr. Mudd, and even if its many procedural errors did not annul its judgment, Dr. Mudd's conviction should nevertheless be overturned because the record cannot satisfy the government's burden of proof.

According to Captain M'Naghten, a military court must provide the highest level of justice available under the circumstances.[38] Notions of due process and fundamental fairness require the government to carry the burden of proving Dr. Mudd was guilty of the charges beyond a reasonable doubt. The government's evidence linking Dr. Mudd to the late President's assassination clearly fails to satisfy this burden of proof. Accordingly, this court should set aside the commission's judgment.

Both the common law and the Fifth Amendment of the Constitution impose on a felony prosecution the strictest standard of proof, that which is sufficient to produce in the decision maker certainty beyond any reasonable doubt. Indeed, many reported decisions in the United States establish that a person accused of a crime must be found guilty beyond a reasonable doubt. In *State v. Roe*,[39] the Supreme Court of Vermont declared that "the only degree of certainty known to the law and recognized, is this: conviction beyond a reasonable doubt." Decisions of the highest courts of New York, Pennsylvania, and Massachusetts confirm the position of the court in *State v. Roe*.[40] In the words of Chief Justice Shaw, writing for the Massachusetts Supreme Court in *Commonwealth v. Webster*:

> What is reasonable doubt? ... The evidence must establish the truth of the fact to a reasonable and a moral certainty; a certainty that convinces and directs the understanding, and satisfies the reason and judgment, of those who are bound to act conscientiously upon it.[41]

The highest courts of New Jersey and of California have specifically relied upon *Webster* when insisting that the prosecution offer proof beyond a reasonable doubt.[42] Both Greenleaf and Halsted,[43] in their celebrated works on the law of evidence, acknowledge the prevalence in American law of the reasonable doubt standard. That a similar — or even more stringent standard — applies in cases governed by the military law of the United States is clear from General Macomb's observation that no person may be convicted by court martial "unless upon the strongest and most satisfactory evidence."[44]

If the charge and specification against Dr. Mudd amounted to treason, the government had to prove Dr. Mudd knew

Booth was a public enemy when he gave him aid and comfort; if the charge and specification amounted to conspiracy, the government had to prove Dr. Mudd knew Booth and the others had agreed to murder the President; if the charge and specification amounted to aiding and abetting a felon, the government had to prove Dr. Mudd knew Booth had murdered the President. Judged by the most lenient of proof standards, the government's evidence, as set forth in the commission's record, would prove wanting; judged by the applicable reasonable doubt standard, the government's evidence is wholly inadequate. Therefore, the Court should overturn the commission's judgment for its failure to find proof of an essential element of any of the crimes derivable from the charge and specification.

Before the commission, witnesses for the government, as well as those for the defense, testified that Dr. Mudd had met with Booth when he visited Charles County in December of 1864, some months prior to the President's murder. The record thus shows that the doctor was acquainted with the actor. It does not show, however, that they joined in a conspiracy. Regarding that Charles County meeting, the only testimony that went directly to the substance of Dr. Mudd's conversations with Booth came from defense witnesses Thompson and Bowman, both of whom reported conversation of lawful and innocuous business.

Only one government witness, Weichmann, placed Dr. Mudd again in the company of Booth or any of his alleged gang during the several months before the assassination. Weichmann testified that he witnessed a meeting between Dr. Mudd and Booth in Washington's National Hotel on January 15. On the stand, Weichmann offered to fix this date with greater certainty using the register of the Pennsylvania House, the hotel at which he said Dr. Mudd had registered. The defense later showed that the only time the doctor had stayed in the Pennsylvania House was on December 23, not January 15, calling into question the accuracy of Weichmann's testimony. As to the business between the actor and the doctor on that occasion, Weichmann's testimony was that he was out of earshot, but that the doctor and the actor afterwards told him they discussed a real estate transaction.

Two other government witnesses placed Dr. Mudd in the

city of Washington in the first three days of March, when the government claimed Booth was meeting with his henchmen. Evans testified that he saw Dr. Mudd enter Mrs. Suratt's house on March 1 or 2. Norton placed the doctor in the National Hotel on March 3. Defense witnesses, however, insisted the doctor was in and around Bryantown, Maryland during that period. Even if the commission accepted the testimony of Evans and Norton, and rejected the testimony of the doctor's five alibi witnesses, the most that the testimony of Evans and Norton can prove is that Dr. Mudd passed through Washington's National Hotel at a time when Booth was registered. Neither of these witnesses could put the two men together, much less report the nature of the business they might have conducted had they met.

Of all the crimes that might be construed from the charge and specification against Dr. Mudd, the only two that remained capable of proof when the government closed its case were conspiracy to commit murder and aiding and abetting the assassin. As to the conspiracy charge, the record was devoid of direct evidence of Dr. Mudd's involvement, since it contained nothing as to whether Dr. Mudd had learned, much less embraced, the object of the alleged conspiracy before April 15. Any inference regarding Dr. Mudd's knowledge of, and commitment to, Booth's intentions drawn from the circumstantial evidence of one or more meetings between Dr. Mudd and Booth, must come, if at all, from the doctor's actions after the assassination. If the doctor knew Booth had killed the President when he sheltered Booth after the assassination, then the commission might infer that his meetings beforehand had been to plan such an object. If the doctor did not know that Booth and Herold were connected with the assassination until after they left his care, then there is no basis in the record for assuming Dr. Mudd's part in Booth's conspiracy. The government's case for conspiracy is therefore inextricably intertwined with its case for aiding and abetting.

Before turning to the state of the record regarding a case against Dr. Mudd for aiding and abetting in Booth's escape, there remains to be addressed one more weakness in the government's case against Dr. Mudd for the charge of conspiracy with Booth to murder the president and other officers.

Even if it were accepted that Dr. Mudd conspired with Booth as early as November of 1864 or earlier, the record shows that the object of such a conspiracy was not the murder of the President. A conspirator may not be held accountable for the acts of a co-conspirator which were beyond the scope of the conspiracy's common purpose. Wharton writes that:

> while the parties are responsible for consequent acts, growing out of the general design, they are not for independent acts growing out of one of the particular malice of individuals. Thus, if one of the party, on his own hook, turns aside to commit a felony foreign to the original design, his companions do not participate in his guilt.[45]

The record contains uncontradicted evidence of the gov-ern-ment's own witness, Chester, that Booth at first planned only to kidnap the President and take him to Richmond. Chester testified that Booth did not abandon his intention to kidnap in favor of one to murder *until mid-February*. There is no evidence at all that Booth communicated with Dr. Mudd *after January*. Thus, even if Dr. Mudd had once been a party to Booth's kidnapping plan, the government offered no evidence that Dr. Mudd even knew of the subsequent murder plan. The only charge against Dr. Mudd was conspiracy to murder, not conspiracy to kidnap. As the record clearly shows, Booth's conspiracy underwent a fundamental change of object after Dr. Mudd's last alleged communication with the group. The government has therefore failed to prove — for this defendant — a key element of the crime of conspiracy, *any* commitment of Dr. Mudd to its common object.

Essential to the government's case against Dr. Mudd for both conspiracy and aiding and abetting is whether the doctor recognized Booth and knew he had murdered the President when Booth stopped for help at the farm on April 15. If the government did not prove that Dr. Mudd knew he was help-ing an assassin, there was no basis even in the circumstantial evidence of the record from which the commission could infer an unlawful purpose to Dr. Mudd's earlier meetings with Booth. The record would therefore fail to prove Dr. Mudd knowingly took part in the conspiracy. If the government did not prove that Dr. Mudd knew he was treating and harboring the President's assassin, then the government failed also to prove the doctor intended to aid and abet an escaping felon.

The government called several witnesses to show that Dr. Mudd aided Booth knowing what Booth had done. Lieutenant Lovett testified that, on April 18, Dr. Mudd volunteered to him that two strangers had come to his house on the morning of Saturday, April 15, and that he had treated one of them for a broken leg. Dr. Mudd told Lt. Lovett that he could not identify either of his visitors, and that his patient had shaved a mustache but retained a pair of long whiskers. Lt. Lovett also testified that Dr. Mudd pointed out to him the route by which, the next day, the doctor had directed them through the nearby swamp to Dr. Wilmer's, before Dr. Mudd rode on to church. According to Lt. Lovett, Dr. Mudd said he only learned of the assassination when he spoke with fellow worshippers at church. Colonel Wells testified regarding three conversations with the doctor. According to the Colonel, the doctor told him substantially what the doctor had already told the lieutenant, that Dr. Mudd had entertained two strangers on Saturday, treating one for an injured leg; that his patient arrived with a mustache and whiskers; and that the doctor did not recognize his patient as John Wilkes Booth.

To rebut Dr. Mudd's claim that he neither recognized Booth nor knew Booth had anything to do with the assassination when he treated him, the government offered testimony that the doctor visited Bryantown on Saturday afternoon, after news of the assassination and of Booth's role had been broadcast. That Dr. Mudd traveled that afternoon to town and heard of the assassination was never disputed. The issue is whether he heard on that trip that Booth was wanted as the assassin. Three government witnesses testified that they learned of the assassination in Bryantown on Saturday afternoon. Only one of these was able to discover the name of the alleged assassin; the others were not. There was testimony that Bryantown rumors that Saturday afternoon otherwise identified the murderer, including some that named Boyle, a locally notorious outlaw. Ultimately, however, the government failed to produce evidence directly contradicting the doctor's statements to the government's investigators, Lieutenant Lovett and Colonel Wells. At best, the government proved that Dr. Mudd had an opportunity to learn Booth was being sought earlier than the doctor claimed. It failed to prove that Dr. Mudd took that opportunity.

Review of the record before the commission shows that the government failed to offer any evidence which could be said to prove Dr. Mudd's intentional participation in any conspiracy, much less in one for murder as to which he was charged. It also shows that the government failed to offer any evidence which could be said to prove Dr. Mudd knew he was harboring a felon when he set Booth's leg and sent his travelers back on the road that fateful Saturday. For this failure of proof respecting essential elements of the crimes of conspiracy and aiding and abetting, the commission's judgment should be set aside and the case against Dr. Mudd dismissed.

CONCLUSION

The conviction of Dr. Mudd should be overturned because the record shows that the commission which tried him committed many errors of sufficient gravity to warrant correction on appeal. The commission's first and most serious error was trying him at all. Under the United States Constitution, a military tribunal cannot try a civilian resident of a free state when the civil courts are functioning normally. That martial law may be in force makes no difference. Nor may the law of war justify military jurisdiction over a civilian resident of a loyal state. The military commission which tried Dr. Mudd had no power to do so.

Trial by military commission cost Dr. Mudd his rights under the Constitution to action by a grand jury, trial by a petit jury, and trial in an appropriate venue. These rights may not be denied a civilian resident of a free state by the unilateral action of the government. The attempt to do so in this case warrants reversal of Dr. Mudd's conviction and dismissal of the charge against him.

The charge against Dr. Mudd was so vague as to prevent the fashioning of a specific reply. By proceeding on such a defective charge, the government denied Dr. Mudd's right to due process. By arraigning him and demanding his plea before allowing him to seek counsel, the government denied Dr. Mudd's right to due process. By refusing him the opportunity to elicit testimony beyond the scope of the government's case in chief, the government denied Dr. Mudd's right to due process. By excluding his wife's testimony, the government denied Dr. Mudd's right to due process. By refusing his request for a separate trial, the government denied Dr. Mudd's right to due process. Any of these violations of rights recognized by the Constitution as applicable to criminal trials generally, and by military law as applicable to trial by military commission, warrants reversal of Dr. Mudd's conviction and dismissal of the charge against him.

Finally, the government completely failed to prove Dr. Mudd even knew of the conspiracy to kill the President or of Booth's commission of the crime. This failure of proof of criminal intent on the part of the defendant warrants reversal of Dr. Mudd's conviction and dismissal of the charge against him.

Notes

[1] 11 Op. Att'y Gen. 297, 305 (1865).

[2] The Prize Cases, 67 U.S. (2 Black) 635, 667 (1862).

[3] 6 Parker Cr. R. 675, 681 (N.Y. 1866).

[4] 48 U.S. (7 How.) 1, 45 (1849).

[5] 63 Ky. (2 Duv.) 193 (1865).

[6] 1 SIR WILLIAM BLACKSTONE, COMMENTARIES ON THE LAWS OF EN-
GLAND (London, W. Strahan and T. Cadell, Oxford, D. Prince 1783) *reprinted in*
1 SIR WILLIAM BLACKSTONE, COMMENTARIES ON THE LAWS OF ENGLAND
413-14 (New York & London, Garland Publishing, Inc. 1978); SIR MATTHEW
HALE, THE HISTORY OF THE COMMON LAW OF ENGLAND (3d ed. 1739)
reprinted in SIR MATTHEW HALE, THE HISTORY OF THE COMMON LAW OF
ENGLAND 27 (Charles M. Gray ed., 1971).

[7] 71 U.S. (4 Wall.) 2 (1866).

[8] HENRY WHEATON, ELEMENTS OF INTERNATIONAL LAW § 54 (Richard
H. Dana, Jr. ed., 8th ed., Boston, Little, Brown & Co. 1866) *reprinted in* 19 THE
CLASSICS OF INTERNATIONAL LAW 68 n.31 (James Brown Scott ed., 1983).

[9] 11 Op. Att'y Gen. 297 (1865); BENN PITMAN, THE ASSASSINATION OF
PRESIDENT LINCOLN AND THE TRIAL OF THE CONSPIRATORS 403 (New York,
Moore, Wilstach & Baldwin 1865) (*facsimile ed.* 1954).

[10] WHEATON, *supra* note 8, § 57.

[11] 1 JAMES KENT, COMMENTARIES ON AMERICAN LAW 52-53 (New York,
O. Halsted 1826).

[12] WHEATON, *supra* note 8, § 297 (emphasis in original).

[13] 27 F. Cas. 292, 297 (E.D. Mo. 1862) (No. 15,945).

[14] 5 U.S. (1 Cranch) 137, 177 (1803).

[15] 71 U.S. (4 Wall.) at 123.

[16] *Id.* at 122.

[17] WILLIAM C. DE HART, OBSERVATIONS ON MILITARY LAW, AND THE
CONSTITUTION AND PRACTICE OF COURTS MARTIAL 20-21 (New York, Wiley
and Putnam 1846).

[18] ALEXANDER MACOMB, THE PRACTICE OF COURTS MARTIAL §§ 31-38
(New York, Harper & Bros. 1841).

[19] 27 F. Cas. 1041 (C.C.D. Pa. 1815) (No. 16,264).

[20] 26 F. Cas. 1118, 1120 (S.D.N.Y. 1843) (No. 15,690).

[21] WILLIAM WHITING, WAR POWERS UNDER THE CONSTITUTION OF THE
UNITED STATES (Boston, Little, Brown & Co. 1864).

[22] 11 U.S. (7 Cranch) 32 (1812).

[23] WILLIAM C. DE HART, OBSERVATIONS ON MILITARY LAW, AND THE
CONSTITUTION AND PRACTICE OF COURTS MARTIAL 83 (New York, D. Appleton
& Co. 1862).

[24] MACOMB, *supra* note 18, § 32.

[25] DE HART, *supra* note 17, at 83.

[26] MACOMB, *supra* note 18, § 62.

[27] *Id.* § 31.

[28] CAPT S.V. BENET, A TREATISE ON MILITARY LAW AND THE PRACTICE OF COURTS-MARTIAL 65 (New York, D. Van Nostrand, 2d ed. 1862).

[29] MACOMB, *supra* note 18, § 43.

[30] DE HART, *supra* note 17, at 134.

[31] MACOMB, *supra* note 18, § 90.

[32] 25 F. Cas. 682 (C.C. Pa. 1827) (No. 14,883).

[33] 9 N.H. 271 (1838).

[34] 25 U.S. (12 Wheat.) 480 (1827).

[35] DE HART, *supra* note 23, at 308.

[36] DE HART, *supra* note 23, at 396; BENET, *supra* note 28, at 237.

[37] 1 SIMON GREENLEAF, A TREATISE ON THE LAW OF EVIDENCE 490 (Boston, Little, Brown & Co., 9th ed. 1858).

[38] CAPTAIN M'NAGHTEN, ANNOTATIONS ON THE MUTINY ACT, WITH SOME OBSERVATIONS ON THE PRACTICE OF COURTS-MARTIAL 175 (London, Stevens and Sons 1828).

[39] 12 Vt. 93 (1840).

[40] *See* People v. White, 22 Wend. 167, 178 (N.Y. Sup. Ct. 1839); Commonwealth v. Dana, 43 Mass. (2 Met.) 329, 340 (1841); Commonwealth v. Harmen, 4 Pa. 269 (1846); Vaiden v. Commonwealth, 53 Va. (12 Gratt.) 717, 726-29 (1855).

[41] 59 Mass. (5 Cush.) 295 (1850).

[42] Donelly v. State, 26 N.J.L. 601, 615 (1857); People v. Strong, 30 Cal. 151, 155 (1866).

[43] 1 SIMON GREENLEAF, A TREATISE ON THE LAW OF EVIDENCE 115-18 (Boston, Little, Brown & Co., 11th. ed. 1863); 1 JACOB R. HALSTED, HALSTED'S DIGEST OF THE LAW OF EVIDENCE 244 (New York, Jacob R. Halsted 1856).

[44] MACOMB, *supra* note 18, §§ 129-30.

[45] 1 FRANCIS WHARTON, WHARTON'S CRIMINAL LAW § 524, at 767 (12th ed. 1932).

Brief for the United States in Reply

Bradford Clark Jacob,* Sarah Christian Johnson,** and Lisa S. Spickler†

On April 14, 1865, Abraham Lincoln, the sixteenth President of the United States and the Commander in Chief of their armies was assassinated at Washington, D.C. Elsewhere in the capital that night, William H. Seward, the Secretary of State, was assaulted with a knife. It would later be learned that simultaneous attacks were planned for the Vice President, Secretary of War, and General Grant.

The President was struck down in his box at Ford's Theater, by the bullet of an assassin who was observed by a horrified audience as he escaped across the stage. Eyewitnesses had no trouble identifying the killer as the actor John Wilkes Booth. He left the scene on horseback.

In the early morning hours of the next day, two riders, one of them Booth, visited Samuel A. Mudd at his farm outside Bryantown, Maryland. Mudd, a physician, treated Booth for a broken leg, sheltering him and his companion until later in the day, when Mudd led the pair to a secret path through the nearby swamp. Meanwhile, numerous federal officers and agents were conducting an active manhunt for the President's assassin, issuing the hue and cry for Booth in Bryantown;

* J.D., 1993, University of Richmond; B.S., 1989, University of Richmond.
** J.D., 1994, University of Richmond; B.A., 1989, University of Virginia.
† J.D. *cum laude*, 1994, University of Richmond; B.A. *cum laude*, 1990, Bucknell University.

indeed, across the breadth of Charles County. Mudd visited Bryantown in the afternoon after the assassination, and there discussed it with others, but concealed his visitors from the authorities.

Eventually, federal officers interviewed Mudd. His answers and those of his wife, as well as the discovery of Booth's damaged riding boot in Mudd's home, led to Mudd's arrest. While he was in custody, additional evidence came to light of his clandestine meetings with Booth and John Surratt, a known Confederate agent, in the period preceding the assassination. In addition, witnesses reported other acts by Mudd revealing his sympathy for the rebels. Consequently, President Johnson ordered Mudd to appear on charges related to the assassination before a military commission in Washington in May 1865. During a lengthy trial, two experienced counsel represented Mudd and sixty-four different witnesses took the stand in his defense. Nevertheless, the nine senior officers comprising the commission found him guilty and sentenced him to prison for life. He remains incarcerated at Fort Jackson in the Florida Keys.

Counsel for Mudd petitioned this honorable court for review of his conviction, claiming that the military commission lacked jurisdiction to try Mudd, that it had denied him a variety of procedural rights, and that the government had failed to carry its burden of proof. The court granted Mudd's Petition for Review by an order dated October 21, 1866.

For the murder of our nation's supreme military commander, Mudd was lawfully — and fairly — tried in time of war by the military commission in Washington. To petitioner's numerous claims of error, the government replies with greater specificity in what follows.

PART ONE: JURISDICTION

A military commission, convened on May 8, 1865, could try Mudd for conspiring to murder the nation's Commander in Chief. According to international law to which the United States subscribes, a military commission has jurisdiction in time of martial law to try offenses against *jus belli*, the law of war.

As we all know only too well, at the times of both the assassination and the trial, civil war raged in the United

States. This bloody conflict arose from the attempt to secede by several states, including one whose borders touched both the District of Columbia and Charles County, Maryland. The war took the lives of hundreds of thousands, and destroyed the lives of countless more. Although Lee had surrendered his forces on April 9, and Johnston his on April 26, other rebel armies fought on. The rebel leader, Jefferson Davis, was not apprehended until two days after Mudd's trial began, and the rebels prevailed in battle at San Jacinto on the very day the prosecution opened its case. Rebel warships continued to attack Union vessels as late as November, long after Mudd's sentence had been approved. The city of Washington, seat of government and national headquarters of its armed forces, for four years faced the constant threat of rebel attack. During Mudd's trial, the city remained the fortified center for directing military operations against the rebels. As they had since 1862, soldiers guarded the city's gateways and policed its streets. The Commander in Chief was thus killed within his own camp. These are undisputed facts of common knowledge, and are properly considered by this court in its review. They are more than sufficient to support a finding by the commission that a state of war existed and that the zone of war embraced the place of the crime, the place of the petitioner's arrest, and the place of his trial.

Like courts martial, military commissions are quasi-judicial military tribunals. Courts martial try persons of the armed forces; military commissions try civilians accused of criminal acts during wartime. In England, from whence our law, military and civil, has come, the authority of military commissions has been recognized since the twelfth century. According to Hale, the Court of the Constable and Marshal was established at that time for control over the King's army, for appeals of death for murder committed out of the country, and for determination of prisoners' rights.[1] General Washington ordered the earliest trial in the United States by a military commission, that of the spy John André in September 1780. A military commission tried Arbuthnot and Ambrister in Florida in 1818 for inciting the Indians to war against the United States.[2] General Scott convened military commissions to try offenses against the law of war by civilians during the Mexican War of 1847. On September 24, 1862, the Commander in

Chief ordered that "all rebels ... be subject to martial law and liable to trial and punishment by a court martial or military commission." Congress ratified this Presidential proclamation by the third Act of March 3, 1863.

Application of the law of war (or martial law) to displace or supplement civil law depends upon the condition of war. According to Professor Parker,

> Martial law is that military rule and authority which exists in time of war, and is conferred by the laws of war, in relation to persons and things under and within the scope of active military operations in carrying on the war, and which extinguishes or suspends civil rights, and the remedies founded upon them ... . Founded on the necessities of war, and limited by those necessities, its existence does not necessarily suspend all civil proceedings.[3]

In his Instructions for the Government of Armies of the United States in the Field, later promulgated by Presidential direction as Union Army General Orders No. 100, Professor Lieber wrote, "Martial law is simply military authority exercised in accordance with the laws and usages of war." Whiting has written that the laws of war are the laws that the Constitution expressly authorizes and requires to be enforced when martial law has been declared.[4] Captain Benet observed that, "Many offenses which in time of peace are civil offenses, become in time of war military offenses and are to be tried by a military tribunal, even in places where civil tribunals exist."[5] That the recent war was not international but internecine does not bar the authorization of military commissions by martial law. As the Supreme Court observed in *The Prize Cases*, "It is very evident that the common laws of war ought to be observed by both parties in every civil war."[6]

Mudd was accused of conspiring to assassinate the Commander in Chief of the armed forces of the Union, his immediate Constitutional successors in the chain of command, the Vice President, the Secretaries of State and War, and the general officer in charge of the Union armies in the field. Mudd was thus accused of plotting, in effect, the destruction of the national command authorities of the Union, as effectively as if he had shelled the headquarters tent where they gathered in pre-battle council. Although it has not been shown that Mudd ever donned a uniform of the insurgent forces, or took a place in the ranks of its field armies, he nevertheless became a combatant by plotting against such a military target in time of war. As the Attorney General recently advised the President in his opinion on the power of a military commission to try those who conspired to kill the Commander in Chief, "An Army has a right to protect its own existence by the means and mode usual among civilized nations when at war."[7] Adopted by the President, who ordered military trial for the conspirators, this expression of the inherent power of the army in time of war ought to be afforded great weight.

The decision of the United States Supreme Court in *Ex parte Milligan*[8] is not to the contrary. In that case, it was conceded that Indianapolis, the seat of both the military district and the military commission, had never been seriously threatened by insurgent armies. Indiana was properly regarded more as a military staging area for support of Union forces than as a military target threatened by rebel attack. No such concession is offered here regarding Washington, where the taking of the national capital was always a rebel military objective and rebel armies came distressingly close on several occasions. Only the valiant defense of Fort Stevens blunted General Early's invasion of the District of Columbia less than a year before the trial of this case. The District and the State of Maryland were truly war zones in the recent conflict. In both, the constant threat of attack amounted to a serious military emergency. The late President, by our Constitution both chief executive and supreme military commander, concluded such conditions warranted imposition of martial law, establishment of military commissions, and suspension of the writ of habeas corpus. Congress soon ratified these decisions by legislation, and the Supreme Court has acquiesced. The decision of his successor regarding the trial of this particular case ought to be treated with the same respect.

The Constitution does not prohibit either application of the law of war or trial by military commission. Surely, it is beyond peradventure after *The Prize Cases* that the law of war, as part of the law of nations, is also part of the law of the

United States. The Framers of the Constitution left administration of the law of war to Congress, not to the federal
judiciary. Article I, section 8, clause 10 authorizes Congress
"to define and punish offenses ... against the law of nations."
That Congress may have reassigned, from time to time, some
of that power to civil courts does not mean that Congress is
foreclosed from assigning it also, or instead, to other tribunals, including military commissions.

Congressional authorization of trial by military commission for offenses under the law of war no more intrudes upon
the grant of federal judicial power in Article III than does
Congressional authorization of trial by court martial, a practice uninterrupted since promulgation of the Articles of War
by the First Congress. In the Act of July 17, 1862, Congress
referred approvingly to trials by military commissions, and in
the Act of March 18, 1863, Congress explicitly authorized trial
by military commission of "any person" for spying, an offense
against the law of war.

The law of war and its customary tribunals precede the
Constitution. To the extent that the Constitution might be
said to limit preexisting customary law regarding the power
of the Commander in Chief to employ military commissions,
the Constitution implicates the Congress, not the judiciary.
Congress has lent its approval to trial by military commission
of civilians for violations of the laws of war. No further
approval from the federal courts is required. As Justice Story
wrote in his Commentaries on the Constitution of the United
States,

> in measures exclusively of a political, legislative, or
> executive character, it is plain, that as the supreme
> authority, as to these questions, belongs to the
> legislative and executive departments, they cannot be
> reexamined elsewhere.[9]

Careful assessment of the allocation of federal powers in the
Constitution leads to the conclusion that petitioner's trial by
military commission comported with the supreme law of the
land.

Nothing in the Bill of Rights alters this conclusion. The
assassination of the Commander in Chief by Booth and the

assault on the second in succession to that office by his
henchman were attacks on military commanders and therefore offenses against the laws of war. So, also, were the related
conspiracy and subsequent acts aiding and abetting the perpetrators. As the Attorney General pointed out to the President, infractions of the laws of nations are offenses, to be
distinguished from crimes. In Article I, the Constitution
refers to offenses against the laws of nations, whereas in
Article III and in the Fifth and Sixth Amendments, the Constitution refers to crimes and criminal trials. Mudd was charged
with offenses against the laws of war; he was not charged with
crimes in violation of Federal law. His trial was therefore
beyond the scope of Article III and the Fifth and Sixth Amendments. Justice Story cautioned that the construction of a
power conferred in the Constitution ought

> not be enlarged beyond the fair scope of its terms,
> merely because the restriction is inconvenient,
> impolitic, or even mischievous. If it be mischievous,
> the power of redressing the evil lies with the people by
> an exercise of the power of amendment. If they do not
> choose to apply the remedy it may fairly be presumed,
> that the mischief is less than what would arise from a
> further extension of the power; or that it is the least of
> two evils.[10]

The same principle ought to govern judicial construction
of procedural entitlements in the Bill of Rights. Just as the
guarantee of a jury in the Seventh Amendment has been held
by the Supreme Court in *Shields v. Thomas*[11] to apply only to
those cases that arise from common law, as the text of that
Amendment specifically provides, and not from equity, so,
too, should the guarantee of a jury in the Sixth Amendment be
held to apply to cases arising from common law crimes, and
not from offenses against the law of nations.

The law of war applies in this case even though the United
States never formally recognized the late confederacy as a
belligerent state. First, belligerency is the prerequisite not for
a sovereign's assertion of power under *jus belli*, but for any
assertion of legal limits to that power. Second, belligerency
applies only to civilized and separate sovereignties at war

with each other, not to one sovereign beset by civil war. Finally, even if mutual recognition of belligerency were held to be prerequisite to the application of the law of war in a domestic insurrection, it would not lead to a finding of error in this case, for only legitimate combatants may assert the rights of a belligerent.

With the legal state of belligerency is associated restrictions on the savage power of a sovereign at war. Wheaton, in his Elements of International Law, illustrates the point when he discusses prisoners of war:

> According to the law of war, as still practised by savage nations, prisoners taken in war are put to death. Among the more polished nations of antiquity, this practice gradually gave way .... The present usage of exchanging prisoners was not firmly established in Europe until sometime in the course of the seventeenth century.[12]

As this passage makes clear, the mutual consent of European sovereigns has produced limits on the customary or natural law of war. Without that mutual consent, such limits do not apply. In internal war, "the government must decide whether the municipal or the international code, in whole or in part, shall be adopted."[13] As President Woolsey of Yale has put it, "There is a difference between belligerents and belligerent states, which has been too much overlooked."[14] Petitioner is correct in asserting that the record is devoid of any formal act of the United States sufficient to communicate recognition of the confederacy as a belligerent state. Petitioner is also correct in asserting that the government's discretionary resort to certain customs of prisoner parole and exchange is insufficient to establish a state of belligerency between the Union and the confederacy for other purposes when it was not so intended by the United States. Absent a state of belligerency, the law of war still applies, but the limitations for belligerent states do not.

Belligerency's limits on the law of war have been withheld, again by the mutual consent of sovereigns, from murderous persons not enrolled in the armed forces of a consenting sovereign. Citing Vattel and Kluber, Wheaton noted:

The horrors of war would indeed be greatly aggravated, if every individual of the belligerent states was allowed to plunder and slay indiscriminately the enemy's subjects without being in any manner accountable for his conduct. Hence it is, in land wars, irregular bands of marauders are liable to be treated as lawless banditti, not entitled to the mitigated usages of war as practiced by civilized nations.[15]

In his essay "Guerrilla Parties Considered with Reference to the Laws and Usages of War," Professor Lieber referred to recent European military law and history when he refined the point made by Wheaton. Lieber distinguished various armed bands, including brigands, freebooters, and bushwhackers. None are entitled, as would be the captured soldier of the conventional army of a belligerent, to the privileges of the law of war, but only to its force.

According to Professor Lieber,

the armed prowler, the so-called bushwhacker, is a simple assassin, and will thus always be considered by soldier and citizen; and ... the armed bands that arise in a district fairly occupied by military forces, or in the rear of an army, are universally considered, if captured, brigands, and not prisoners of war.[16]

From Wheaton and Lieber, therefore, it may be concluded that, by international law, a bushwhacker is subject to the full force of the law of war, unmitigated by the actions of sovereigns mutually respecting their armies as belligerents.

As charged before the commission, Mudd and his co-defendants constituted an armed band of bushwhackers. The record shows that they were recruited and led by Booth, who held no commission from the confederacy. Forsaking uniforms and identifying badges, they operated secretly in the rear of the Union army to murder its most senior officers. Against such a band, as against spies, the law of war operates unmitigated by privileges associated with the status of belligerency. So, even if a state of belligerency was necessary to mitigate for regular soldiers the full force of the law of war, its absence has no bearing on the decision in this case.

PART TWO: PROCEDURE

Petitioner had ample opportunity to request a more definite statement of the charge and specifications before trial began. Now that his counsel have presented an extensive, if ultimately unsuccessful, defense, his claim that the vagueness of the charge and specifications left him unable to defend should fall on deaf ears. The record shows that petitioner made no objection to the charge and specification at his arraignment, and only requested a restatement near the end of the government's case in chief. Nevertheless, petitioner now argues that the charge and specification were so vague as to prevent him from making an adequate defense. The government readily concedes that an accused should be apprised of the extent and degree of guilt with which he stands charged, and of the particular facts on which the prosecutor plans to base the evidence against him. The government also agrees that, as Captain Benet observed, if a charge is found to be so defective in all legal respects that it is impossible to confirm a finding of guilt thereon, no sentence of punishment could be properly adjudged or enforced.[17] The issue here, however, is whether, considering petitioner's failure to object earlier, he really was forestalled as he now claims. If Mudd did not understand the charge, he could have called upon the prosecution to specify the particular facts, a request that, Captain De Hart noted, the commission could not refuse.[18] Since neither Mudd nor his counsel requested a clearer statement until the government's case was nearly complete, this court is entitled to assume that, at the time, Mudd understood well enough the charges under which he was indicted. Even if his failure to make a timely objection is excusable, the court ought to find that such an objection is nevertheless meritless, because the charge and specifications left no doubt as to the persons accused and the crimes in question.

As presented at petitioner's arraignment, the charge and specifications were sufficiently clear as a matter of law. According to General Macomb and Captain Benet, the charge and specification are too vague only when they fail to point to any specific crime.[19] Captain De Hart has noted that, while in framing charges of military offenses, precision and conciseness should be observed, it is not necessary to follow technical strictness. De Hart has concluded that a requirement for technical strictness would encumber the proceedings of military courts to an inconvenient extent without any substantial benefits and make necessary a body of lawyers to provide guidance and administration of military justice.[20] All that should be necessary to satisfy basic fairness is enough precision and certainty in the description so that the defendant may know the nature of the crime charged.

The specifications to the charge must be brief, clear, and explicit. Captain Benet wrote that, in general, they must give the facts, circumstances, and intent in specific terms.[21] In particular, when conspiracy is charged, the accused must be named and informed of the offense, as well as the time and place of its commission. In this case, the general conspiracy specification reported that petitioner, with Booth and John Surratt, on or before March 6, 1865, and from then to April 15, 1865, did "combine, confederate, and conspire together ... unlawfully, maliciously, and traitorously to kill and murder within the Military Department of Washington, and within the fortified and entrenched lines thereof" Abraham Lincoln and other named officers. The specification then described the assassination in detail, including the time, place, and circumstances. An additional paragraph recounted the individual involvement of the petitioner, stating that he did "advise, encourage, receive, entertain, harbor, and conceal, aid, and assist" certain listed people with "knowledge of the murderous and traitorous conspiracy aforesaid ... ." Thus, the charge and specifications presented the case against petitioner in sufficient detail as to leave no question in a reasonable mind about what he was called upon to answer.

When petitioner's counsel finally did request that the charge and specification be stated more clearly, the government fully complied. The record shows that, although the Judge Advocate replied that the charge and specification could not be stated "with more certainty, or with more appropriateness or terseness of language, than has been already employed," he did reiterate that the general allegation was conspiracy and that the applicable law would be the common law. When defense counsel continued to ask whether the accused were charged with conspiracy, both the Judge Advocate and Assistant Judge Advocate Bingham answered affirmatively. In particular, Bingham stated that they were indicted for a conspiracy and would be held accountable for as many overt acts in the execution of that conspiracy as they were guilty of.

It strains credulity that petitioner's counsel did not understand the charge and specification, when he proceeded without clarification for much of the government's case. Any complaint as to the charge and specification should properly have been made at arraignment or as the trial began, yet petitioner made no motion to quash, offered no plea in abatement, and never presented a demurrer.

However, assuming for the sake of argument that there were ambiguities in the charge, the explanations given by the Judge Advocate and the Assistant Judge Advocate should have eliminated any remaining uncertainty. From the charge and specification introduced at arraignment, as well as from amplifying responses by the Judge Advocates, petitioner should have learned all he needed to know and all that the law required the government to inform him. No error sufficient to justify reversing the judgment of the commission ought to attach to the communication made by the charge and specification.

The commission's refusal to sever petitioner's trial from that of his co-defendants denied him neither a procedural right nor an adequate opportunity to defend himself. Where several persons are jointly indicted, the common law is clear that the accused have no right to insist upon separate trials. If the court, in its discretion, chooses not to separate the trials, it commits no error. *United States v. Marchant*[22] stands as authority for the applicability of this rule in federal courts. Other precedents supporting its universality at common law include *Maton v. People*,[23] *Whitehead v. State*,[24] and *State v. Soper*.[25] Bishop[26] and Starkie[27] concur in their works on criminal law.

The same rule applies in military law. General Macomb and Captain Benet distinguish between cases in which the defendants are named in a common charge and those in which they are named in separate charges.[28] According to both learned commentators, where defendants are named in a common charge, they are tried together. In this case, petitioner was named in the same charge and general specification as his co-defendants. The commission therefore adhered to customary practice when it tried the eight together, and it did not abuse its discretion when it denied petitioner's request to be tried separately.

The fact that Mudd's wife did not testify on his behalf does not support the claim that he was denied an adequate chance to defend. His counsel never called Mrs. Mudd to testify. The defense's failure to call a witness cannot later be deemed an error by the tribunal. By not even attempting to call Mrs. Mudd, the defense waived whatever right it might have to her testimony.

Had the defense called Mrs. Mudd to testify, the commission would have been well justified in refusing to admit her testimony. Neither common law nor military law admits husbands and wives as witnesses *for* or *against* each other, in any trial where one of them may be a party. Roscoe and Greenleaf, in their treatises on evidence, both present as the common law the rule here stated.[29] General Macomb, Captain De Hart, and Captain Benet in their treatises on military law, present as the customary law of military tribunals the same rule.[30] The United States Supreme Court confirmed the rule's applicability in federal court in *Stein v. Bowman*.[31] It has not seen fit to revisit the matter since.

Any argument for admission of the testimony of a spouse can therefore be based on no more than wishful thinking. As Greenleaf notes, the identity of interest between husband and wife makes a wife's testimony as vulnerable to claims of improper interest as the testimony of the defendant himself. Petitioner fails to point to anything that might justify reassessing the policy balance of public and private life that has long persuaded the courts to adhere to such a rule.

PART THREE: EVIDENCE

The prosecution furnished more than enough evidence to sustain Mudd's conviction. The charge against him was proven sufficiently to satisfy the understanding and conscience of the commission. The government recognizes the long-settled principle that the obligation of proving any fact lies upon the party who asserts the affirmative of that fact, and accepts that this principle applies to trials by military tribunals. According to Captain De Hart, in military courts, "He who makes the charge is bound to prove it."[32] "Proof," however, is nothing more than, as De Hart puts it, the legal credence that the law gives to evidence. The government readily concedes, therefore, that it bore the burden of proof at petitioner's trial. Thus the dispute here is not about which party bore the burden of proof but about how heavy a burden it had to be. Petitioner is really calling on this court to determine the minimum amount of credible evidence necessary for his conviction.

Petitioner makes the novel but misguided assertion that the prosecution had to furnish proof sufficient to meet the common law standard of "reasonable doubt." On this point, military law does not follow the common law, as the lack of citation to military authorities for this point in petitioner's brief makes clear. Moreover, as Captain Benet notes in his treatise, military law does not even require the same proof standard for a military commission as for a court martial.[33] The commission that tried petitioner was free to set for itself the standard of proof. Its findings should not be set aside for failure to follow procedures appropriate to other tribunals. The prosecution need only have provided enough evidence so that petitioner's guilt was a certainty in the understanding and conscience of the commission members.

To assert that the prosecution was not bound to prove petitioner guilty beyond reasonable doubt is not to concede that the government's case fell short of that strictest of standards. The commission heard evidence more than sufficient by any proof measure to find petitioner guilty of conspiracy to murder the President and other officers in the chain of command.

This case presents no issue as to the nature of criminal conspiracy. The government and the petitioner concede that military law ought to define the crime of conspiracy in the same manner as does the common law. Maltby, Benet, and De Hart agree that, in the absence of specific rules found in military law, common law provides a source for principles to guide military trials.[34] It is black letter law that a conspiracy is a confederacy of two or more persons to accomplish some unlawful object, and that the object of the conspiracy need not be accomplished for the crime to be perfected. The confederacy itself constitutes the crime. No further overt act other than the agreement need be proven. The crime is complete when the conspirators enter the agreement. Thus, in this case, the prosecution had only to prove that petitioner agreed with at least one other that one of them would commit a crime.

Whether petitioner intended to personally take part in attacking the President and the others is irrelevant; the issue is whether Mudd agreed with someone else that the attacks should be carried out. Conspiracy, like any other controverted fact, can be proven by circumstances. As the court noted in *United States v. Donau*,[35] the fact finder need only find that the circumstances have been satisfactorily proven as facts. The commission, therefore, could infer petitioner's agreement to Booth's plot from the evidence of petitioner's own words and actions.

Two long-settled principles, originating in the common law and adopted by military law, guide proof of intent. The first, set forth by Captain Benet, is a presumption that a person intends to do what he does, and intends the natural, necessary and probable consequences of his actions.[36] The second, which follows from the first, is that a person's intent can be inferred from his actions. The commission could properly rely on these principles to find that the evidence supported petitioner's conviction for conspiracy.

Petitioner's statement to Daniel J. Thomas that the President, his cabinet, and other Union men would soon be dead surely permitted the inferrence of petitioner's knowing involvement in a plot by those with whom he was repeatedly in contact during the period leading up to their attacks on such officers. Several witnesses testified of petitioner's meetings with the assassin Wilkes Booth, the Confederate agent John Surratt, and other conspirators. Louis Weichmann testified that, on January 15, 1865, he met Mudd and Booth on a Washington street, after Mudd had called out to John Surratt, and that the foursome repaired to the National Hotel for conference. According to Weichmann, Mudd had private conversations at the hotel with Booth and Surratt, during which Booth appeared to draw a diagram. William A. Evans, a minister, testified that he saw Mudd going into Mary Surratt's Washington home in early March. Marcus P. Norton placed Mudd at the National Hotel on March 3, when the doctor entered Norton's room looking for Booth. From this evidence of petitioner's repeated, furtive meetings with Booth and other conspirators, the commission could infer Mudd's willing participation in the planning of the attacks.

Evidence that petitioner was an active and spirited adherent to the cause of secession goes to the purpose of petitioner's meetings with Booth and others implicated in the attacks. Such evidence warrants the commission's finding that petitioner met repeatedly with Booth and the other plotters during the life of the plot to discuss the plot, and not unrelated matters. Witnesses testified that Mudd entertained gatherings of Confederate sympathizers at his home. Several of his former slaves testified of secret gatherings of men, many in Confederate uniform, in the woods surrounding petitioner's home. They told of his instructing servants to provide the men with bedding and food, tend their horses, and serve as look-outs. The record also shows that the Confederate agent, now fugitive, John Surratt was a frequent guest in the Mudd home.

In addition to this circumstantial evidence of petitioner's support for the secessionists, the record contained petitioner's own treasonous utterances. These, too, tend to prove petitioner's felonious purpose in meeting with Booth and his gang in the months and weeks immediately before the assassination. Melvina Washington recalled petitioner telling her, "Lincoln would not be in office for long" and cursing the President as a "son of a bitch" who ought to have been dead a long time ago. Walter Marshall had earlier heard petitioner praise the rebel General Jackson, stating that he had no objection if the General were to "burn Lincoln up in his house." Petitioner was rightly adjudged Booth's co-conspirator.

Evidence of the actions and surrounding circumstances of other conspirators supports the commission's conclusion that Mudd was a party to an agreement to murder the President. The crime of conspiracy requires that an agreement between two or more persons to commit an unlawful act be proven. However, there is no authority stating that the agreement be formal. Indeed, as Federal courts have ruled in *United States v. Hertz*[37] and *United States v. Wilson*,[38] the acts and words of the defendant's co-conspirators can prove a common conspiracy. As the court noted in *United States v. Cole*,[39] this includes their acts both before and after the commission of the object of the conspiracy. The most telling act by petitioner's co-conspirators was the visit by Booth and Herold at the

Mudd home during their flight to avoid capture. From that visit, the commission could infer that petitioner had previously offered his home as a safe house in Charles County and that this contribution explained his several meetings with Booth and other conspirators.

Petitioner's inaction following Booth's stopover also suggests his willing participation in the plot. Informed of the manhunt for the President's assassin, Mudd kept silent about Booth's visit until he and Herold gained a vital head start toward Richmond. As the Indiana Supreme Court said in *McGregor v. State*,[40] when circumstantial evidence is relied on for a conviction, the totality of the evidence must be so conclusive that a reasonable man would believe in the existence of the offense even in view of the most important concerns of life and liberty. In this case, the commission considered the circumstances presented among the totality of the evidence to reach the reasonable conclusion of Mudd's complicity. Thus, the commission permissibly and correctly found that petitioner was party to the agreement to attack the Commander in Chief and the Secretary of State.

That petitioner's witnesses presented a different interpretation of his words and actions does not warrant setting aside the judgment against him. It is black letter law that the credibility of witnesses is the province of the fact finder. As the court noted in *Dickenson v. The Gore*,[41] assessment of the witnesses' demeanor is essential to determining their credibility and assigning weight to their testimony. For this reason, appellate courts, with resort only to written transcripts, have traditionally eschewed overruling a trial court's findings of fact based on the credibility of witnesses offering conflicting versions of the facts. Nothing in this appellate court's organic law suggests that Congress intended this court to proceed otherwise. This court, therefore, ought to defer to the commission's tacit judgment that the government's witnesses were more believable than the petitioner's.

CONCLUSION

Petitioner's several claims of error by the commission are groundless. Because the law of war would have empowered the commission to try Booth, a bushwhacker who killed the Commander in Chief and attempted to kill his successors in the chain of command, the law of war empowered the commission to try that bushwhacker's confederates, including Samuel Mudd. The U.S. Constitution, which recognizes and incorporates the law of war by reference, does not prohibit petitioner's trial by military commission, nor does it require the substitution of a civil court or a common law jury. That the Union denied secessionist state governments formal recognition as belligerent sovereigns does not dictate a contrary conclusion.

Petitioner got the trial to which the law entitled him. He did not deserve a jury. No error resulted from the commission's refusal to try him apart from his co-conspirators, or from the omission of his wife's testimony.

The totality of the evidence presented by the prosecution was sufficient for even the highest burden of proof. For all these reasons, the United States respectfully pray that this court affirm the commission's conviction of Samuel A. Mudd.

Notes

[1] SIR MATTHEW HALE, THE HISTORY OF THE COMMON LAW OF ENGLAND (3d ed. 1739) *reprinted in* SIR MATTHEW HALE, THE HISTORY OF THE COMMON LAW OF ENGLAND 26 (Charles M. Gray ed., 1971).

[2] See Charge to Grand Jury — Neutrality Laws, 30 F. Cas. 1021, 1023 (C.C.D. Ohio 1851) (No. 18,267).

[3] Joel Parker, *Habeas Corpus and Martial Law*, NORTH AM. REV. 471, 501 (1861).

[4] WILLIAM WHITING, THE WAR POWERS OF THE PRESIDENT, AND THE LEGISLATIVE POWER OF CONGRESS IN RELATION TO REBELLION, TREASON, AND SLAVERY 56 (Boston, J.L. Shorey, 4th ed. 1863).

[5] CAPT S.V. BENET, A TREATISE ON MILITARY LAW AND THE PRACTICE OF COURTS-MARTIAL 16 (New York, D. Van Nostrand, 2d ed. 1862).

[6] 67 U.S. (2 Black) 635 (1862).

[7] BENN PITMAN, THE ASSASSINATION OF PRESIDENT LINCOLN AND THE TRIAL OF THE CONSPIRATORS 405 (New York, Moore, Wilstach & Baldwin 1865) (*facsimile ed.* 1954).

[8] 71 U.S. (4 Wall.) 2 (1866).

[9] 1 JOSEPH STORY, COMMENTARIES ON THE CONSTITUTION OF THE UNITED STATES § 374 (Philadelphia, P.H. Nicklin and T. Johnson 1833)

[10] *Id.* § 426.

[11] 59 U.S. (18 How.) 253 (1856).

[12] HENRY WHEATON, ELEMENTS OF INTERNATIONAL LAW 250 (Philadelphia, Carey, Lea & Blanchard 1836).

[13] THEODORE D. WOOLSEY, INTRODUCTION TO THE STUDY OF INTERNATIONAL LAW § 136 (New York, C. Scribner, 2d ed. rev. 1864).

[14] *Id.*

[15] WHEATON, *supra* note 12, at 255.

[16] Francis Lieber, Guerilla Parties Considered with Reference to the Laws and Usages of War, letter to Henry Wager Halleck, General-in-Chief, Union Army, in response to Halleck's letter of Aug. 6, 1862, *in* THE WAR OF THE REBELLION: A COMPILATION OF THE OFFICIAL RECORDS OF THE UNION AND CONFEDERATE ARMIES, ser. III, vol. II, 301 (Washington, GPO 1899).

[17] CAPT S.V. BENET, A TREATISE ON MILITARY LAW AND THE PRACTICE OF COURTS-MARTIAL 107 (New York, D. Van Nostrand, 3d ed. 1863).

[18] WILLIAM C. DE HART, OBSERVATIONS ON MILITARY LAW, AND THE CONSTITUTION AND PRACTICE OF COURTS MARTIAL 101 (New York, Wiley and Putnam 1846).

[19] BENET, *supra* note 5, at 106; ALEXANDER MACOMB, THE PRACTICE OF COURTS MARTIAL 37-38 (New York, Harper & Bros. 1841).

[20] DE HART, *supra* note 18, at 285, 287.

[21] BENET, *supra* note 17, at 54.

[22] 25 U.S. (12 Wheat.) 480 (1827).

[23] 15 Ill. 536, 539 (1854).

[24] 10 Ohio 449 (1850).

[25] 16 Me. 293 (1839).

[26] JOEL P. BISHOP, COMMENTARIES ON THE CRIMINAL LAW § 541 (Boston, Little, Brown & Co., 1st ed. 1856).

[27] THOMAS STARKIE, A TREATISE ON CRIMINAL PLEADING 36 (Exeter, Gerrish & Tyler, 1st Am. ed. 1824).

[28] BENET, *supra* note 17, at 93; MACOMB, *supra* note 19, at 34.

[29] HENRY ROSCOE, A DIGEST OF THE LAW OF EVIDENCE IN CRIMINAL CASES 147 (Philadelphia, T. & J.W. Johnson 1854); 1 SIMON GREENLEAF, A TREATISE ON THE LAW OF EVIDENCE § 254 (Boston, Little, Brown & Co., 9th. ed. 1858).

[30] MACOMB, *supra* note 19, at 56; BENET, *supra* note 17, at 239; DE HART, *supra* note 18, at 397.

[31] 38 U.S. (13 Pet.) 223 (1839).

[32] DE HART, *supra* note 18, at 355.

[33] BENET, *supra* note 17, at 15.

[34] ISAAC MALTBY, A TREATISE ON COURTS MARTIAL AND MILITARY LAW 2 (Boston, Thomas B. Wait & Co. 1813); BENET, *supra* note 17, at 224; DE HART, *supra* note 18, at 334.

[35] 25 F. Cas. 890 (C.C.S.D. N.Y 1873) (No. 14,983).

[36] BENET, *supra* note 17, at 282.

[37] 26 F. Cas. 293 (C.C.E.D. Pa. 1855) (No. 15,357).

[38] 28 F. Cas. 699 (C.C.E.D. Pa. 1830) (No. 16,730).

[39] 25 F. Cas. 493 (C.C.D. Ohio 1853) (No. 14,832).

[40] 16 Ind. 9, 13 (1860).

[41] 7 F. Cas. 673 (D.C.D. Mich. 1855) (No. 3,893).

Oral Arguments

Candida Ewing Steel,* F. Lee Bailey,**
John Jay Douglass,† and John S. Jenkins††

BEFORE THE UNITED STATES SPECIAL COURT OF
MILITARY APPEAL, RICHMOND, VIRGINIA
February 13, 1867

CLERK OF THE COURT: All rise. OYEZ! OYEZ! OYEZ! All
persons having business before the honorable United States
Special Court of Military Appeal are admonished to draw
nigh and give their attention for the court is now sitting.
God save the United States and this honorable court.
JUDGE EVERETT: We have only one matter for hearing this
afternoon and that is United States against Mudd. Is

---

* Attorney at Law; Member, Maryland State Board of Contract Appeals; great-great-granddaughter of Gen. Thomas Ewing, Jr.; court-certified mediator and senior arbitrator; former Assistant Corporation Counsel for the District of Columbia.
** Attorney at Law; lecturer and author; former Marine Fighter Pilot and Legal Officer; partner, Bailey, Gerstein, Carhart, Rashkind, Dresnick & Rippingille, Miami; partner, Bailey, Fishman, Freeman & Ferrin, West Palm Beach; partner, Bailey, Fishman & Leonard, Boston.
† Dean of the National College of District Attorneys and Professor of Law, University of Houston Law Center; former Commandant of the Judge Advocate General's School and past President of the Army Judge Advocates Association; Colonel (ret.), U.S. Army.
†† Associate Dean and Lecturer, George Washington University National Law Center; former Judge Advocate General of the Navy and Special Counsel to the Secretary of the Navy; Rear Admiral (ret.), U.S. Navy.

counsel ready for the appellant? As I understand it, the
time will be divided between the two counsel for appellant?

MS. STEEL: That's correct, Your Honor. I will have fifteen
minutes and [co]counsel will have twenty minutes, and I
would like to reserve ten minutes for rebuttal, if we may.

JUDGE EVERETT: Is counsel prepared to proceed for the
appellee?

DEAN DOUGLASS: Yes, Your Honor.

JUDGE EVERETT: We'll hear argument.

MS. STEEL: Good afternoon. May it please the court. My
name is Candida Ewing Steel and, with Mr. F. Lee Bailey,
I represent Dr. Samuel Mudd who was tried by the Hunter
Commission of acts related to the assassination of President Abraham Lincoln. As the Court will recall, John
Wilkes Booth stopped and received medical treatment
from this Maryland country doctor. General Thomas
Ewing Jr., who was trial counsel below, is unable, for
personal and professional reasons, to prosecute this appeal, and I thank the Court for allowing me, as his granddaughter, to appear in his stead. I will be addressing the
question of jurisdiction (in this case) for the Hunter Commission to try Dr. Mudd, and my co-counsel, Mr. F. Lee
Bailey, will be addressing the violations of procedural
rights guaranteed to Dr. Mudd under the Constitution
and military law traversed by the Hunter Commission.

It is now nearly two years after the cessation of hostilities
between the states and the tragic assassination of our
beloved President Lincoln. On the birthday of this President who will be forever honored for preserving the
Union, it is appropriate to ponder the Constitutional foundation of the Union and its relation to the circumstances
which have brought Dr. Mudd before the Court. Mr.
Bailey will be addressing the direct impact on Dr. Mudd of
the decision to convene a military commission. I will, with
the Court's permission, address the larger question of the
jurisdiction of the military over citizens as it applies to all
citizens in this nation.

Your Honors, the petitioner submits that the military commission did not have jurisdiction under the Constitution
to try a civilian in the circumstances of this case and the

decision to impanel the commission was an unwarranted
and unconstitutional usurpation of power by the presidency.

Petitioner Samuel Mudd was a citizen of the United States and
lived in the Union State of Maryland, a simple physician
and farmer, not belonging to the Army or Navy, and he
was not in the public service. He was in the same shoes as
any other citizen who might fall under suspicion — any
judge, lawyer, or clergyman of the State of Maryland. His
guilt or innocence does not affect the question of the
competence of the tribunal by which he was judged. Mr.
Bailey will address the questions of guilt or innocence, but
for the purpose of my argument, the court must determine
jurisdiction without regard to whether or not Dr. Mudd
may have been innocent or guilty of the charges that were
made against him. The military commission depended
entirely on the executive will for its creation and its court.
Had the President, in the time of war, by his own mere will
and judgment of the emergency, the power to bring before
the military any man or woman to be tried and punished
whether for life or to be sentenced to death? If the President had this power, it must come from the Constitution,
since the President has no power which the citizens have
not granted him through the Constitution that they have
specifically authorized. The President is given the executive power, the execution of those laws enacted by Congress, and the authority to direct the operations of the
military which Congress caused to be raised. If it were
otherwise, Your Honors, in wartime, either foreign or
domestic, the President would become a dictator. The
theory on which the Government rests its argument is that
the Commander in Chief may do whatever is necessary to
promote the success of his armies, and that he is the sole
judge of the necessity. Congress and the courts would be
just as subject to the whim and will of the Executive as Dr.
Mudd and any other citizen that might be taken before a
military court. The essential point, as I am certain Your
Honors are aware, of the Magna Carta, which was the
foundation of the English system which has become the
common law of our country, was to reduce the regal to a
legal power when imprisonment was involved, and the

Magna Carta was treasured and imitated by our founding
fathers and the exemption from military rule for all but the
military and trial by jury were very carefully preserved
and retained.

JUDGE EVERETT: Hasn't there been a traditional basis of
jurisdiction under the law of war with respect even to
civilians if, for example, they are spies or working for an
enemy nation; and doesn't that basis of jurisdiction apply
here?

MS. STEEL: There is, under the law of war, certainly someone
acting as a spy, a citizen of a foreign jurisdiction or foreign
country — there is authority under the law of war and we
do not ask that the court disturb that authority to try that
person in the military court. In this case, however, Dr.
Mudd was not in the employ of a foreign nation, was not
in the employ of a belligerent nation. There is not sufficient proof to show that he was acting as a spy; and even
if that were to be true, because he is a citizen of the United
States and of the State of Maryland, as the Supreme Court
has stated this past December in *Ex parte Milligan*, the
citizen has a right to be tried before a civil court, even
without regard to whether or not he was engaged in
rebellious activities. *Milligan* was a case involving very
much the same circumstances.

JUDGE EVERETT: *Milligan*, I believe, was a case involving
martial law, and the law of war is something different. If
you had a situation where Dr. Mudd was clearly established to have been working, let's say, as a spy for the
insurgents — the Southern forces — wouldn't he be subject to trial by military commission?

MS. STEEL: Your Honor, we would submit that he would not
for the very reason that he is a citizen, as the Supreme
Court stated in *Milligan*. In that case, Lambdin Milligan
was viewed as a spy. He in fact entered an arsenal in the
Union State of Indiana and relieved not only prisoners of
war but arms from this arsenal to carry secretly across the
Indiana state line, and certainly was acting in the interest
of the rebel side in this case. He was, in the Supreme
Court's opinion, very clearly entitled to, and should have
undergone, a civil trial, and that is what we ask for Dr.
Mudd.

JUDGE RE: Ms. Steel, is there any allegation or any proof that at any time Dr. Mudd served in any capacity as a spy?

MS. STEEL: No sir, and there is no proof in any way that he served as a member of any military or army or naval forces either.

JUDGE RE: You would therefore conclude that whatever military powers would exist over a spy would not apply to Dr. Mudd.

MS. STEEL: That's correct, Your Honor. With regard to the statement that I have just made, about the citizenship and requirements of Dr. Mudd, that argument was made in fact on December — I mean on May 10, 1865, on the same day that the trial opened in the Mudd case — the Hunter Commission trial opened. That argument was made however by Mr. Field on behalf of Mr. Milligan, and we would submit that our argument is entirely parallel to that of Mr. Milligan; and the court in *Milligan* stated that the military commission did not and would not have jurisdiction over Mr. Milligan. There is argument or suggestion from the Government that necessity overrides the right of a citizen to be tried by a civil court, and we would submit that, the courts in Indiana, as well as in Maryland and the District of Columbia being open, fully operational, (and, in fact, as Attorney General Speed conceded, the courts were open and operating in the District of Columbia) there was, in fact, no military necessity for overtaking the right of the civil court to try Dr. Mudd or any other person charged with similar crimes.

JUDGE COX: Was there any effort by Dr. Mudd or Mr. Ewing to enjoin this prosecution, relying on *Milligan* — to these courts that were open and in business?

MS. STEEL: I would urge the court to read both the arguments of Thomas Ewing and of Senator Reverdy Johnson, very thorough and very learned arguments on the jurisdictional question, which were made at the outset of the commission and again at the close of the commission before the decision was rendered, and they were ...

JUDGE COX: Was a habeas corpus petition brought in the United States District Court for the District of Columbia or in the original jurisdiction of the United States Supreme Court to release him?

MS. STEEL: Your Honor, I'm not certain — there may have already been a *habeas* petition filed but I'm not sure that a decision has been issued or if it has, if it can be located — on behalf of Dr. Mudd.

JUDGE COX: I didn't mean ... I'm aware of one that may have been filed subsequent to the trial, but I'm talking contemporaneous with the trial.

MS. STEEL: No, I don't believe so. There were, I believe, with regard to other parties and ...

JUDGE COX: Doesn't that belie your argument that the courts were open and in business if Dr. Mudd did not attempt to take advantage of these open courts to give him some relief?

MS. STEEL: Your Honor, there was an attempt made by other parties before the court who declined to do so based on President Lincoln's suspension of the writ, and, as the court is aware, in 1863 Congress ratified President Lincoln's authority to suspend the writ of habeas corpus.

JUDGE COX: But hadn't that suspension been declared illegal by another federal court in the *Merryman* case or some other cases of that era?

MS. STEEL: Whether or not it had been declared illegal, the court, Your Honor, was not able to enforce a writ if it were to be issued. The court can issue a writ and it not be returned.

JUDGE COX: That clearly would be an issue for us ...

MS. STEEL: Right.

JUDGE COX: If one had been issued and they disobeyed it.

MS. STEEL: Right — right.

JUDGE RE: Ms. Steel, would it have not hurt whether or not he took advantage of the civil courts if the commission that tried and convicted Dr. Mudd had no jurisdiction in fact over the subject matter?

MS. STEEL: No. We would submit that it does not and that this court has authority at any time to take a look at the jurisdiction of this commission — jurisdiction is the perennial question that we hope the court will look at now.

JUDGE COX: You urged us to read some material — what might be extremely helpful, I'm sure that you've read, would be the Petition of Mr. David Dudley Field, whose petition I think could have practically been used here.

MS. STEEL: Your Honor, I had just transposed a good portion of that argument before the questions began. Five of those paragraphs were in fact from Mr. Field's argument, because they were so clearly in support of Dr. Mudd.

As stated by Mr. Ewing — in fact in his argument on the plea to the jurisdiction as well, he stated that:

The Judge Advocate has been unable in the cases of *Arnold* and *Mudd* to present any evidence remotely approaching that prescribed by the Constitution and the laws as a condition of conviction. And yet I am led to infer that he will claim a conviction of one or both of them on the proof presented. What is the profession on this and the other side of the Atlantic to think of such administration of criminal jurisprudence? For this, the first of our state trials, will be read with avidity everywhere. I ask the officers of the government to think of this carefully now, lest two or three years hence they may not like to hear it named.

We would submit that we are now two or three years hence from the trial of Dr. Mudd. The court can look back and see that the circumstances which applied at the close of the war — the war, which it is our position, was over at the time of Dr. Mudd's trial — in fact, if there was a danger in Washington, D.C., it was from the Union troops gathering in Washington, D.C. to celebrate the close of war, not a threat from the South. As the *Milligan* court stated, the threat must be immediate and imminent to justify any necessity for taking over from the courts. As the court said in *Milligan*: If Society is disturbed by civil commotion, if the passions of men are aroused and the restraints of law weakened, if not disregarded, these safeguards need and should receive the watchful care of those entrusted with the guardianship of the Constitution and laws. In no other way can we transmit to posterity unimpaired the blessings of liberty, consecrated by the sacrifices of the Revolution.

And we would submit, Your Honors, that the fundamental principles upon which our nation was founded are set forth in the Declaration of Independence. Among the insufferable abuses and and usurpations of the King which required the dissolution of the historical band with England the founders set forth the following: [the King] has obstructed the Administration of Justice, by refusing his Assent to Laws for establishing Judiciary Powers; he has made Judges dependent on his Will alone ... and he has affected to render the Military independent of and superior to the Civil Power.

As stated by our late President, ours is "a government of the people, by the people and for the people;" to replace that principle with the unprincipled doctrine of military necessity would be to abandon our liberties, rendering the deaths of our countrymen in our great civil war truly in vain. And, Your Honor, we would ask that the court uphold the Constitution that was so carefully and painfully and strugglingly achieved, defended in the Revolution, and surviving the Civil War and ask that the court show that this country can maintain a Constitutional government which has a balance of power, the tension between those powers providing the life to that Constitution and protecting the interests and the rights of the citizens of that country.

Thank you very much.

MR. BAILEY: If it please the court, despite the able argument of my distinguished colleague on the vital question of jurisdiction, we would not have it thought that Dr. Mudd seeks to escape conviction on some technicality; because what flowed from the perversion that was involved in abridging the Constitution and using a military commission is one sledge-hammer after another of corruption of the very things the Constitution was intended to protect, and it produced an unjust and inaccurate result. And I shall cover those points. Before doing so, I should like to point out respectfully to Judge Cox that the great writ — the great protector — was totally flaccid in these times. Indeed Mary Surratt's last act before she was hanged was to invoke the great writ only to be told through the court that it was suspended and could not come to her aid. Now, in order to find out what Dr. Mudd confronted because of the course taken by President Johnson (which indeed would have offended President Lincoln very gravely as he was a great lawyer), start with the final argument of that most distinguished counsel who at the age of 34, not only was a brilliant advocate and a general, but a former supreme court justice of the Territory of Kansas. He began by saying to the Commission: I don't know what I'm on trial here for. All I can do is argue the contingencies: If you are trying me for treason you lack two witnesses or an open court confession. If you are trying me for murder I was in Maryland, six hours away. If you are trying me for accessory before the fact, there isn't enough evidence to hang a titmouse on, and if you are trying me for accessory after the fact (obviously they weren't in view of the punishment), you don't have enough there.

John Wilkes Booth could not have known, if it please the court, that he was going to catch his boot and his spur in a flag as he jumped from the box to the stage and break his leg, and therefore had no reason to line up a co-conspiritorial doctor in the State of Maryland to whom he could flee for assistance. The hard evidence in this case shows and shows only that Dr. Mudd was a physician who knew Booth because he had met him once before and to whom he went for help before the news of the assassination or the identity of the perpetrator could possibly have reached Charles County; indeed, so relaxed was Booth about that aspect of his protection, lacking the fast communications which I'm sure some day this country will enjoy, that he even stayed on for a period of hours after being treated.

Now, when defense counsel makes his appearance one day before the evidence starts, there should be a great deal of suspicion in the mind of any appellate court about due process. Or if, as the prosecution seeks to persuade this court, due process does not apply, and reasonable doubt doesn't apply, they at least concede that some degree of fundamental fairness has its place, even in a military commission constituted of subordinates of the much-beloved victim who has just been brutally and senselessly assassinated and who are anything but a fair and impartial tribunal.

What in the world was the Government thinking of when it decided to bypass the judiciary in its zeal to quickly bring someone to the bridge of punishment in order to satisfy an outraged public? To impanel this group in the habit of obedience to the Commander in Chief, whose marching orders were written everywhere but on the paper in front of him to render a fair and impartial judgment and to give the defendants an even shot to defend themselves made no sense at all. The only good that flowed from the use of this military commission, when there was no emergency and no exigency, a condition which must always exist if military commissions are to be used instead of juries, the only good to flow from that was the satisfaction of the monumental embarrassment for the lack of security of the President of the United States that allowed him to be killed by an amateur, and the ineptitude of the Army and the setting of his leg by my client.

JUDGE RE: Mr. Bailey.

MR. BAILEY: Yes?

JUDGE RE: Since you have referred to the exigency which is very important ...

MR. BAILEY: Yes, sir.

JUDGE RE: To what extent would you say that this tribunal owes a deference to the determination of the military that says there is a necessity notwithstanding the cessation of hostilities, notwithstanding the fact that the war is physically over — do we owe a deference or may we look into that fact independently, as a matter of standard of review?

MR. BAILEY: Deference must be carefully given from one branch to another; when the judiciary will allow the executive to take over its functions on some ground they boot-strap is ever a danger. So if they can prove with evidence a real exigency why then you can at least undo what they did in haste if it were done unjustly. But I do not believe that my distinguished colleagues have enough to satisfy you that they could not have tried Samuel Mudd before a jury, as, I hasten to point out, John Surratt (captured last November in Europe) is going to be tried by a jury. Would it not look rather terrible, distinguished judges, if in a civilian court the prosecution is unable to convict John Surratt who certainly has evidence allayed against him far more deadly than that looked at for Dr. Mudd? I predict that that is exactly what will happen and any affirmance of these convictions will hold the military tribunal in even lower esteem in this country — something we do not need. This case has rubbed so much lustre from the fledgling jurisprudence of this great country that it needs to be dismantled and put to rest and never used as precedent for anything in the future.

JUDGE EVERETT: You know, in your catalogue of offenses ranging from treason through accessory after the fact, there was one it seemed to me that you omitted, and that's conspiracy. Doesn't the evidence persuasively tie together to show, even using a reasonable doubt standard, that there was a conspiracy and that Dr. Mudd, as one of the co-conspirators, is responsible for the consequences — all of the consequences?

MR. BAILEY: Once again, in a civilian court, had the same result obtained, based on the evidence submitted, one might have confidence that a dispassionate judgment was made. But when the prosecution will bring forward witnesses of the calibre of one Thomas (against the duty of bringing the truth to the court), when twenty of his neighbors testified he's a congenital liar, when his stories were inconsistent, and use that as evidence to convict Dr. Mudd, then I say the evils of the Commission have visited themselves on the procedure and you cannot trust the findings of fact.

JUDGE EVERETT: I want to see if I understand you correctly then. You're conceding basically — I gather — the evidence would be sufficient if presented before a civilian jury, the jury chose to disbelieve the twenty-seven witnesses in favor of the one, they would be empowered to do that and that an appellate court could properly affirm. You're saying that the evidence is insufficient because it is before a military tribunal, is that the position?

MR. BAILEY: No. I'm saying that the military tribunal was too insensitive to perjured testimony because it wanted to reach a certain result no jury would ever accept of that witness and, even if they had, this court, on the totality of the evidence, would have concluded that reasonable men could not have found beyond a reasonable doubt that that evidence was sufficient to support a conspiracy conviction with a sentence of life hanging from it. And reasonable doubt, if it please the court, is the Achilles heel of my opponent. Nowhere is it shown that that standard was applied and yet it is universal in criminal cases in this country and can never, never be abridged.

JUDGE RE: Mr. Bailey, even if the proof were to be conclusive, that would in no way justify or make legal — or am I wrong in my belief — the conclusion that would inevitably follow if your co-counsel's point is correct: that there was no jurisdiction to try him, and there was no jurisdiction, regardless of the crime, regardless of the nature of the offense, regardless of the proof. It would be *non coram judice*. Forgive the Latin, but I use that because reference was made to Magna Carta, which is also the Latin phrase there, "Per Legem Terrae," which means the law of the land, and under the law of the land, if this tribunal had no jurisdiction over Dr. Mudd — he was to be tried by the civil courts where the offense was allegedly committed.

MR. BAILEY: I certainly concede the fact that the argument of my co-counsel should have mooted mine by now; however, I think it fair to point out that this is a real evil that flows from the use of these commissions and not a technical evil of which we are trying to take advantage. This was a hurry-up, slam-dunk proceeding. Dr. Mudd should have stood trial alone. Had he done so, even this commission might have not had the temerity to find him guilty. I say they were ...

JUDGE RE: Mr. Bailey, you'll have to forgive me. The only reason I take this view is because — a view that I must admit that I have arrived at that would have absolutely nothing to do with the total integrity and faith and loyalty of the officers and the others that presided. My question really would in no way cast any aspersion upon either motives or the genuine contribution made by military officers who believe they are carrying out their duty. Isn't that why we have the independent judiciary to which Ms. Steel refers? It's interesting. She referred to the Declaration of Independence because that did nothing more than bring to the United States something that had happened in Great Britain in 1701 with the Act of Settlement that made the British judges independent — something that we find enshrined in Article III of our Constitution.

MR. BAILEY: Yes, sir. No attack whatsoever of an *ad hominem* nature is visited upon any member of the commission or the prosecutors. It is the institutional evil that I attack and that is giving the executive the power to seek retribution for an insult to the executive. That's what tripartite government is all about: the safeguards, such as you three gentlemen on the bench who say, "Hold on here. Have you overacted? Have you too swiftly exacted your punishment when this is to be a cool, calm, dispassionate and balanced procedure before we deprive a citizen of life or liberty?" — both of which have occurred here. This was the wrong road to take and, in retrospect, I think there are few arguments that can countervail that notion.

JUDGE COX: Mr. Bailey, if I could return to the morning of April the 15th, I believe it was, when Dr. Mudd treated Mr. Booth. Had there been evidence of record that he knew of the assassination, and that — not because he treated him, but because it is alleged and evidence is there he showed him a secret route out of the swamp, or something of that nature — wouldn't a reasonable inference be drawn that he was aiding and abetting after the fact?

MR. BAILEY: I would say that that would satisfy ...

JUDGE COX: Had he expressed an opinion earlier that he wanted — that he had no problems with the President being killed and so forth, and knew Mr. Booth, and now knew of the assassination?

MR. BAILEY: We overlooked the fact, perhaps historically, that not everyone loved President Lincoln. And he wasn't required to, as long as he didn't take action against him. Now your specific question is, of course, right on the money. If he knew that he was dealing with an assassin — it didn't have to be of a President ...

JUDGE COX: But isn't it reasonable to infer, based upon his prior conversations with Booth, his familiarity with the Surratts, and the fact that Booth was there for some time, that Booth would have revealed to him exactly what he had done?

MR. BAILEY: No, it isn't reasonable, Your Honor, because Booth continued to wear his beard throughout the encounter, and if they were in league together, he hardly needed to try to disguise himself from his confederate. I think the evidence is that this doctor was awakened at four in the morning, confronted by an injured man with a broken leg — there is no suggestion that assassination is the reason for this injury; this was no gunshot wound — and he obeyed his Hippocratic oath, and that is what he has maintained ever since that event. He only learned after Booth was on his way — of course with his assistance — that the President was dead, and the name of the suspected assassin. You will recall from the record it is clear that it was first thought that an assassin, a professional named Boyle, had done the deed, and that was the talk in Bryantown initially and that's what Mudd would have heard.

JUDGE RE: Mr. Bailey, one thing about that, though, gives me concern. The doctor wakes up at 4:00 a.m. He takes care of the patient pursuant to the Hippocratic oath; but then the patient says, "Can you show me a secret route?" That's not the ordinary patient-physician relationship. What sort of inference can be drawn from that — a secret route through a swamp?

MR. BAILEY: I most respectfully, Your Honor, must nitpick your choice of one word. David Herold, not Booth, said, "Can you show me a *short* route" — not a *secret* route; and in the days before we had faster transportation, short routes were always to be coveted. So I think that, in and of itself, would not be enough to tip a man into the state of *mens rea* necessary to the conviction of a crime.

Now, in summary, many criminal cases that look like they have some substance to them and, if you believe all the witnesses that the prosecution rousted up, despite the many more witnesses that said they were not believable at all and despite the inconsistencies in their stories, you might be suspicious that Samuel Mudd was something more than a friend of the cause of the South. Indeed, history shows that he attended Georgetown as did many Confederates; in those days it was handy to hang people just for going to Georgetown. But, the fabric of any criminal proceeding is that which deserves the overview — the calm, deliberate, combined wisdom in the overview of an appellate court. This is simply a safeguard which the military has finally learned, that, when there is no need for immediate action — there is no battlefield requirement for a firing squad to stop a wave of desertions (not present here) that if, in scrutiny, there is doubt on the part of the court that the system has been played to the melody rather than discord, the price is simple. The re-trial of Samuel Mudd before his jury, as his colleague — John Surratt — is about to be tried, will not disrupt the United States, bring it to the brink of war, or bankrupt its coffers. And if he is re-convicted on some definable charge, having had the opportunity to know the charge, prepare his case, and confront the charge before what this country was formed for — a jury of his peers — then, should the case go to another appellate court, they may, with somewhat greater comfort than I think anyone here should feel, say maybe indeed there is enough and Samuel Mudd is a criminal. If he is a criminal, the life sentence he has received — and I don't concede that for a minute — the life sentence he has received is totally disproportionate to that which was shown, and that is that he fixed the leg of the most notorious and vile assassin in the history of this country. If you find that he knew, or should have known — and this is a dangerous standard to use in criminal cases, but it occasionally creeps into our law —knew or should have known because he cannot be an ostrich — that this was an assassin — he gave him aid and comfort — he fulfills the common law elements of accessory after the fact and that is what he should be tried for and nothing more. I respectfully suggest that this record will not support such a conclusion and that, even if it would, the numerous abridgements of the very rights that the Constitution sought to safeguard such as trial for treason — bear in mind those who wrote the Constitution were very mindful about that offense because they expected they might be tried for it, if we lost the war, and so they carefully cracked it out — an elaborate set of safeguards. That was their state of mind. If we're to give all of those up because in reaction to an angry populus, a successor and not terribly popular President and Attorney General decide to move swiftly in a definitive way to assure that justice will have someone to fry, then we have simply given up a large chunk of what the Revolutionary War was all about.

Thank you.

JUDGE EVERETT: We will pause for a moment before hearing from Appellee.

JUDGE EVERETT: We'll hear now from the Government.

COLONEL DOUGLASS: May it please the court. I'm Colonel
Douglass, and I am representing the Government as a
respondent and will be assisted by Admiral Jenkins in part
of the argument.

On April 2, 1865, the valiant men of the Army of Northern
Virginia withdrew from the fortifications around this city
in which we now sit. And a few days later, on April 9th,
their gallant leader, Robert E. Lee, surrendered his army at
Appomattox Court House. General Lee and his army
were treated with the honor they deserved for their coura-
geous and chivalrous struggle during the years of war.
There remained other armies in the field. At that same
moment, a sinister and despicable group of men and
women, who scorned to fight in uniform, were clandes-
tinely and secretly plotting and planning to continue the
war, not as honorable soldiers, but as assassins and kid-
nappers who strike in the night. Their plans were long
considered. And their purpose was not to seek victory on
the battlefield but rather to achieve their goals by treach-
ery, deceit, kidnapping and murder. Their plans were
more than a reversal of the loss suffered by General Lee
and his troops but were schemes for revenge. They conspired to destroy the very fabric of government and to
create chaos and disorder. The conspirators acted not
with the gallantry, the integrity, and the honor and the
courage of Robert E. Lee and his generals, but as assassins.

Who were these who plotted to destroy the structure? Who
were these despicable characters who designed a blue-
print to murder the Commander in Chief? Who were these
who schemed to kill all of those in the line of succession?
Who were these who planned the death of the very military commander who had granted the Army of Northern
Virginia surrender terms with honor? Who were these
who conspired to betray and besmirch the reputation and
respect of the soldiers? These conspirators were John
Wilkes Booth, Mary Surratt, John Surratt, David Herold,
George Atzerodt, Lewis Payne, and Dr. Samuel Mudd.
They committed no ordinary crime as it is defined in the
brief. They instead conspired and committed an offense

decried by every civilized nation on the earth. They planned and committed an offense which placed them under the jurisdiction of a military commission, like thousands of others who had committed similar offenses in violation of the law of war during the terrible years of conflict.

The petitioner in his arguments to this honorable court would lead the court down not one but several rabbit trails in arguing against jurisdiction of the military commission. Petitioner has asserted the accused were charged with treason, and therefore the Constitution changes the venue of jurisdiction. Petitioner asserts that there was no state of war to authorize the establishment of the commission, and to the contrary then argues that the war had been concluded. Petitioner asserts that as a citizen of Maryland, the petitioner could not be tried in the city of Washington. Petitioner argues that no overt act of the conspiracy was committed in Maryland and thereby separated him from the other conspirators. Let us not be misled. The issues are clear. The commission was an Article One court. This court before whom we stand today is an Article One court. The petitioner was charged with conspiracy to kill the Commander in Chief, his successor Vice President, the Secretary of State, and the General-in-Chief of the Army. The petitioner was tried before a military commission which liberally granted him rights: the right to counsel, to an open and speedy trial, with the right to bring competent witnesses before the tribunal, and the right to argument by counsel. And, finally, the petitioner was tried by a tribunal recognized by the Constitution, by the Congress, by the executive and by the courts of the United States as the appropriate and proper tribunal for violations of the law of war committed by one not in military service.

Let us begin by reminding the court that petitioner was charged with conspiracy. A reading of the charges and specifications is clear and unambiguous. In a colloquy between counsel for defendant and the Judge Advocate, the Judge Advocate was unequivocal that this was a charge of conspiracy. Significantly, General Ewing did not seek an explanation of the charge against which he must defend until after he had presented his case in the defense of Dr. Mudd. Were General Ewing and the defendant confused, surely they would have made this inquiry before presenting the case to the Commission. The petitioner in his brief seeks to define the charge by extrapolating from the words "treacherously" and "traitorously" to change the charge to treason. Making this incredible leap, he would then insist that there are Constitutional provisions for the trial of treason which are required for the trial of this petitioner. Manipulating the words does not change the charge, nor change the jurisdiction. When a conspiracy has been created, each of the conspirators is bound by the acts, declarations and crimes of each other member done or made in furtherance of that criminal agreement. The conspirators sought to destroy the leadership of the Union government by destroying the effectiveness of the Presidency and the Commander in Chief. And it was against that agency that the conspiracy was directed.

JUDGE EVERETT: Let me ask you this, however. Was there any showing or any allegation that any of these alleged conspirators were acting in behalf of the rebel forces of the South — the erstwhile insurgent government in the South — was there any allegation of a connection?

COLONEL DOUGLASS: There was an allegation, yes, that they were acting in conjunction with numerous members of the government of the Confederacy.

JUDGE EVERETT: So is it your contention they were in the same position as a spy would be? Is there any evidence of that, as for example, Major André who was acting in behalf of the British government in Revolutionary times? I think you cited his case as a precedent.

COLONEL DOUGLASS: I would point out that there were two thousand cases tried by military commissions during the late war. They were tried for all sorts of violations of the laws of war, whether it was spying or whatever the violation of the law of war, when they were non-combatants, as were these conspirators. They fit, therefore, in the jurisdiction of a military commission.

JUDGE RE: Dean Douglass, you have to forgive me. I listened most attentively to what you have said as to the importance of facts and the period of history. Suppose, for purpose of my question, I were to concede that what you say as to the nature of the charges — am I not correct that there was a surrender on April 9th — you have made reference to that very significant day in the history of our country. Is it not also true that on April 29th the President revoked the proclamation dealing with a blockade? Now that would seem to be some evidence that perhaps the war was over, and therefore I return to the question that was asked previously: What was the basis of the military trial?

COLONEL DOUGLASS: The war, Sir, had not been completed. Hostilities had not ceased. During the ... the leadership of the Confederacy had not yet at this time ever conceded the surrender. It was only the surrender of the Army of Northern Virginia. General Kirby Smith remained with an army; General Hood remained with an army ...

JUDGE RE: Excuse me then — because this to me is tremendously important, and even more important than I had imagined when you tell me that this happened to two thousand others. That really requires that we read and re-read the opinion in *Ex parte Milligan* as to the proper division of authority between the military and the civilian courts. What was there that you wished to bring to our attention that would indicate that it was not possible to have granted Dr. Mudd a proper trial as required by the Constitution before a jury at the place where the crime was allegedly committed — because that goes back to the question of the applicability of *Ex parte Milligan*? And you will forgive me for that if it is going to be covered by Admiral Jenkins, I do not know, however. That to me is the question.

COLONEL DOUGLASS: There is no question that this commission was convened by the highest authority of the Union Army — the commander in chief of that army. And so the jurisdiction was not limited to the city of Washington but included all the theater of operations.

Let me talk for a moment about *Ex parte Milligan*. *Ex parte Milligan* was a case brought on a habeas corpus as you well know. The question was asked by your colleague as to why this was not done in the case of Dr. Mudd. It should be pointed out that in *Ex parte Milligan* the court presented two prongs as denying the authority of a military commis-

sion. One, that the civil courts were open; but the other
prong was that it not be a locale of war. Certainly the area,
the city of Washington, even in the days of April and May
and June of 1865 continued to be a locale of war. The very
purpose of this conspiracy was to continue the war; to
make it possible for the Confederacy to continue to seek
the separation that they desired; to continue the operation
to break up the Union. There were armies still in operation. There were sea battles still being fought as late as a
year later. There were still fights. There were still con-
flicts. There were still battles in Texas well after the end of
this trial.

JUDGE RE: I'm not familiar with the situation in Texas. I
should like to ask what were the battles and where were
they being fought on June 28, 1865 when Dr. Mudd, a
civilian, I would gather not a spy, not an insurgent, yet, a
sympathizer of different point of view, was convicted and
found guilty of charges that sound pretty much like treason although you are absolutely right, it was a conspiracy.
What can you tell us as a factual matter that would warrant a disruption and dislocation of the ordinary procedure, namely the civil courts within the meaning and
express language of *Ex parte Milligan* ? Were the courts
operating in Washington, D.C. and in Maryland where the
offense allegedly ...

COLONEL DOUGLASS: The courts were operating in the
city of Washington and had operated throughout the
period of the war. As a matter of fact, they had tried, as is
pointed out in the brief of Dr. Mudd, that these courts
were trying "ordinary crimes" during all this entire period. Hostilities had not ceased throughout. There was a
surrender of the Army of Northern Virginia, but there was
not a surrender of the army of General Hood; there was
not a surrender of the army of General Johnston; there was
not a surrender of the army of General Kirby Smith.

JUDGE RE: Are you telling this court that the surrender by
General Lee did not effectively represent a surrender of
the insurgent forces, if I may use that phrase?

COLONEL DOUGLASS: It did not end the insurrection. It
did not end the establishment of the Confederacy. Yes, sir,
I am telling you that it did not end the hostilities which

were between the South and the North in the period from 1861 to 1865.

JUDGE EVERETT: Would it be correct, Colonel Douglass, after the Confederate government left Richmond, they went to Greensboro, there were still operating forces in the Carolinas and elsewhere at that point. Was that true as of the time of the attempted assassination?

COLONEL DOUGLASS: Yes. And there were battles fought by Union and Southern forces well into the period after the conclusion of this trial.

JUDGE RE: In Maryland?

COLONEL DOUGLASS: Not in Maryland.

JUDGE RE: In the District of Columbia?

COLONEL DOUGLASS: Nor in the District of Columbia. But there was no evidence that there would not be an attempt by Southern forces to attack one of the sixty forts surrounding the State of Maryland. And you read the *Ex parte Milligan*, they make clear that there was never a locale of war in Indiana. This is not true of Maryland. This is not of the city of Washington. It was not a situation that involved ... it was not the same situation as in *Ex parte Milligan* and this particular military commission which tried these conspirators.

JUDGE COX: Dean Douglass, one concern I have had throughout this. None of the authorities that I've seen cited, or none of the argument, has focused on the fact that we're talking about a rebellion within the territory of one country.

COLONEL DOUGLASS: Yes, sir.

JUDGE COX: We're not talking about one recognized sovereign at war with another recognized sovereign.

COLONEL DOUGLASS: Yes, sir.

JUDGE COX: It would seem that these principles that we're grappling today would be equally applicable for a civilian insurrection in the city of Washington where — or anywhere — where there was no civil law functioning.

COLONEL DOUGLASS: That's correct, sir.

JUDGE COX: The leader could declare martial law.

COLONEL DOUGLASS: Let me make that clear, sir.

JUDGE COX: If that were the case, it seems that your best argument is that within the boundaries of what was then the United States of America, the civil authorities had not yet been settled.

COLONEL DOUGLASS: That's correct.

JUDGE COX: And while you might have a court in the District of Columbia, throughout the nation as a nation, civil obedience still had not been restored. We were still ... and therefore the military commission still had a constitutional place.

COLONEL DOUGLASS: The danger still existed for the people, for the Union and its continuance during this period. The troops of the South had not totally surrendered; there was not a capitulation by all of those involved.

JUDGE EVERETT: What if the assassination had occurred, let's say, in July of 1865, at a time when all the effective opposition from Southern forces had ceased, even General Smith down in Texas, and there were only a few privateers or vessels sailing around. Would you still maintain that there was jurisdiction ... of a military tribunal at that point?

COLONEL DOUGLASS: You present to me a hypothetical situation, Your Honor, that I am unprepared really to determine, not knowing the situation which had developed that had convinced these particular conspirators to continue their operation and to seek to continue the hostilities. What they were seeking to do was make certain that those Southern forces could be rejuvenated and continue the battle. This was the whole idea of the destruction of and the killing of the President and the Vice President. They were seeking not merely revenge. They weren't doing this for some purpose of merely killing the President. They were seeking to do this in order to continue the war ... and to continue the battles, and to continue the hostilities, so that their side — the side which they supported — could be continued in office.

JUDGE EVERETT: So you would concede then, that, under your law of war approach, there would have to be some relationship of this particular activity to organized Southern resistance in an attempt to overthrow the Union government.

COLONEL DOUGLASS: I don't think there's any question

that there has to be a continuation of the possibility of hostilities which would create the necessity for a continuation of military service and military forces to protect the Union.

JUDGE EVERETT: So the fact that President Johnson did not terminate martial law until some months later would really be irrelevant. It would be the question of how the defendants, the alleged conspirators, viewed themselves as participating in an effort to continue hostilities.

COLONEL DOUGLASS: Correct.

JUDGE RE: This would be quite independent of the honorable surrender by General Lee. In the minds of some this would cast some serious doubt as to the nature and the honor of the surrender. You mean, notwithstanding the surrender, there were still pockets that were going to keep fighting?

COLONEL DOUGLASS: That is correct.

JUDGE RE: You surely would not have us infer with the consent and approval of General Lee that ...

COLONEL DOUGLASS: There's no question that General Lee had surrendered the Army of Northern Virginia, but he had no authority to surrender the armies of other commanders. He had no authority to give up the government of the Confederacy which escaped from Richmond and did not continue with him, but evacuated to the South.

JUDGE RE: Let me ask you this factual question, since you obviously know more about it than I do: As of the time of the trial, and as of the date of conviction of Dr. Mudd, what was the state of the public danger, as that phrase is known, in either Washington, D.C. or Maryland? What was the public danger that warranted the supplanting of the normal usual civil authority by the military forces, bringing about what is in fact, what might be properly called, a dictatorship by the military ... warranted because of the necessity?

COLONEL DOUGLASS: We have a tendency to walk down another rabbit trail when we become concerned about "dictatorship of the military." It was the civilian President of the United States who ordered this military commission. It was not a military commander who ordered this. It was ... Under the Constitution, it was provided that the

Commander in Chief is a civilian and is the President.
Now, to get back to your question, your original question
was what was the danger of hostilities? There was considerable danger that — those people in charge (the military
forces) were concerned that — still there remained a viable
and possible Confederate force which might attack any
place across the country. Granted that it was not close to
Washington at this point, but it had not been close to
Washington when they surrounded ... two years before
when they came up behind and attacked Gettysburg,
which is far to the north.

JUDGE RE: You speak of potential, my question was: What
was there that warranted depriving this citizen, this resident of a state loyal to the Union, the rights guaranteed to
him by the Constitution — including trial by jury?

COLONEL DOUGLASS: Well, that, if I may say so, tends to
beg the question, because first of all we have to decide
whether he is being ... he is subject to trial by a military
commission and then we have the question ...

JUDGE RE: On whom does that burden fall, Colonel Douglass?

COLONEL DOUGLASS: Pardon, Sir?

JUDGE RE: On whom does that burden fall? Need he prove
that there is no jurisdiction or may the Government prove
that there is jurisdiction to try a civilian — not a spy, not
any of the other things — by a military commission?

COLONEL DOUGLASS: There's no question that he was a
civilian. There's no question that he was a non-combatant.
There is no question that he was charged with a conspiracy to violate the law of war. No one can argue these
points. It seems clear. Based thereon, he is then subject to
trial before a military commission in a time in which there
is still a danger to the continuation of the government of
the United States. And there was that danger because this
was the very purpose of the conspiracy.

JUDGE RE: I hate to repeat my question — and I do not wish
to belabor the point, but we are used to dealing with
burdens of proof. Need I prove myself innocent or must
you prove me guilty? Then we go to the next question of
by what standard? What is the case that can be made by
the government that he could have been lawfully tried by
a military commission, at that time and at that place?

COLONEL DOUGLASS: There remained an insurrection; there remained the fact that he was charged with a violation of the law of war; there remained the fact that he was a non-combatant who sought to continue the war and to continue it with the aim of supporting those in insurrection.

JUDGE RE: You say the necessity continued?

COLONEL DOUGLASS: Yes, Sir.

JUDGE COX: Don't the very facts of this case prove your point?

COLONEL DOUGLASS: I thought I was saying that ...

JUDGE COX: The military was viewing that there were pockets of conspirators still out to destroy the government.

COLONEL DOUGLASS: Yes, Sir.

JUDGE COX: And therefore they founded their jurisdiction on that public danger?

COLONEL DOUGLASS: Yes, Sir.

JUDGE COX: Let me ask you a question. You made a very eloquent opening argument about the despicable nature of the conspirator and so forth. What evidence could a rational fact-finder in this case pin his or her hat on?

COLONEL DOUGLASS: Pardon me, I'm sorry.

JUDGE COX: What evidence could a rational fact-finder in this case say shows that Dr. Mudd was participating in a despicable conspiracy? Is there anyone who says he was there at the planning? Any evidence?

COLONEL DOUGLASS: We know that the law of conspiracy can be proved by circumstantial evidence.

JUDGE COX: Granted.

COLONEL DOUGLASS: Those who commit a conspiracy do not do it in the open and provide us with the kind of open evidence — so we have to go on circumstantial evidence. We know that Dr. Mudd met with John Wilkes Booth on more than one occasion in Maryland.

JUDGE COX: That was a year or so before the ...

COLONEL DOUGLASS: No, it was only several months before, Sir.

JUDGE COX: Okay.

COLONEL DOUGLASS: Ah, if I may — Dr. Mudd talked to Mr. John Wilkes Booth in his own home. Booth came to

Maryland on some flimsy excuse of buying real estate for doing some oil exploration — the kind of thing that people talk about when they're seeking to hide their real purpose. Dr. Mudd met with Mr. Booth and introduced him to John Surratt, another member of the conspiracy, in the city of Washington.

Dr. Mudd's home, which was pointed out, is off the main road, was found by John Wilkes Booth and Mr. Herold at four o'clock in the morning as they rode through, trying to escape. Does one find a doctor that he never has heard of or met before, has no relationship to, at that time of day off the main road? Does one take a patient and put him upstairs in his upstairs bedroom and take care of him over night and into the next day? Does one who does not have any relationship with a patient point out that he should go across a swamp, tear down a fence, in order to move to the next safe haven? I say that these facts all show the relationship of John Wilkes Booth and the other conspirators with Dr. Mudd. I think it is plainly obvious from these relationships that he was a part of the conspiracy.

JUDGE COX: But if you're using circumstantial evidence and there is a contrary inference of innocence, to what extent can we use that circumstantial evidence? Where there is no direct evidence to corroborate any of this — there's no statement by Mudd that he was aware of the assassination, there's no evidence at all to tie it all back together.

COLONEL DOUGLASS: We need no direct evidence to prove the conspiracy because the law provides that we may do this by circumstantial evidence, and it seems abundantly clear that there's much circumstantial evidence to tie Dr. Mudd to the conspiracy.

JUDGE EVERETT: Now, *apropos* the conspiracy, I gather from your earlier remarks, your earlier argument, that the purpose of the conspiracy is material in establishing jurisdiction. It has to be more than a conspiracy to exact vengeance; there has to be a conspiracy to interfere with the government and the military operations of the United States government.

COLONEL DOUGLASS: Sir.

JUDGE EVERETT: All right. And that something would have to be established as a jurisdictional fact at trial. Would that be true?

COLONEL DOUGLASS: Yes, Sir.

JUDGE EVERETT: Now, what is there that shows that this was a conspiracy for that particular purpose, as distinguished from mere vengeance?

COLONEL DOUGLASS: They sought to kill the President of the United States. The conspirators attacked the Secretary of State in his bed. Another conspirator stalked the Vice President of the United States, and there was a plan clearly by one of the members to kill the General-in-Chief of the Armies, General Grant. This was the top leadership of the entire Union government in the executive branch. It was not simply vengeance against Abraham Lincoln. It was an attempt to kill President Lincoln, the Vice President, the Secretary of State, and the General-in-Chief of the Armies — all of those who could bring order out of chaos should only the President have been killed.

JUDGE COX: And your contention is that Dr. Mudd's role in the conspiracy was to provide a safe haven for the conspirators? They certainly, as Mr. Bailey argues, could not foresee that he would break his leg. I mean, did they say: "If anybody gets injured, Dr. Mudd, then you will agree to treat him?" Is that what he did in the conspiracy?

COLONEL DOUGLASS: No. Obviously that was fortuitous. He could well have agreed. I don't know all of his participation, but once one joins a conspiracy, then he becomes responsible for all of the acts of any of the conspirators. We don't need an overt act, but, here, this case abounds in overt acts committed by the various conspirators. And he is responsible therefore for whatever took place under that conspiracy.

JUDGE COX: I agree with you that it abounds with overt acts, but where in the record can we point to with some comfort, much less beyond reasonable doubt, as to what Dr. Mudd's participation and agreement was in the conspiracy. What did he agree to do? What did he agree to contribute?

COLONEL DOUGLASS: Dr. Mudd was one station on the route from Washington to Surrattsville to Bryantown to Port Tobacco to Virginia, at which place ...

JUDGE COX: Because he was a safe haven?

COLONEL DOUGLASS: He was a safe haven. And one that

was easily found, apparently, by [Mr. Booth] and Mr. Herold as they escaped at four o'clock in the morning off the main road.

JUDGE COX: What testimony proves this?

COLONEL DOUGLASS: This again is proven by the very fact that Booth and Herold were able to find this safe haven in the middle of the night when they were escaping down through Maryland into Virginia, and that's the way they were going. We know that during this whole period of the war this part of southern Maryland was the highway for those spies and for contraband from Washington into Virginia and into Richmond.

JUDGE EVERETT: No indication that Dr. Mudd was involved in any of that, was there? With that particular route?

COLONEL DOUGLASS: There is no indication ... there is nothing in this record of trial which presents Mr. Mudd as a part of that route or participating in it.

Thank you, gentlemen.

ADMIRAL JENKINS: May it please the court. I am Rear Admiral John Jenkins, and I appear with my friend, Colonel Douglass, on behalf of the United States. I wonder if it might be helpful for the court if, in view of some of the questions that have been asked, we fall back just one step or two and look at the issue as I see it presented to us. We have talked, we have answered questions on both sides with respect to the appropriateness, if you will, of an Article I military commission having heard this case as compared to an Article III civil court operating normally.

I would call the court's attention to the language first of Section 8 of Article I of the Constitution, which provides that there be rules made for the government of the land and naval forces. It also provides in Section 8 a reference to the law of nations. Article I stands for the proposition that the executive can create a system of courts, tribunals, commissions — call them what you will — when Article I is applicable with respect to, for instance, a situation involving martial law.

JUDGE EVERETT: Let's just pause for a second, Admiral Jenkins. That Article I, Section 8 provision requires, as I recall, an action by Congress, doesn't it? And what is the Congressional action that would be the basis for this particular court, and to whatever extent you are invoking law of war jurisdiction?

ADMIRAL JENKINS: In this case, and I think the authors and the treatises in the early 30s and 40s — 1830 — 1840 — would stand for this proposition. Indeed Congress did enact the Articles for the Government of the Navy and the Articles of War, but there is a common law of military law which applies here. And if the court will look back, for instance, to the British tradition, the British court martial system came from the Crown as the Commander in Chief. The British judicial system came from the Crown as the fount of grace and mercy. So there were two tracks, even in the British system. One, the military track, the sovereign as commander-in-chief. The other, the track to the courts, as the fount of grace and mercy. And that applies in our situation here.

JUDGE EVERETT: There is no federal common law of crime, at least in the Article III courts, is that correct?

ADMIRAL JENKINS: I would agree with that.

JUDGE EVERETT: So you're contending that even though in Article I, Section 8, clause 10, there's a provision for Congress to make provision for offenses against the law of nations, and even though I gather there's no specific reference thereto in either the Articles of War or the Articles for the Government of the Navy, you're saying that, in some way, there exists this common law for which there is no provision in the U.S. Constitution which gives jurisdiction to a military court. Is that the argument?

ADMIRAL JENKINS: I am suggesting to the court that, in addition to the statutory law, there is a common law of military tradition which supports the proposition that there be commissions and indeed expands the law in the area of martial law. The court will note that martial law can be declared in the event, for instance, of a hurricane, or a major flood. It doesn't necessarily require a state of war. So martial law, the law of nations, and military law all merge together to provide a basis under Article I of our Constitution for something such as the military commission.

JUDGE EVERETT: Well, I think we need to separate these out. The military law would apply only to a military person,

which this defendant was not. Martial law, as I understand the *Milligan* case, is a law of necessity. And to
establish that, wouldn't you have to show that the civilian
courts were not functioning — that it was necessary to
proceed in this way?

ADMIRAL JENKINS: Not totally, Your Honor. There is
language in *Milligan* which suggests that, for ordinary
crimes, we look to the issue of the functioning of civilian
courts. We submit, for the matter concerned here, we're
not dealing with an ordinary crime. We know that during
the entire period of hostilities between the states, the civil
courts in the District of Columbia were functioning for
certain purposes. We also know that during that entire
time, there was modified martial law in the District of
Columbia. So I submit that it is not solely a question of one
or the other, but there are situations where both can apply
at the same time.

JUDGE EVERETT: Well, let me ask you this, then. Martial law
can mean many things. It can mean the authority to take
people into custody, but maybe would not require their
being tried. Were there trials of civilians going on under
martial law in the District of Columbia during the recent
war?

ADMIRAL JENKINS: There were, as we have heard from co-
counsel, over two thousand trials by military commission.

JUDGE EVERETT: Not in the District of Columbia though?
Let me be more specific. Was there a single trial that you're
aware of in the District of Columbia predicated on martial
law or the rule of necessity?

ADMIRAL JENKINS: History tells me yes. There were some
simple trials with respect to drunkenness, and disrespect,
which were based on martial law.

JUDGE RE: And those persons were deprived of the Constitutional protections set forth in the Constitution?

ADMIRAL JENKINS: They were tried by Article I institutions
to which the panoply of protections with respect to Article
III do not necessarily apply.

JUDGE RE: So Article I, Section 8, which sets forth the powers
of the Congress were used to deprive... You're telling us
that that provision of the Constitution was used to deprive
American citizens, civilians, of Constitutionally protected

rights, such as a trial by jury, civilian courts with all the protections that were ...

ADMIRAL JENKINS: ... opinion of the Attorney General of the United States with respect to these Article I courts. They are simply an instrumentality for the more efficient execution of the war powers. Congress has generally left it to the President and the military commanders to employ the commission for investigation and punishments of the law of war.

JUDGE RE: Well, you know the opinion of *Milligan* also says that the Constitution applies in time of war as well, and you merely indicate how important this case is, so, if it is part of the war powers, I ask again the question I asked before: What was the war going on in Maryland and in Washington, D.C. at that time?

ADMIRAL JENKINS: I submit that it was a question of fact for the tribunal to establish jurisdiction by ascertaining, as a matter of fact, those indicia which support the Article I military commission having jurisdiction over the case, and I submit on the record that the tribunal did consider enough matters to conclude that it had appropriate Article I jurisdiction. We know, for instance, that there were still naval actions taking place.

JUDGE RE: Where?

ADMIRAL JENKINS: Throughout the Atlantic, there were ...

JUDGE RE: Dr. Mudd was not tried throughout the Atlantic.

ADMIRAL JENKINS: For the purpose of the commission determining that it had jurisdiction, its jurisdiction flowing from the law of nations and the law of war, it is not unreasonable for the commission to consider the fact that there are still naval elements deployed at sea; that there are still Union army elements deployed in battle formation against the insurrectionists, and therefore the commission could conclude under the law of nations and the law of war that there were the kinds of facts available to them to support the conclusion of jurisdiction.

JUDGE RE: Well, Admiral Jenkins, it was precisely for that reason that I asked earlier upon whom is the burden of proof as to the question of necessity which would warrant — and we admit that the necessity exists, no one questions the existence of the power to declare martial law, and we also concede the applicability of the law of nations and the laws of war — the question is, did that apply here, or were there, in this case, what in the *Milligan* case are called distractions, such as the emotions of the moment, the clamor of the moment, and for that reason the Constitution guarantees to civilians the safe haven of independent judiciary?

ADMIRAL JENKINS: I would say to the court that any tribunal does have the responsibility of making a conclusion with respect to the application of its jurisdiction and I would submit to the court that the tribunal below did make such a conclusion.

JUDGE RE: And what is the standard of review? Because that of course was my first question. The second inevitably flows, what is the standard of proof? To what extent do we defer is the question I asked.

ADMIRAL JENKINS: Let me first address His Honor's question with respect to the standard of review. Again, I think we can look to the collection of Anglo-American common law on this issue, as we question the standard of review in a case such as this. I will borrow His Honor's Latin, and say that we might look at a court's approach, admittedly in the civil side, to a judgment *non obstante veredicto*. What would a trial judge do with respect to examining a verdict and changing that verdict? The test seems to be that we would ask ourselves whether any rational jury can come up with the finding. And I submit that that is the test that ought to be applied on appeal of the Article I commission to this Article I appeal court.

JUDGE RE: Admiral Jenkins, you would apply that on the question of jurisdiction?

ADMIRAL JENKINS: I would apply that on your review of the finding of the law.

JUDGE RE: But our review of whether there was jurisdiction ... could, since you use Latin, I'd like to have you tell me whether or not this standard ought not to be de novo?

ADMIRAL JENKINS: No, it should not.

JUDGE RE: And whether there was a basis for the exercise of the jurisdiction by a military commission over a civilian at the time and place in question.

ADMIRAL JENKINS: It should not, Your Honor, because the

court below had to find sufficient facts to conclude it has jurisdiction. I think it is inappropriate for this court of appeals to evaluate those facts ...

JUDGE RE: There ought to be a deference?

ADMIRAL JENKINS: There ought to be a deference.

JUDGE EVERETT: Admiral Jenkins, I am disturbed about one distinction you seem to draw. You seem to distinguish *Milligan* with the ordinary crimes and then some category of extraordinary crimes. Wasn't *Milligan* a fairly extraordinary case itself? They gave him a death sentence, as I recall.

ADMIRAL JENKINS: I think *Milligan* was extraordinary in terms of the death sentence, but I don't think the crime in *Milligan* can be compared to the crime here in terms of the parties involved — that is, the Commander in Chief, the Vice President, the Secretary of State, and the General of the Armies — and indeed I don't think in *Milligan* you had the potential for the continuation of hostilities and the disruption of the state of the Union if the four parties involved in this conspiracy had been killed. So, I use ordinary crime in the sense of the crime *qua* crime and not the punishment, as compared to the extraordinary crime, conspiracy to kill the Commander in Chief, the Vice President, and the other parties involved.

JUDGE EVERETT: So you think of extraordinary consequences for the national security, then?

ADMIRAL JENKINS: Yes, Sir.

JUDGE EVERETT: I see.

ADMIRAL JENKINS: And I think that that is the kind of thing that has to be taken into consideration as a decision is made with respect to the appropriateness of a military commission as compared to the appropriateness of trial in an Article III court. All of those things combined to provide the commission with jurisdiction and the extraordinary nature of the crime in this case is of some significance.

JUDGE EVERETT: Proceed.

ADMIRAL JENKINS: I thank the court.

• • •

JUDGE EVERETT: Ms. Steel.

MS. STEEL: Thank you. Your Honor, first of all, I would state

to Judge Re that I think it certainly must be review *de novo*.
Jurisdiction must be raised or can be raised at any point in
the proceedings and for such an essential and elementary
function of a court, the court should have the full range of
ability to review the question; and for specific reference
for Your Honor, *Matter of Egan* addresses the question of
the burden of proof of the necessity that must be shown by
the military if it chooses to take jurisdiction over this kind
of a crime, and, as the court there stated, "this necessity
must be shown affirmatively by the party assuming to
exercise this extraordinary and irregular power over the
lives, liberty and property of the citizens whenever called
into question."

JUDGE EVERETT: Let me ask you this, though. President
Johnson, the President of the United States, was the one
that established this court by his proclamation. Isn't there
some presumption of correctness? Isn't there some deference that has to be given to the determination of the
President of the United States that such a military tribunal
should be assembled? Wouldn't it be inappropriate on
our part to make a de novo determination as to the necessity for this type of tribunal, given the determination by
President Johnson?

MS. STEEL: Your Honor, the President is elected and serves
to execute the laws of Congress. He is not placed as Regent
or King to determine the law or the effects on the citizenry
itself. The President has a specific range of obligations
and responsibilities, and it is our position that he has
overstepped that bound by impaneling [the Hunter Com-
mission]. His Attorney General recommended that he do
so, and I would think that the argument presented by
Attorney General Speed, particularly in the *Milligan* case,
is quite shocking to legal scholars of the establishment of
the Constitution in this country. The President has limits.
If he did not, we would have a despot for president, and as
my co-counsel has stated, we presume that President
Lincoln would have been horrified at the action taken by
President Johnson.

JUDGE EVERETT: Well, President Lincoln suspended the
writ of habeas corpus on his own initiative, before Congress gave approval. Do you really think he would have

been shocked by an attempt to establish a tribunal to provide swift justice to a group of conspirators who had tried to overturn the national war effort — who had tried to, in effect, continue a disastrous war of rebellion that had gone on for four dismal years? Do you think President Lincoln would have been shocked by that, Ms. Steel?

MS. STEEL: Your Honor, yes, in light of the fact that the war, in fact, was now over; that we had accepted the surrender of Lee; that the blockade had been lifted by Andrew Johnson. There was no longer a war. In fact, there had not been a war declared and this was argued with regard to the law of war that belligerent rights have ascribed in this case and therefore the law of war would apply.

JUDGE EVERETT: What was the date when President Johnson issued the proclamation establishing the court?

MS. STEEL: I believe it was sometime the end of April or the first week of May; the end of April — and within a week or so — May 1st.

JUDGE EVERETT: So we have to look at the situation as of that time, don't we?

MS. STEEL: Your Honor, I believe he was at that moment preparing to bring Union troops into Washington for celebration.

JUDGE EVERETT: And yet, on the other hand, wasn't there a large Southern force still operating under General Smith in Texas, to the west of the Mississippi?

MS. STEEL: Which I imagine would have taken many, many days to get from Texas to the city of Washington, D.C. in 1865.

JUDGE EVERETT: But don't we still have to consider the fact that there was this continuing effort, that President Johnson took this into account when he established the [commission]?

MS. STEEL: I'm certain that he took it into account, Your Honor. It's our position that he was wrong in doing so. With regard to belligerent rights, I just want to quickly answer the issue of whether or not, under the laws of war, Dr. Mudd could be tried. Belligerent status is not applicable in this case. There has never been a declaration that there was war by the Congress in this instance.

JUDGE EVERETT: But didn't, in 1862, our Supreme Court say

in *The Prize Cases* that there is the phenomenon of imperfect war, that you do not have to have a declared war? For example, for seizures?

MS. STEEL: We would submit that this case is quite distinguishable from *The Prize Cases*. In *The Prize Cases*, there was property at stake, and the courts have held quite differently in cases such as this where lives are stake, Your Honor, and I would like to give time now to my co-counsel to complete this rebuttal.

JUDGE COX: May I just ask one question?

MS. STEEL: Certainly.

JUDGE COX: In a rebellion, as opposed to dealing with a recognized foreign nation, is there any difference between the rebel soldier who is wearing the uniform, and the rebel civilian who is on his own adventure?

MS. STEEL: Yes, Your Honor. And the court has said ...

JUDGE COX: How could that be? If we don't recognize the rights of rebellion to begin with? We don't recognize him as a soldier, do we?

MS. STEEL: Belligerent rights are ascribed for the purpose of decency in war.

JUDGE COX: If you say it's one who's carrying a gun and shooting, then John Wilkes Booth fit that definition.

MS. STEEL: Yes, but Dr. Mudd was not carrying a gun nor shooting, and he was a victim and not a rebel. Your Honors, I would simply finish with saying that the court stated that the laws of war cannot be applied to citizens in states which have upheld the authority of the government and the State of Maryland as a Union state.

Thank you, Your Honors.

JUDGE EVERETT: Mr. Bailey.

MR. BAILEY: If it please the court, I should like to most respectfully suggest that the court give deep thought to giving deference to a President who claims jurisdiction and thereby satisfies his burden. We are greatly disturbed about the fact that a President might, by using the power of pardon, shut down the investigation to protect himself. Should we not be much more disturbed about the notion of a President granting jurisdiction in order to get the result he desires? Now, ...

JUDGE EVERETT: We are concerned there, too, but yet he is

the premier magistrate of the country. We have to give respect to him.

MR. BAILEY: Give him a little respect, but make him prove he's got the jurisdiction. When a towering tower of advocacy like my distinguished colleague Douglass is in heavy weather on the central question, I find great comfort; and the central question is, once you go by jurisdiction, and you cannot go by it but you can look at the other aspects of the case, what was it that should uphold this conviction of conspiracy to commit murder?

The decision to commit murder by the testimony of the prosecution witness Chester on May 12, the second day of trial, was made on Friday, April 7th. The decision prior to that was to kidnap the President and swap him for prisoners in gray uniforms. Dr. Mudd was never in contact with any of the alleged conspirators between April 7th and 14th on any of the evidence. And he can at best have known nothing about a plan to kill the President until it was done — he cannot be guilty of that conspiracy. Furthermore, it is suggested that the oil deal was a scam; and yet the prosecution's own witness said, "Booth backed off the oil deal because his colleagues lost interest." It was a very real deal. Same witness, Mr. Chester. Mr. Ewing said to that tribunal, "You say you are trying this person under the common law of war." There is no common law of war. I have looked for it in the books — it's not there. We all know it's not there. What you're saying is, the law is what you say it is even though you won't tell me so I can disprove the allegations. That flaw in this case is so telling and so penetrating that it cannot and should not survive.

JUDGE EVERETT: Mr. Bailey, I have one question I want to ask you.

MR. BAILEY: Yes.

JUDGE EVERETT: Suppose John Wilkes Booth had himself been seized and had been brought before a military tribunal for trial after the assassination of President Lincoln. Would you be here making the same argument to us?

MR. BAILEY: Absolutely. Because absent the exigency ... absent the exigency, the only thing that can ever justify transferring judicial power to the executive, John Wilkes Booth should have been tried and would have been convicted and hung by a jury of his peers.

Thank you.

JUDGE EVERETT: The court's going to take this matter under advisement, since it deals with a number of very serious issues with great implications. We do, however, plan to render our opinions today and make a decision, so if counsel are willing, we would request that they stand by and we will attempt to announce our decision in the immediate future.

• • •

CLERK OF THE COURT: The United States Special Court of Military Appeal is back in session.

JUDGE EVERETT: Each of the judges has a brief opinion. Before we announce the decision, I'm going to call first on Judge Re to express his opinion on the merits of this case.

JUDGE RE: I should like to make an informal statement at this time, and a formal opinion will follow, and I know it will become part of the proceedings of this case. Before I do so, I should like to state the tremendous privilege of sitting with a dear friend and colleague of many, many years, Judge Everett, and Judge Cox, and I should like to set forth my great admiration for the remarkable argument that has been made by all counsel. I deemed it a great privilege to have heard the wonderful arguments, the splendid arguments that have been made.

I explain at the outset that the facts were known and need not be recited, and proceeding to the power of this court, I have no difficulty in saying that we have the power to not only look into the guilt or innocence, but also the question of jurisdiction. It's true that we have been appointed by the President, but clearly our mandate is to do justice, however swift, and, therefore, if doing that justice brings us to a conclusion that the court that tried Dr. Mudd had no jurisdiction, it is our duty to say so. And there is no deference to be shown under circumstances where the Government has not and cannot succeed in showing the necessity which would warrant a displacement of the civil court and the civil authorities under the circumstances of the case of Dr. Mudd.

Proceeding to the actual merits of the jurisdictional question, it is my firm opinion that the military commission had no

jurisdiction to try a civilian at the time and place that he
was tried. Therefore, I would hold that all of the proceedings of the commission were a nullity. And this would be
regardless of the nature of the offense. And the reason is
because we start with a fundamental postulate that the
Constitution is the supreme law of the land. Article VI
says so expressly, and the importance of the Constitution
being paramount was set forth in the tremendously important opinion — the seminal opinion — of Chief Justice
Marshall in *Marbury v. Madison*. So in the words of
Madison, the fundamental and paramount rule of the nation is our Constitution.

Commencing with that I must express that our determination
really is determined by what is said in the holding of *Ex
parte Milligan*. *Ex parte Milligan*, were we to read it with the
care that it deserves, is a great landmark for the expansion
of human freedom and liberties in our nation. It shows
that, unless there is the necessity that warrants a declaration of martial law, martial law is extraordinary, and
cannot be applied. During the able argument, reference
was made to the fact that President Lincoln declared
martial law and that it applied in Indiana — it's true. But
Ex parte Milligan said that it was a nullity and that the writ
of habeas corpus freed *Milligan*. The petitions in that case
could very well have been used here, because whether or
not a military commission could have tried a conspirator
or anyone else in Texas or anyone else was not before this
court. The question was, could Dr. Mudd, a civilian, not
a spy, not coming within any of the categories over whom
the military courts would have had jurisdiction, could he
have been tried in Maryland, where the alleged offense
took place, because as I understand the basic facts of this
case, it all stems from some services he rendered as a
physician — he set the leg of a patient.

Whether he was a conspirator or not really is not the question
that I should like to address. The question is, did you have
jurisdiction to try the individual? If there is no jurisdiction, again, you are not a court. The Latin phrase, *non
coram judice* — you are not a judge — and indeed if there
is no jurisdiction there's a very serious question as to
whether these judges themselves have any judicial immu-

nity. So I find that the *Milligan* case determines the outcome of this case and, on jurisdictional grounds, I would hold that the proceedings below were a nullity. I do not address the guilt or innocence of the individual because, regardless of the nature of the offense, the Constitutional provisions say that he is entitled to a trial by jury and there are other protections set forth in our amendments, all of which ... and the authorities for my statements will be set forth in an opinion that I will submit in due course.

Having determined that there wasn't jurisdiction, it follows that Dr. Mudd should be released forthwith, which was the order issued by Chief Justice Chase on May 3rd, 1865 in the *Milligan* case, and you remember that, in that case, the opinion followed on December 17, 1865. The reasons were set forth much later. So having said that, it would be dicta for me to comment on all of the evidentary questions that have been raised. Nonetheless, I cannot resist the temptation of saying that I have serious doubts as to whether an impartial mind, removed from what in the *Milligan* case I refer to as distractions of the moment — tempers ... feelings ... emotions ... clamor — whether on the evidence presented, and I say this with great deference because I could not help but be moved indeed by the remarkable argument by Colonel Douglass and Admiral Jenkins. This still is a very tenuous reed to do away with all of the civil rights that flow from that great document which attempted to give legal status to the ideals of our Declaration of Independence. It is all but forgotten that in our Declaration of Independence we speak of such lofty ideals but they did not become principles of law until our Constitution was enacted. And that speaks of we the people who want to form a more perfect union. It is more relevant for us today to say that the next two words are "establish justice." So I considered my mandate not only to hear this case but also to do justice because I assume that is precisely what the President would wish. So, in dicta, I would say that applying an appropriate standard of proof and in view of the nature of the charges, I would have no hesitation in venturing the additional dicta that there would have to be guilt beyond a reasonable doubt.

For that not to be so, we would be doing an injustice to the
thousands of courts martial and military commissions
that have properly exercised their jurisdiction and have
performed valuable service. However, if the necessity
doesn't exist, if the public danger doesn't exist, our system
requires that, when the courts are open and functioning,
trials should be before the civil courts, with trial by jury,
and with all of the protections guaranteed by the Constitution.

JUDGE EVERETT: Judge Re, thank you. Judge Cox, would
you lend us your opinion?

JUDGE COX: Thank you, Chief Judge Everett.

I do not concur in the opinion, albeit the scholarly opinion, of
my brother, Judge Re, that *Ex parte Milligan* is dispositive
of this case. You know, one of the great ironies of this case
is that the war that was going on at this time in our history
was being fought, as I understand it, to preserve and
protect the very Constitution of the United States that we
are now dealing with. It was armed resurrection throughout the land, pitting brother against brother and sister
against sister, and so on and so forth, and as I understand
the law and believe it to be, that one must look at the state
of insurrection, the state of war, because we were not at
war with a foreign power. We were at war among ourselves. And given that state of insurrection, which was
going on throughout the South, and indeed if the facts of
this case as they have been argued by the Government are
like they are, it was still being continued by conspirators
in the State of Maryland and throughout the District of
Columbia. And given that state of affairs, I do not believe
that it was an unreasonable exercise of the powers of the
President to call into [being] a military commission to hear
the evidence and decide the case before us. Therefore I
would not set aside this case for a lack of jurisdiction.
Which leads me inevitably to the next question, and that is
whether the Government has maintained its burden of
proof.

Now, what is the standard of review that this court should
apply to the facts of this case? I believe that this court must
give every reasonable inference that can be drawn from
the evidence on behalf of the Government to the Govern-

ment. I likewise, like Judge Re, agree that fundamental norms of due process in this country, whether it be a Constitutional court such as the Article III courts, or whether it be a military tribunal, such as this Commission, the standard of proof should be beyond a reasonable doubt. I think that is the fundamental underpinning of due process in this country. So therefore I look to the charge in this case to try to determine what it was that the Government was required to prove beyond a reasonable doubt.

Now Mr. Bailey, in his argument, suggested, and I believe that I agree with him, that the charge, at the outset at any rate, suggested the possibility that Dr. Mudd was guilty of treason; that Dr. Mudd was guilty of becoming an accessory before the fact to the homicide of President Lincoln; that Dr. Mudd was indeed the killer of President Lincoln; or that Dr. Mudd became an accessory after the fact and gave aid and comfort knowing that Booth had been the assassin; and lastly, as the Government argues, that this was a sinister conspiracy among Dr. Mudd and the other defendants to wipe out the leadership of the United States at that time.

Having said that, though, I turn to the evidence and say what evidence is here to prove what Dr. Mudd did in further-ance of this awesome conspiracy that Colonel Douglass has painted for the court? And I find from the evidence taken in light most favorable to the Government suggests the following: That Dr. Mudd was acquainted — ac-quainted is the word I believe best describes it — with John Wilkes Booth at some time prior to the night in question. I find that, in light most favorable to the Govern-ment, that at the time Dr. Mudd treated John Wilkes Booth he knew who he was, notwithstanding his disguise, and notwithstanding some hearsay evidence denying that. However, I must say that I find nothing in this evidence which suggests that Dr. Samuel Mudd agreed, partici-pated in, or aided and comforted in the assassination of President Lincoln. I just don't find that proof in the record. As the Government suggests, perhaps you could find that he was providing a safe haven along a spy route. But were that the case, I think he nevertheless would have to understand that he was providing a safe haven for an assassin of President Lincoln to be found guilty of that conspiracy, and I can't find that in the record. Accordingly, I would reverse this case and order a new trial. I do think that, as a matter of law, on this day the necessity is over, that a reasonable tribunal could not find military necessity and so any trial would have to be in a civilian tribunal. That's what I would hold. Again, an opinion will be rendered in due course.

JUDGE EVERETT: I have focused on the jurisdictional issue because, if in fact there was no jurisdiction on the part of the military commission, then the disposition of the case is rather obvious in light of the view taken by Judge Re.

It seems to me clearly to be the fact that there was no jurisdiction predicated on a theory of martial law. Martial law is a doctrine of necessity as the Supreme Court has recently reiterated in the *Milligan* case and there really was no necessity to use a military tribunal under these circumstances. There was opportunity to try Dr. Mudd in a civilian court.

There is, however, another rationale for jurisdiction which deserves attention. I think this was the one that was being expounded with particular vigor and conviction by Colonel Douglass. And that is the jurisdiction predicated on the law of war. This is a doctrine that has been affirmed over the years by our jurisprudence. It goes back, for example, to the trial of Major André and admittedly that was prior to the Constitution. But nevertheless, it evolves as principle that a spy or certain other types of individuals, be they of foreign nationality or American, be they military or civilian, can be tried by military tribunal. That ground of jurisdiction was used by our courts, by American authorities, during the Mexican war. It has apparently been used in some two thousand cases, I infer from what Colonel Douglass said, and have little doubt it would sustain the trials in those two thousand cases.

However, given the circumstances of this particular case, it seems that the law of war rationale was not sufficiently articulated in the pleadings nor sufficiently established by proof, and that it is too tenuous a basis on that theory. Given the time, the circumstances, I'm really not con-

cerned by the fact that hostilities were concluded because
I think it would be true that under certain circumstances
jurisdiction can be exercised by a military tribunal, even
though hostilities have come to an end. But looking at all
the circumstances it seems to me that here that basis of
jurisdiction also fails and therefore I come to the same
conclusion that Judge Re did — namely, that jurisdiction
of the military commission was lacking. That being the
case, there is no need for me to deal with the issues of
sufficiency of the evidence that Judge Cox discussed. I
think clearly the standard would be one of proof beyond
reasonable doubt, whether a military tribunal is involved
or a civilian tribunal. That's certainly a well-accepted,
well-established premise of American jurisprudence. I
think the law of conspiracy has many aspects and it can be
persuasively argued that even if Dr. Mudd did not know
all the purposes of the conspiracy, if he engaged in the
conspiracy and if a particular act was a reasonably foreseeable consequence of the conspiracy, then he would be
responsible for that act. So I think there is at least very
substantial basis for the argument that was presented by
Colonel Douglass. But, as I indicated, I need not make a
determination in that regard because I do conclude that
the military tribunal had no jurisdiction.

That being the case, although two of us have one rationale and
one has a third, the members of the court have unanimously come to the conviction that Dr. Mudd's conviction
by the military tribunal must be set aside and the corollary
of that is that an order must be entered at this time that he
forthwith be discharged from custody.

There being no other matter to come before the court today,
the court is now adjourned.

CLERK OF THE COURT: All rise.

The Judgment and Opinions by the Court

OPINION

EDWARD D. RE, Judge:*

At the outset I should like to note the great pleasure of sitting with a dear friend and colleague of many years, Judge Robinson O. Everett, and with my esteemed colleague, Judge Walter T. Cox. I should like also to express my appreciation and admiration for the extremely helpful arguments that have been made by the distinguished and able counsel who represented Dr. Mudd and the Government. I deem it a great privilege to have heard the splendid arguments that have been made in the course of this appeal.

The salient facts surrounding this case are well known, and need not be recited at length. Before this court, Samuel A. Mudd of Charles County, Maryland appeals his conviction by a military commission of conspiracy to murder the President of the United States, the Vice President, the Secretaries of State and War, and the General commanding the Union Army. Although John Wilkes Booth, the person said to have shot President Lincoln, died resisting arrest, Mudd and seven others were apprehended. On May 1, 1865, President Johnson

---

* Chief Judge Emeritus, U.S. Court of International Trade; Distinguished Professor of Law, St. John's University School of Law.

ordered their trial by a military commission. The trial began on May 9 and ended on June 30. Mudd was sentenced to life imprisonment, and that sentence was approved by the President on July 5. Before this court, Dr. Mudd challenges both the military commission's jurisdiction to try him and the sufficiency of the Army's evidence against him.

I commence by stating that I have no difficulty in finding that we have the power not only to look into the soundness of the commission's findings regarding the appellant's guilt or innocence, but also into the question of the commission's jurisdiction. It is true that we are not an Article III court, but an Article I court, having been appointed by the President at the direction of the Congress. Clearly, however, our mandate is to do justice. What else could we presume the President and Congress to have wished or intended in establishing this court? If doing justice brings us to a firm conclusion that the Army tribunal that tried Dr. Mudd had no jurisdiction, it is our duty to so declare, and to order the error corrected. Moreover, the question of a tribunal's jurisdiction is one of law, in this case, Constitutional Law. Hence, as to such a question, we need pay no deference to either the prior decision of the tribunal, or to the present opinion of the United States as appellee.

Proceeding to the actual merits of the jurisdictional question, it is my firm opinion that the military commission had no jurisdiction to try a civilian like Mudd at the time and place that he was tried. Because I conclude that there was no military jurisdiction over the defendant, I need not address appellant's other constitutional objections.

At trial, Dr. Mudd's counsel objected to a trial by a military commission because his client was a civilian resident of a free state, over whom a military tribunal could not exercise jurisdiction without violating the Constitution. Counsel for Dr. Mudd renew that objection before this court. There is evidence in the record, introduced by the United States, which shows that Mudd was a physician and a planter, residing outside Bryantown in Charles County, Maryland. On the other hand, there is no evidence that Dr. Mudd enlisted in the armed forces of the insurgent states, or that he otherwise took up arms against the Union. On such a record, the issue is whether the Army may try a civilian resident of a loyal state for the offenses of which Dr. Mudd was accused.

On the record before us, I hold that all of the proceedings of the commission were a nullity, and this conclusion would apply regardless of the nature of the offense or offenses. I start with the fundamental postulate that the Constitution is the supreme law of the land. Article VI says so expressly, and the paramount importance and supremacy of the Constitution was subsequently confirmed in the tremendously significant opinion — the seminal opinion — of Chief Justice Marshall in *Marbury v. Madison*.[1]

In the words of the great Chief Justice for a unanimous Court in *Marbury*, "those who have framed written constitutions contemplate them as forming the fundamental and paramount law of the nation,"[2] and the "constitution is to be considered, in court, as a paramount law."[3] Therefore, I must reject any assertion or contention that a rule or principle derived from international law, or, more precisely, the law of war, could disturb the legal order established by the Constitution. What remains for us to determine is the extent or limits of military jurisdiction over civilians that is permitted by the Constitution.

In the basic document, the Framers were silent as to the propriety of military jurisdiction over persons or crimes. In Art. I, Sec. 8, Cl. 10, Congress is authorized to define and punish offenses against the law of nations. This provision may reasonably be interpreted as authorization to define and punish offenses against that subdivision of the law of nations called the law of war. Appellant, however, has not called into question Congress' power to define and punish but, rather, has challenged the Army's power to adjudicate. On the power to adjudicate, the Constitutional provisions are found in Article III which declares that the judicial power of the United States is vested in the Supreme Court and in such inferior courts as Congress may from time to time ordain and establish. This article also provides that the judges, both of the Supreme Court and the inferior courts, shall hold their offices during good behavior.

In this case, the appellant was tried by a military commission known as the Hunter Commission. The commission was established by order of the Commander in Chief, not by Act of the Congress, and the commission's members, general and field grade officers on active service with the Army, did not hold their offices as commission members during good behavior, but only *pro illa vice* ("for that turn"). As these commissioners cannot be said to have held their offices in accordance with Article III, they may not be regarded as having had jurisdiction described in Article III.

The Bill of Rights reveals that the First Congress contemplated different adjudicative treatment for crimes of a military nature, but it falls far short of validating military jurisdiction over a civilian as in this case. The Fifth Amendment guarantees that no person may be held to answer for a capital or otherwise infamous crime, unless upon presentment or indictment of a grand jury, *"except in cases arising in the land or naval forces, or in the Militia, when in actual service in time of war or public danger ... ."*[4] Thus, the Fifth Amendment permits a criminal conviction without the involvement of a Grand Jury only for crimes arising in the armed forces. Here, the specific exception of the Fifth Amendment cannot apply, for, as the government must concede, Mudd was neither a soldier nor a militiaman.

In the face of the one exception for military crimes explicitly set forth in the Fifth Amendment, I am loathe to assume that the Constitution contains or permits any other exception which its Framers failed to articulate. On this point I am guided by a firmly established tradition of interpretation summarized in the canon *inclusio unius est exclusio alterius.* Hence, no implicit exception ought to be read into either the federal jurisdiction set forth in Article III, or the guarantee of a jury of the state and district wherein the crime shall have been committed, as provided in Article III and in the Sixth Amendment of the Constitution.

This brings me to the recent decision of the United States Supreme Court in *Ex parte Milligan.*[5] In light of the overwhelming persuasiveness of that decision, I have no doubt regarding its proper influence in this case. Indeed, I believe our decision today is really determined by the reasoning and holding of that case. I venture to add that if *Ex parte Milligan* were to be read with the care it deserves, it would be viewed as a great landmark for the expansion of human freedom and liberties in our nation. Even though that decision admits that the military, in exceptional circumstances, may adjudicate offenses by civilians, it limits the exercise of that power to cases arising out of true and absolute national necessity, and not merely for the Army's convenience.

Ex parte Milligan indicates clearly that, unless there exists that "public danger" or necessity that warrants a declaration of martial law, martial law can neither be declared nor applied to empower a military commission to judge civilians. *Ex parte Milligan* also teaches that a finding by the executive of the prerequisites for imposing martial law is not controlling upon the judiciary in determining whether the necessity warranted the exercise of military jurisdiction over civilians.

Whether a military commission could have tried one of these conspirators, or anyone else, within the territory of a secessionist state is not before this court. The events which led to the trial of Dr. Mudd and his co-defendants occurred in the District of Columbia and in the State of Maryland, areas which stayed with the Union and remained loyal to its lawful government.

During the oral argument before us, able counsel for the government noted that President Lincoln declared martial law and that it applied in Indiana, the state in which Lambdin Milligan resided and in which his offenses were committed; that much is true. But *Ex parte Milligan* held that the declaration by the President was a nullity, and that the writ of habeas corpus was available to free Milligan, a civilian resident of a loyal state. The Supreme Court concluded that, as long as the courts of the State of Indiana were open and operating, the military courts of the United States Army could not usurp their jurisdiction over civilian defendants.

Consequently, as long as the courts of Maryland were open and operating, the Hunter Commission could not try Samuel A. Mudd, a civilian.

While the record of the Hunter Commission, completed before *Ex parte Milligan* was decided, is justifiably barren of evidence on this essential matter, I find sufficient proof in the Maryland Reports that the courts of that state were open and operating at the time of Dr. Mudd's arrest. Indeed, I find particularly compelling evidence that Maryland's courts were capable of hearing and properly deciding his case in the reported decision in *Anderson v. Baker*,[6] heard and decided by the Court of Appeals during its October Term in 1865. In that case, Maryland's highest court affirmed a judgment of the Circuit Court of Montgomery County denying a petition for a writ of mandamus which had been requested by persons refused registration as voters in accordance with Maryland's registration law because they had been in "armed hostility to the United States."[7] Clearly, the courts of Maryland were open, operating, and loyal to the Union.

The specific question presented is whether the Hunter Commission had jurisdiction to try the appellant. If there was no jurisdiction, the commission was not properly a court, and could not try the appellant. The Latin phrase *coram non judice*, before one not a judge, expresses the principle and signals the consequence — that any decision such a simulacrum may render is null and void. Indeed, if there is no jurisdiction, there is a very serious question as to whether the judges themselves enjoy any judicial immunity. I have concluded that the *Milligan* case determines the outcome of this case and, on jurisdictional grounds, I hold that the proceedings below were a nullity. It follows that Dr. Mudd should be released forthwith, which was the order issued by Chief Justice Chase, on April 3, 1866, in the *Milligan* case.

As I understand the crucial facts of this case, the charges against Dr. Mudd stem from services that he rendered as a physician — when he set the leg of a patient. Whether he was a co-conspirator in the assassination is not a question that needs to be addressed. Having concluded that the military commission over which this court has supervisory authority acted without jurisdiction in passing on the appellant's guilt, I need not pass on what persuaded the commission in its judgment. Nonetheless, from a study of the entire record, I have serious doubts as to whether an impartial mind, removed from what might be called the distractions of the moment (i.e., the tempers, feelings, emotions, and clamor surrounding this case), applying an appropriate standard of proof as to the evidence presented, and in view of the nature of the charges, could conclude that there was guilt beyond a reasonable doubt.

It is my decision that the military commission that tried Dr. Samuel A. Mudd had no jurisdiction to try him, that the proceedings before that commission were a nullity, and that Dr. Mudd should be released forthwith.

ROBINSON O. EVERETT, Chief Judge** (concurring):

If it were necessary for me to decide as to the sufficiency of the evidence, I might be persuaded by the incisive arguments and briefs on behalf of the Government that Samuel Mudd's guilt of some crime had been established. Even if Booth's slaying of the President were outside the scope of any plot in which Mudd might have been involved, there is evidence suggesting that he was an accessory after the fact. However, I need not reach the issue of evidentiary sufficiency because — for the reasons ably set out by my esteemed brother Judge Edward D. Re — I also am convinced that the military commission lacked jurisdiction to try Dr. Mudd.

Three bases of military jurisdiction are consistent with the Constitution. The first is derived from Art. I, Sec. 8, which authorizes Congress to "make rules for the Government and Regulation of the land and naval Forces." Clearly this provision of the Constitution — under which Congress has enacted the Articles of War — is inapplicable. In no sense can Samuel Mudd be considered a member of the "land and naval Forces."

A second possible basis for military jurisdiction is martial law, which was unsuccessfully relied upon by the Government in *Ex parte Milligan*.[8] As the principal opinion in that case makes clear, martial law — which is nowhere specifically mentioned in the Constitution — is predicated on necessity. Absent necessity, no basis exists in martial law for trying a civilian by a military commission or other military tribunal. Because the civil courts were open in Indiana where Milligan was tried, the Supreme Court ruled that the military commission there lacked jurisdiction to try him and to impose a death sentence. Even though martial law still applied in Washington when President Lincoln was assassinated and later when the Hunter Commission tried Dr. Mudd, it seems undeniable that the civil courts were open and that, if Federal authorities had been so inclined, Dr. Mudd could have been tried in a civil court by a jury upon an indictment rendered by a grand jury.

Any argument for military jurisdiction based on martial law would be stronger if the trial of Samuel Mudd by a military commission had been specifically authorized by

---

** Senior Judge (ret.) and former Chief Judge of the U.S. Court of Military Appeals; Professor of Law, Duke University School of Law.

Congress — just as the Congress has created our Special Court and authorized it to review Mudd's conviction. However, in my view, even a legislative mandate would not be sufficient to establish military jurisdiction based on martial law.

That leaves only an argument based on Art. I, Sec. 8, Cl. 10, which confers on Congress the power to "define and punish . . . Offenses against the law of nations." In my view, neither the accessibility of civil courts nor Mudd's American citizenship is decisive as to the legality of any exercise of military jurisdiction pursuant to Clause 10. However, because trial by a military tribunal deprives an accused of many safeguards, such as indictment by grand jury and trial by petit jury, Clause 10 should not be given a novel or extraordinarily broad construction. Moreover, I am troubled because it is unclear that Congress has attempted to exercise the power granted it by Art. I, Sec. 8, Cl. 10. Nonetheless, I shall proceed on the premise that, in some way, Congress did authorize military authorities to utilize whatever power might stem from this clause.

A question also may be raised as to whether the law of war — within the "law of nations" — justifies trial by military commission for acts which took place in Maryland on April 14, 1865. The Army of Northern Virginia had surrendered on April 10, 1865. General Johnston was about to surrender to General Sherman in North Carolina. However, a sufficient residue of military operations at the time of the assassination permits the law of war to punish Mudd and the other alleged conspirators. Moreover, as to conduct punishable by a military tribunal under the authority of Art. I, Sec. 8, it probably makes no difference whether hostilities abate after the offense is committed and prior to trial or the execution of a sentence.

Even so, I conclude that the military commission lacked jurisdiction. Had the conduct of Mudd and the other alleged co-conspirators occurred in one of the States which had attempted to secede and join the Confederacy, a different result might be called for. The use of military tribunals to maintain order in occupied countries appears to be well-accepted[9] and I would draw no distinction between the power of American military commanders to establish courts in the occupied territory of a foreign government — such as Mexico two decades ago — and their power to establish military commissions to administer justice in the occupied territory of rebellious States.

Admittedly, at the outset of the recent conflict, Maryland, where Samuel Mudd resided, exhibited secessionist tendencies. However, even though some military operations took place within the State, its constituted authorities never undertook to withdraw from the Union. Washington, where the assassination was carried out, always remained under Federal control. Furthermore, no evidence has been offered that the assassination plot was encouraged, organized, or condoned by the persons in charge of military operations for the secessionist States.

No one can minimize the gravity of the crimes committed by those who were responsible in any way for the slaying of President Lincoln and thereafter for shielding the assassin. Indeed, those involved may have been guilty of treason. However, even that most aggravated of offenses is not subject to summary trial by a military tribunal; to the contrary, the Constitution at Art. III, Sec. 3 provides special safeguards to assure that a person accused of treason is protected against conviction on the basis of hearsay and innuendo. With this in mind, I cannot subscribe to the proposition that the exigencies of the situation created by the assassination of the President authorized trial in a forum where the usual safeguards for trial of a civilian would be absent.[10]

The conclusion I have reached seems most consistent with the language and spirit of our Constitution. Moreover, it precludes a rush to judgment before a tribunal whose unfamiliar procedures and rules of evidence will inevitably result later in claims of arbitrariness, bias, and hysteria. Thus I join Judge Re in holding that the military commission sitting in Washington lacked jurisdiction to try Dr. Samuel Mudd — a citizen of Maryland, a State which remained with the Union — for any misconduct on his part in connection with the assassination of President Lincoln or with the harboring and assisting of those who perpetrated this dastardly crime.

WALTER T. COX, III, Judge[†] (concurring in the judgment):
My learned colleagues make compelling arguments that

[†] Judge of the U.S. Court of Military Appeals; former Judge of the 10th Judicial Circuit of South Carolina.

the military commission was without jurisdiction to try Dr. Samuel Mudd for the crimes arising out of the assassination of President Abraham Lincoln and the assault on Secretary of State William H. Seward, relying on the Supreme Court's recent decision in *Ex parte Milligan*.[11] I respectfully disagree. However, for the reasons set forth, I agree that the judgment of guilty must be reversed.

In reaching these conclusions, I first ask whether *Milligan* stands for the proposition that a civilian may never be tried by a military commission — or does that case merely establish those essential elements which must be present in order for a military tribunal to require a civilian to answer to criminal charges before such a body? I read *Milligan* as permitting jurisdiction over civilians under certain circumstances. I do not read it as an absolute bar to jurisdiction.

It is true that no civilian may be tried by a military tribunal absent extraordinary and compelling circumstances. *Milligan* makes it clear that a civilian cannot be tried for ordinary offenses arising out of state or federal laws if the civil government is functioning and in control, and if the civil courts are open and capable of doing justice. Likewise, *Milligan* makes it clear that the exercise of jurisdiction by a military tribunal is a corollary to martial law. Furthermore, martial law must exist out of "necessity actual and present, the invasion real, such as actually closes down the courts and deposes the civil administration."[12]

These are seductive words which, if taken literally, belie the truth. I view our duty as an appellate court in a much broader sense than one which merely asks if the doors to the local courthouse are physically open. We must look beyond that simple fact to the true state of affairs. We, as an appellate tribunal, must resolve the question of jurisdiction, as we must in every case, as a question of law — certainly one mixed with facts, but nevertheless a question of law.

When we examine the jurisdiction of a military tribunal, we are not hidebound to the traditional questions of criminal jurisdiction, albeit they remain important. In addition to the traditional questions — Did the tribunal have jurisdiction over the subject matter? Did the tribunal have jurisdiction over the person? Where was the situs of the crime? — we must also examine the time, place, and circumstances pertaining to the alleged offenses. We must likewise look at the offenses to determine if they are against military order and discipline or against the common citizenry. In other words, necessity is a much broader concept than an open civil courthouse.

This broader view of jurisdiction is alien to our normal view thereof. Normally, all we ask is: (a) Whether the crime occurred in the county or district? (b) Do the charges allege an offense? (c) Was the defendant properly before the court by information or arraignment? and (d) Was the indictment returned a true bill by the grand jury? These questions are fairly routine and easy to answer. Necessity as an element of jurisdiction presents quite another question.

In my view, when we peel away the constitutional platitudes surrounding the debate over the issue of jurisdiction in this case, resolution of the question boils down to consideration of the *time, place,* and *circumstances* surrounding the crime and trial.

Unlike my colleagues, I find that an examination of the record of the proceedings supports a finding of jurisdiction. As recited in the Charge and Specification, Washington was a city "fortified and intrenched." The offense occurred on the night of April 14, 1865. The intended victims were Abraham Lincoln, President of the United States and Commander in Chief of the military forces of the United States; Andrew Johnson, Vice President of the United States; William H. Seward, Secretary of State; and Lieutenant General Ulysses S. Grant, then in command of the Armies of the United States. Martial law had been previously declared in the city of Washington, D.C. *Habeas corpus,* which had been suspended, was not restored until February 1867, long after the trial in question.

A very important fact supporting jurisdiction is that the war between the Union and the Confederacy was not over. It is true, as Petitioners argue, that General Robert E. Lee had surrendered the Army of Northern Virginia in early April 1865, but hostilities continued throughout the South. Rebellious renegade groups flourished and Jefferson Davis, President of the Confederate States of America, was eluding capture. Indeed, he was not captured until May 10, 1865, the day after this trial commenced.

The most important factor demonstrating the appropriateness of this military commission can be found in the very facts of the case. The offenses themselves demonstrate the very grand and immediate danger to the military leadership in the District of Columbia. Prompt investigation of the charges, swift trial of those believed to be involved, and speedy rendering of punishment were unquestionably necessary to convince the local populace of the avowed determination of the military to instill discipline and control in the community. That is the purpose of martial law and military tribunals, to maintain control and order when the civilian populace is in disarray.

It is easy to look backward to find some evidence that the courts of Maryland or the District of Columbia were open. However, given the time, place, and circumstances of this case, it is my view that the exercise of jurisdiction by the military commission was justified and proper, in order to ensure the safety of the military leadership and peace and harmony within the District of Columbia and, indeed, the nation. A military force must, as a matter of common sense and necessity, be capable of protecting itself and its leaders from such heinous crimes against it. In my judgment, that is the necessity required by *Ex parte Milligan* and the Constitution in order for a military tribunal to exercise jurisdiction over civilians. Accordingly, I am of the opinion that Dr. Mudd was subject to the jurisdiction of the commission.

Whether or not the verdict of guilty against Dr. Mudd, for conspiring to murder the President and others, should stand is quite another question. Petitioner questions whether the evidence against him supports a finding of guilty as charged. I conclude that the evidence is insufficient, and, therefore, I would reverse his conviction on this basis.

I agree with the Petitioner as to the burden of proof. It is a fundamental principle in Anglo-American jurisprudence that no man shall be punished for a crime unless the state (or, in this case, the United States) shall prove the defendant guilty by legal and competent evidence which shall prove each and every element of the criminal offense beyond any reasonable doubt.

The legal test is, the sufficiency of the evidence to satisfy the understanding and conscience of the jury.

On the one hand, absolute, metaphysical and demonstrative certainty, is not essential to proof by circumstances. It is sufficient if they produce moral certainty, *to the exclusion of every reasonable doubt.* Even direct and positive evidence does not afford grounds of belief of a higher or superior nature. The rule, even in a capital case is, that should circumstances be sufficient to *convince the mind and remove every rational doubt*, the jury is bound to place as much reliance in such circumstances as on direct and positive proof.[13]

Thus, an appellate tribunal reviewing a record of trial regarding a claim of insufficient evidence must ask itself two questions:

1. Is the evidence of record legal and competent? Evidence erroneously admitted into the trial cannot be considered.

2. Does the evidence of record, if true, offer proof of each and every element of the charged offense?

Of course, an appellate court must view the evidence in a light most favorable to the Government, unless the appellate court is convinced that no reasonable juror would do so. After all, even appellate courts are not bound by absurd, arbitrary, or capricious views of evidence. Furthermore, unlike historians and even legal scholars, an appellate court is bound by the record of trial before it and the laws and precedents pertaining to the case; it may not consider evidence developed outside the record.

My starting point for review of this record is, therefore, the charge against Petitioner. It is clear from the Charge and Specification that the prosecution's theory regarding Dr. Mudd's role in the case was two-fold. First, Dr. Mudd was an active conspirator in the plot *to assassinate* the President, Vice President, Secretary of State, and Lieutenant General Grant. Second, in support of that murderous compact, Dr. Mudd gave aid, safe harbor, and comfort to the injured assassin, John Wilkes Booth; and he assisted Booth and his colleague to escape from Maryland into Virginia.

It is certainly an inescapable conclusion that Dr. Mudd did indeed aid, comfort, and assist John Wilkes Booth in his flight from Washington, D.C., to Virginia. Such conduct may well have constituted some offense against the United States, in the same manner as providing food and shelter to retreating Confederate soldiers or escaped prisoners of war. But such is not the nature of the crime for which Dr. Mudd stands convicted.

Rather, he stands convicted for willfully, knowingly agreeing to kill and murder the President of the United States, for assaulting the Secretary of State, and for knowingly providing aid and comfort to the President's actual killer. In my view, the record is entirely void of any evidence from which a finder of fact, honestly seeking the truth, could conclude that Dr. Samuel Mudd conspired to *murder* the President.

Viewing the evidence presented to the military commission in May 1865, in a light most favorable to the prosecution, I find the following:

1. Dr. Mudd knew the assassin, John Wilkes Booth, prior to April 15, 1865, and recognized him on the morning that he treated his leg.

2. Between November 1864, and March 1865, John Wilkes Booth and others conspired to kidnap President Lincoln, Vice President Johnson, Secretary of State Seward, and Lieutenant General Grant.

3. In early March 1865, Booth and certain of his fellow conspirators modified the plot and decided, instead, to assassinate the victims.

4. The witness Weichmann observed Dr. Mudd meeting with Booth and others in a Washington hotel on January 15, 1865, and he saw them discussing a map.

5. Dr. Mudd was seen in Washington on March 3, 1865, looking for Booth.

6. Dr. Mudd was sympathetic to the cause of the Confederate States of America, and he operated a safe house for anti-Union operatives at his farm in southern Maryland.

7. President Lincoln was killed by John Wilkes Booth on April 14, 1865, and Secretary of State Seward was assaulted on the same night by a fellow conspirator of Booth.

8. Dr. Mudd provided aid and comfort to Booth and his companion during the daylight hours of April 15, 1865.

9. When Dr. Mudd was given the opportunity to explain the presence of Booth at his farm to Lieutenant Lovett, a Union Army officer investigating the case, he denied having

recognized Booth.

These are powerful items of circumstantial evidence that Dr. Mudd was involved in a conspiracy, his particular role being to cover and assist in the escape of the perpetrators to the South. However, it is the following lack of evidence, rather than the evidence, direct or circumstantial, that causes me to conclude that the prosecution failed to meet its legal burden — that is, to prove *every* element of the offense charged:

a. Even assuming Dr. Mudd participated in the original conspiracy to *kidnap* the President and others, it is clear that the plot later was fundamentally changed. There is no evidence of record showing that Dr. Mudd agreed to *kill* the President and others or to be a part of such a plot.

b. There is also no evidence of record to indicate that, at the time Dr. Mudd aided Booth, he knew that Booth had killed the President. In fact, there is no evidence that even Booth knew the President was dead at that point, only that he had fired a shot at him. Based upon the prosecution's evidence, it was not established that Dr. Mudd learned of the assassination of the President until April 16, 1865, one day after Booth made his escape.

I know of no rule of law that would hold a conspirator vicariously liable for crimes which are independently committed by a principal and outside the foreseeable scope of the conspiracy. For example, if two men conspire to steal a farmer's horse — one to commit the theft, the other to aid and abet in the thief's escape — and the thief changes his mind and decides to rape the farmer's daughter instead of stealing the horse, the rape is without the conspiracy, and the actor alone must suffer the punishment. On the other hand, if the farmer were killed in an attempt to stop the thief from taking his horse, the co-conspirator would be liable for the homicide. When two or more persons set out on a criminal enterprise, each is liable for the acts of the other, for it is true that the "hand of one is the hand of all."[13]

As to aiding and abetting the escape in general, the Government's case is considerably stronger. Certainly, given Dr. Mudd's sympathetic views of the Confederacy, his previous acquaintance with Booth, and the fact that Booth was attempting to go covertly in the middle of the night to the South, a reasonable, prudent man would realize that he was aiding and abetting some endeavor, perhaps even an illicit one. However, there is still no evidence which proves, directly or indirectly, that Dr. Mudd knew of the murder at the time he rendered aid.

Be that as it may, Dr. Mudd was not charged with being an accessory after the fact. His conviction must be based upon evidence of his knowing participation in the plot to murder the President, not upon his political views or his willingness to provide comfort and aid to travelers along the covert route to the South. The proof fails as to the charged offense.

In retrospect, the complete record before us shows that the assassination of President Abraham Lincoln was an extraordinary and sensational crime, committed by a well-known actor and southern sympathizer, John Wilkes Booth. The murder was obviously part and parcel of a grander scheme, which included the murder of other important officials of the United States, a fact well proved by the simultaneous assault on Secretary of State Seward and the attempts on others.

There was most certainly probable cause to believe that Dr. Mudd was an active conspirator. Nevertheless, based upon the evidence presented to the military commission, stripped of speculation and conjecture rising out of the heat and passions inflamed by the death of the President, the prosecution failed to prove that Dr. Mudd ever conspired to commit the offense charged.

Accordingly, with due respect to the members of the military commission, I would reverse Petitioner's conviction and order him released forthwith from his confinement.

The findings of guilty and the
sentence are set aside.

Notes

[1] 5 U.S. (1 Cranch) 137 (1803).

[2] *Id.* at 177.

[3] *Id.* at 178.

[4] U.S. CONST. amend. V.

[5] 71 U.S. (4 Wall.) 2 (1866).

[6] 23 Md. 531.

[7] MD. CONST. of 1864, art. I, § 4, *quoted in* Anderson v. Baker, 23 Md. at 580.

[8] 71 U.S. (4 Wall.) at 2.

[9] CAPT S.V. BENET, A TREATISE ON MILITARY LAW AND THE PRACTICE OF COURTS-MARTIAL 11-13 (New York, D. Van Nostrand, 2d ed. 1862); Francis Lieber, Guerilla Parties Considered with Reference to the Laws and Usages of War, letter to Henry Wager Halleck, General-in-Chief, Union Army, in response to Halleck's letter of Aug. 6, 1862 *in* THE WAR OF THE REBELLION: A COMPILATION OF THE OFFICIAL RECORDS OF THE UNION AND CONFEDERATE ARMIES, ser. III, vol. II, 301 (Washington, GPO 1899).

[10] *Cf.* ISAAC MALTBY, A TREATISE ON COURTS MARTIAL AND MILITARY LAW 36, 38-39 (Boston, Thomas B. Wait & Co. 1813).

[11] 71 U.S. (4 Wall.) at 2.

[12] *Id.* at 127.

[13] BENET, *supra* note 9, at 283 (emphasis added).

[14] 1 SIR WILLIAM OLDNALL RUSSELL, A TREATISE ON CRIMES AND MISDEMEANORS 28-29 (Philadelphia, T. Johnson & J.W. Johnson, 6th Am. ed. 1850). Russell's account on aiders and abettors is analogous:

> If a fact amounting to murder should be committed *in prosecution of some unlawful purpose,* though it were but a bare trespass, all persons who had gone in order to give assistance, if need were, for carrying such unlawful purpose into execution, would be guilty of murder. But this will apply only to a case where the murder was committed *in prosecution of some unlawful purpose,* some common design in which the combining parties were united, and for the effecting whereof they had assembled; for unless this shall appear, though the person giving the moral blow may himself be guilty of murder, or manslaughter, yet the others who came together for a different purpose will not be involved in his guilt. [Footnote omitted.] Thus where three soldiers went together to rob an orchard; two got upon a pear-tree, and the third stood at the gate with a drawn sword in his hand; and the owner's son coming by collared the man at the gate, and asked him what business he had there, whereupon the soldier stabbed him; it was ruled to be murder in the man who stabbed, but that those in the tree were

innocent. It was considered that they came to commit a small inconsiderable trespass, and that the man was killed upon a sudden affray without their knowledge. But the decision would have been otherwise if they had all come thither with a general resolution against all opposers; for then the murder would have been committed in prosecution of their original purpose.[w]

[w] Fost. 353. Case at Sarum Lent Assizes, 1697, MS. Denton & Chapple, 2 Hawk. P.C. c. 29, s 8. And see Rex v. Hodgson and others, 1 Leach, 6; and an Anon. case at the Old Bailey, in December Sessions, 1664, 1 Leach, 7, note *(a)* where several soldiers, who were employed by the messengers of the Secretary of State to assist in the apprehension of a person unlawfully broke open the door of a house where the person was supposed to be; and having done so, some of the soldiers began to plunder, and stole some goods. The question was, whether this was felony in all; and Holt, C.J., citing the case, says, "That they were all engaged in an unlawful act is plain, for they could not justify breaking a man's house without making a demand first; yet all those who were not guilty of the stealing were acquitted, notwithstanding their being engaged in one unlawful act of breaking the door; for this reason, because they knew not of any such intent, but it was a chance opportunity of stealing, whereupon some of them did lay hands."

Part Two

Commentary

His Name Was Mudd

Frederick Bernays Wiener*

INTRODUCTION

At about 9:30 p.m. on Good Friday, April 14, 1865, John Wilkes Booth fatally shot President Abraham Lincoln in the head. The shooting took place in Ford's Theater, located on 10th Street, N.W., in Washington, D.C. Jumping out of the box in which the President, Mrs. Lincoln, and two others sat, Booth caught the spur on his left boot in a decorative flag, with the result that he broke his left leg as he landed on the theater's stage.

Early on the next day, Booth and his companion David E. Herold rode up to the home of Samuel A. Mudd, M.D., near Bryantown in Charles County, Maryland, some thirty miles from Washington. Booth had earlier visited Charles County and had been with Dr. Mudd there and in Washington; Mudd

---

* Ph.B., Brown University, 1927; LL.B., Harvard University, 1930; Hon. LL.D., Cleveland-Marshall Law School, 1969. Practiced law privately, in government service, and in the Army, 1930-1973. Lecturer and Professorial Lecturer in law, The George Washington University, 1951-1956. Guggenheim Fellowship, 1962; Brown University Bicentennial Medallion, 1965; Selden Society, Member of Council since 1961, Lecturer at Lincoln's Inn, 1962, Vice-President for the U.S. 1978-1984. Colonel, Army of the U.S., Retired, 1966; Distinguished Member, The Judge Advocate General's Corps Regt., 1989. Author of *Briefing and Arguing Federal Appeals*, 1961, *Civilians Under Military Justice*, 1967, and many publications on legal, military, and historical subjects over a period of more than 60 years.

would later admit that he recognized Booth when the assassin appeared at his home on April 15.

Dr. Mudd cut the boot from Booth's broken leg, set the break, and furnished the injured man with crutches. Mudd also provided food and shelter for both visitors. The next day, after trying to find a carriage that would have facilitated Booth's travel, Mudd directed Booth and Herold across Zekiah Swamp to the Potomac River and Virginia. He also gave them a map of Virginia's Northern Neck.

Eleven days later, on the Garrett farm beyond Port Royal, Virginia, Booth died, whether by his own hand or by that of one of the Union soldiers who surrounded Garrett's tobacco barn, still remains unclear to this day.

Mudd and seven others linked with Booth were then placed on trial before a military commission comprised of nine field-grade and general officers of which the senior and president was Major General David Hunter. The eight in the dock were charged with conspiring to murder President Lincoln, Vice President Johnson, Secretary of State Seward, and Lieutenant General Grant.

Originally, some time in 1864, Booth had planned only to abduct the President and to hold him as ransom for the return of the thousands of Confederate prisoners then in Union hands, thus making possible a peace on Confederate terms. But after Lee's surrender, this was no longer possible. Accordingly, Booth turned to a mass killing that would paralyze the victorious Union government. He would kill the President, George A. Atzerodt was to do in the Vice President, and Lewis Payne would kill the Secretary of State, next in succession under the law then in force. General Grant (with his wife scheduled to be the Lincolns' guests that night at Ford's Theater) would also be disposed of because he was the highest ranking officer in the Union Army.

The specification under the general charge that was solely applicable to Mudd alleged that he advised, encouraged, received, entertained, harbored and concealed Booth and aided the other conspirators in escaping from justice.

After a trial that lasted from May 9 to June 30, 1865, and deliberations for two more days, the Hunter Commission found Mudd guilty and sentenced him to life imprisonment at Fort Jefferson in the Dry Tortugas, Florida. While imprisoned there, he sought three writs of *habeas corpus*, all of which were denied. But, because of his medical assistance to other prisoners during a yellow fever epidemic, Mudd was pardoned by President Johnson on March 1, 1869, just before the latter's term came to an end.

Dr. Mudd's oft asserted innocence became a cause that has been pursued over the years with virtually theological fervor. Finally, in 1991, a grandson of Dr. Mudd applied to the Army Board for Correction of Military Records to set aside his grandfather's conviction. That Board, on January 22, 1992, recommended that this be done, on the sole ground that the military commission that convicted Dr. Mudd lacked jurisdiction to try him in the first place.[1]

Exactly six months later, however, the Acting Assistant Secretary of the Army rejected the Board's recommendation and denied the Mudd family's application, on the ground that it was not the Board's role to settle historical disputes by rewriting history, even though the matter might have been decided differently today.[2] Thereafter, on February 12, 1993, a three-judge "Special Court of Military Appeal" presided over a moot court hearing at which were debated the questions deemed by the Secretary to be beyond the reach of the Board.

I. FUNDAMENTALS FREQUENTLY OVERLOOKED

A. Incompetence of the Accused as Witnesses

Before the Board and again before the Special Court, Dr. Mudd's family and their counsel attacked the Hunter Commission's refusal to permit any of the accused to take the stand in his or her own defense. Indeed, the Board formally found that "Dr. Mudd and the other defendants were not permitted to testify in their own behalf,"[3] as if this constituted a denial of due process on the part of the Hunter Commission. Actually this finding reflected simple ignorance on the part of the Board, because, at the time of Mudd's trial, in May and June 1865, no one accused of a crime before any tribunal of the United States, civil or military, was legally entitled to testify. That disqualification was not removed until 1878, when it was also provided that the accused's "failure to make such request shall not create any presumption against him."[4] Some States permitted the prosecution to make adverse comments on the accused's failure to testify, and that course was originally upheld.[5] But both decisions were overruled in *Malloy v. Hogan*,[6] decided in 1964 during the rewriting of the Constitution of the United States *tempore* Warren, C.J.[7]

Two other preliminary matters also need to be noted. Reading a record is inadequate to determine which of two conflicting witnesses is the one to be believed, because "[One] cannot now recreate his tone of voice or the gloss that personality puts upon speech."[8]

Second, even uncontradicted testimony must be ignored when it runs counter to settled rules of law. Thus, when Herold told Willie Jett, "We are the assassinators of the President,"[9] and when Booth immediately afterwards said of Herold, "I declare before my Maker that this man here is innocent of any crime whatever,"[10] it is plain that Booth knew nothing either of the law of conspiracy or of the law governing accessories. Similarly, while it has been suggested that the shift in Booth's plan from abduction to assassination meant that there were two separate conspiracies, one to abduct and the other to kill,[11] this distinction will simply not stand. For it is the law that, so long as the original objective is unchanged, there is still only a single conspiracy as long as the purpose of both plans is to inflict an unlawful deed upon the victim.[12]

B. Strength of Secessionist Sentiment in Maryland

Only good fortune and ruthless action kept Maryland from joining the Confederacy. Maryland's complete military subjection by northern troops, not the sentiment of its native people, kept the state in the Union. Maryland, particularly its southern counties, was territory hostile to the Lincoln administration and to the Union Army that occupied it.

In the 1860 election, Maryland gave the Republican ticket of Lincoln and Hamlin less than 3,000 votes, and some counties did not deliver a single vote to that slate.[13] The Democratic party was split in 1860. Stephen A. Douglas and Herschel V. Johnson, representing the more moderate pro-slavery group, received 1,376,957 votes in the nation, but received only twelve in the Electoral College. Vice President John C. Breckinridge and Senator Joseph Lane of Oregon, representing the more extreme pro-slavery views, received only 849,781 popular votes, but secured seventy-two electoral votes. The latter number included Maryland's.[14]

When, in April 1861, Fort Sumter was fired on and soon surrendered, President Lincoln called for 75,000 troops to put down the insurrection. Among the first regiments to head south for the defense of the Union was the 6th Massachusetts. It was cheered in Boston, New York, and Philadelphia, but received a quite different welcome in Baltimore.

In that city, the railway depot for the track from the north was one and one half miles away from that for the track to Washington. Military planners had taken note of the strong pro-Secessionist feeling in Baltimore. To reduce the disorder certain to ensue when the regiment moved from one depot to the other on April 19, the troops were carried between the two depots in horse cars. Nevertheless, an attack was mounted on the Massachusetts troops which escalated into a city-wide riot that left sixteen dead: twelve civilian and four military.[15] Maryland's Governor and Baltimore's Mayor both begged President Lincoln not to send any more troops through the city, the Mayor saying that while he did not believe in secession, he did believe in the right of revolution on the part of the oppressed people of the South. Soon, Baltimore effectively seceded from the Union. All available units of the State militia were called out, all telegraphic communication with the North was cut off, and all bridges connecting the city with the North were destroyed.[16] One of those bridges, connecting the city with Pennsylvania, was destroyed by members of the Baltimore County Horse Guards, commanded by Lieutenant John Merryman.[17] We shall hear more of him later.

Obviously, by April 20, the Union was in dire straits. Washington, the national capital, could not communicate by wire or by rail with the loyal states. If the secessionists of Virginia south of the Potomac were joined by those of Maryland north of the river, their troops could easily surround and conquer the District of Columbia that lay between the two. Fortunately, this "worst case" contingency never materialized. Union troops reached Annapolis by sea and soon branched out to occupy the area around Baltimore. Track repairs were effective, and, by midday April 25, "just six days after the Battle of Baltimore, the first trainloads of troops reached Washington. The road from the north had been reopened."[18] Soon General Winfield Scott formulated a plan for the capture of Baltimore, which "was no longer that ferocious tiger that had deliberately baited the Union. ... For Baltimore, in cutting the rail line to Washington, had succeeded only in cutting its own jugular vein."[19]

Baltimore rejoined the Union. The militia, after a showy parade, soon disbanded. The 6th Massachusetts reentered the city where it had been so violently attacked; vast quantities of arms were seized by the Union forces; and, by way of summary, "[a] combination of political, economic and military factors very quickly wrenched control of Maryland from the secessionists and turned the state back into the arms of the Union."[20]

We return now to John Merryman, the Baltimore militia officer who had destroyed the railway bridge between Maryland and Pennsylvania. On April 27, the President suspended the privilege of the writ of *habeas corpus* along "the military line ... used between the city of Philadelphia and the city of Washington."[21] Nearly a month later, at 2:00 a.m. on May 25, in consequence of an order from the commander of the Pennsylvania troops along the railroad line between Harrisburg and Baltimore, Merryman was arrested and taken from his home near Cockeysville to Fort McHenry in Baltimore.

He sought his release by applying for a writ of *habeas corpus*, an application that came before Chief Justice Roger B. Taney in the United States Circuit Court in Baltimore. Taney, then 84, had written the *Dred Scott v. Sanford*[22] decision which had denied Congress authority to outlaw slavery in the territories. He was a strong believer in states' rights and favored "a peaceful separation" of North and South.[23]

Justice Taney issued the writ, requiring General Cadwalader to produce Merryman in court. When the General politely replied that he had been authorized by the President to suspend the writ of *habeas corpus* for the public safety, the Chief Justice ordered that an attachment issue against the General for contempt. When the marshal went to Fort McHenry, he was told that there was no answer. The Chief Justice then concluded that, since the power refusing obedience was far superior to any posse the marshal could summon, the marshal was excused from doing more.

The opinion later filed holds that the President, under the

Constitution, cannot suspend or authorize suspension of the writ of *habeas corpus*, that a military officer has no right to arrest or detain a person not subject to the Articles of War, and that if the military authority makes an arrest, it is its duty immediately to deliver the prisoner to the civil authorities, to be dealt with according to law. Merryman was therefore entitled to be set at liberty.[24]

> The opinion concluded:
> I shall, therefore, order all the proceedings in this case, with my opinion, to be filed and recorded in the circuit court of the United States for the district of Maryland, and direct the clerk to transmit a copy, under seal, to the president of the United States. It will then remain for that high officer, in fulfillment of his constitutional obligation to take care that the laws be faithfully executed, to determine what measures he will take to cause the civil process of the United States to be respected and enforced.[25]

Inasmuch as the Constitution's provision on *habeas corpus* [26] appears in Article I, relating to Congress, rather than in Article II, dealing with the President, the latter officer lacked power to effect suspension on his own; it was a legislative function. Modern views accordingly concur with the Chief Justice on this point.[27]

More than half a century ago, the late Professor Fairman noted that "[i]t has become something of an article of liberal faith to regard this opinion as a great classic of liberty."[28] Indeed, Taney's latest biographer has rung the changes on that theme.[29]

But, in fact, the *Merryman* decision was worse than wrong; it was wrong-headed, and had it been obeyed it might well have been calamitous. As was observed by a contemporary pro-Union commentator, Professor Joel Parker of the Harvard Law School: "If the marshal had summoned the posse, the Secessionists would have had a better chance to capture the fort by volunteering under his banner than they are likely to have under any military commander."[30]

Fortified by a sensible opinion by Attorney General Edward Bates,[31] President Lincoln never admitted that he had acted unconstitutionally. Indeed, he told the Congress that, "[T]he whole of the laws which were required to be faithfully executed were being resisted and failing of execution in nearly one-third of the States. ... Are all the laws but one to go unexecuted, and the Government itself go to pieces lest that one be violated?"[32]

Following the disastrous defeat of Union forces at Bull Run in July 1861, secessionist sentiment in Maryland became stronger, and anti-Union riots and disorders multiplied.[33] Secretary of State William E. Seward directed widespread military arrests of those who publicly sympathized with the South or criticized President Lincoln and his cabinet.[34] Both houses of the Maryland legislature passed a resolution condemning such actions and then adjourned to meet at Frederick on September 17, 1861. The President's response was to make it impossible for such a meeting to take place. Orders went out to Major General John A. Dix in Baltimore and to Major General Nathaniel P. Banks in western Maryland to arrest all non-Union members of the Maryland legislature. There followed the suppression of pro-secession newspapers and the imprisonment of their editors. Journalists joined lawmakers as inmates at Fort McHenry. The pro-secession resolutions earlier passed by the Legislature and multiplied to the extent of 25,000 copies, were simply burned.[35]

By the time that Generals Dix and Banks had carried out their orders, virtually all of the leaders of the Peace Party in Maryland were in prison, the newspapers supporting them had been suppressed, and their editors were also in captivity.[36] More military arrests preceded the regular elections for members of the Legislature in November 1861. Election officials were warned by General Dix not to allow the ballot boxes to be "polluted by treasonable votes."[37] This, of course, was not a free election, because, in 1861, instead of secret ballots each party offered a ballot with its own distinctive color. As a consequence, every legislative seat in Baltimore was won by the Unionists, and the Unionist candidate for Governor won the city with a margin of about five to one:[38]

It was in Maryland that the orgy of suppression reached its apex. For here were pitted two irreconcilable forces, the historically mercurial temperament of a Southern city, and the absolute necessity for survival of the federal government. Temporarily the insurrectionary audacity of Baltimore had been triumphant, and during this phase the blockade of Washington had been complete. But in time, the overwhelming resources available to the North overcame this lone city and the ultimate subjugation of Baltimore was as complete as the blockade had been. As a result, Maryland was to stand through the war as a symbol of oppression, and its martyrs were to provide unlimited ammunition to those who criticized President Lincoln for his 'tyranny' and his Administration for its abuse of freedom.[39]

Finally, President Lincoln's general amnesty in February 1862 brought about the release of most of the Maryland prisoners who still remained in custody. Some prisoners refused to accept a parole on the ground that it would imply their guilt. Indeed, two were not freed until they had served seventeen months in detention.[40]

In short, in Maryland as well as in Kentucky and Missouri, the one step that kept three slave states from seceding with their eleven neighbors, was their effective military occupation by the Union Army.[41] As a practical matter, Maryland was hostile territory, militarily occupied.

C. Strength of Secessionist Sentiment in Charles County

Nowhere in Maryland were secessionist sympathies stronger than in Dr. Mudd's home county. Not by chance did Booth recruit many of his conspirators from that rural county, planned his escape across it to the Potomac, and avoided a massive Union manhunt for nine days through the connivance of Mudd's seditious and disloyal neighbors.

Charles County, Maryland, named for Charles Calvert, the third Lord Baltimore,[42] was in the middle of the 19th century an agricultural area with a tobacco economy founded on slavery. At a meeting in December 1860, those who had supported the Republican ticket were deemed to have committed an indiscretion, but one individual, Nathan Burnham, who had been "a Black Republican emissary," was given until the first of the new year to leave the county, and that in default thereof a designated committee of four would "expel him *vi et*

armis from our county."[43]   Some ten thousand to twelve
thousand Union troops were sent into Charles County. At
Port Tobacco, their commander reported that most inhabit-
ants were secessionists and that the post office was the me-
dium through which contact with the South was conducted.
Indeed, at his residence at Pope's Creek, Thomas A. Jones
helped boat loads of people illegally passing to the South. He
was arrested in September 1861 and confined for six months.
However, returning home after his release, he agreed to act as
Chief Signal Agent for the Confederacy north of the Potomac.
After the war, he asserted that he had never lost a letter or a
paper.[44]

As is reasonably well known, it was Booth's original plan
to kidnap the President, and to hold him hostage for the
release of all Confederate prisoners of war in Union hands.
He changed his plan to assassination only after Richmond fell
on April 3, 1865, and Lee surrendered on April 9.[45] Indeed,
according to Booth's diary, he did not change his mind until
the very day of the murder.[46]

Most of Booth's co-conspirators in both aspects were residents of Charles County. Dr. Mudd lived there, and the
county was Mrs. Surratt's home also. Indeed, what is now
Clinton, Maryland, was known in 1865 as Surrattville. The
tavern in Surrattville was owned by Mrs. Surratt and leased to
John M. Lloyd. The day before the assassination, she left at the
tavern for Booth's future use, a set of field glasses and told
Lloyd to have ready two carbines left in his care previously by
her son, Herold, and Atzerodt.[47]

Atzerodt lived at Port Tobacco in Charles County, where
he had often ferried Confederate spies and contraband across
the Potomac to Virginia. He signed a hotel register on April
14 giving his address as Charles County, Maryland.[48]

After Dr. Mudd set Booth's leg and put him up as a house
guest, he tried to procure a carriage for him. Failing to find
one, he gave Booth a chart of the Zekiah swamp and a map of
Virginia's Northern Neck. Booth and Herold then rode off,
eventually killing their horses lest one should neigh and
disclose their location to patrolling Union soldiers.[49] Herold
then found a black man to guide them to the home of Captain
Cox, whose Southern sympathies were well known.[50]

Next to Cox's house was that of his brother-in-law, Thomas A. Jones, who as already indicated was the Confederacy's Chief Signal Agent. Cox hid the two men in a thicket until he could arrange for Jones to take them across the Potomac.[50] Actually, although the area was virtually crawling with Union cavalry, Booth and Herold went undiscovered for some nine

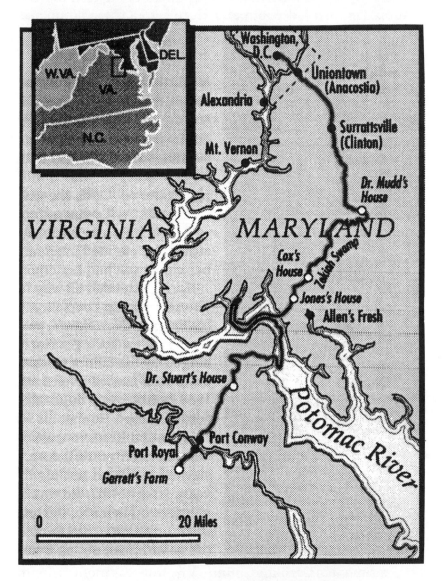

The escape route traveled by John Wilkes Booth and David Herold.

days. When Jones went to Port Tobacco, then the county seat, he heard one detective in the barroom of the Brawner Hotel say that he would give a $100,000 reward for information leading to Booth's capture.[52] A week after the assassination, when new rumors sent the federals hurrying into St. Mary's County, Jones decided that the time had come to move his guests. He then led Booth and Herold to a rowboat he had hidden at Dent's Meadow about a mile north of Pope's Creek on the Potomac.[53]

On the night of April 21, Booth was helped into Jones' rowboat with Herold at the oars. By morning they had not reached the Virginia shore. They put in at a creek on the Maryland side during daylight and when night came they pushed off again and finally made the Virginia shore. There they found a guide to the home of Dr. Richard H. Stuart, the richest man in King George County and a relative of General Robert E. Lee. However, Dr. Stuart wanted no part of these visitors. He gave them a meal in the kitchen, "where they ate in the fashion of a tramp given a handout,"[54] and then had them put up for the night in a black man's cabin. Dr. Stuart declined to attend to Booth's swollen and blackened leg.[55]

When the two fugitives reached Port Conway, they learned that the ferry to Port Royal would not come until the tide rose. Meanwhile, three young Confederate soldiers rode up, whereupon Herold identified himself and Booth: "We are the assassinators of the President."[56]

Across the Rappahannock, in Port Royal, the two Peyton sisters at first agreed to take in the fugitives, but then declined and suggested that Booth and Herold move on to the farm of Richard Garrett, who might take them in.[57]

While Booth and Herold were guests at the Garrett property, Mr. Garrett said at the family's dinner that he did not believe the assassination story. But a son, just back from Appomattox, knew the facts from a Richmond paper. "One hundred thousand dollars reward! That man had better not come this way, for I would like to make $100,000 just now!"[58] Whereupon his father asked, "Would you do such a thing? Betray him?"[59]

Sentiment in Caroline County, Virginia was identical with that in Charles County, Maryland: no one in either area would betray the assassin. But the pursuers, Colonel Everton J.

Conger and a detachment from the 16th New York Cavalry under the command of Captain Edward Doherty, nevertheless soon acquired information that led them to the Garrett property. There they found Booth and Herold. Herold was taken alive; whether the former was shot by himself or by Sergeant Boston Corbett has never been determined.[60]

II. FACTS BEARING ON MUDD'S GUILT

A. The Accusation
The charge against all eight of the alleged conspirators whose trial commenced on May 9, 1865, was that they conspired with a number of others to kill and murder President Abraham Lincoln, Vice President Andrew Johnson, Secretary of State William E. Seward, and Lieutenant General Ulysses S. Grant within the fortified and entrenched lines of the Military Department of Washington.[61]

The specification pertaining to Mudd alone alleged that Mudd, at Washington City and within those military lines, did, between March 6 and April 20, "advise, encourage, receive, entertain, harbor, and conceal, aid and assist"[62] Booth and the others[63] with knowledge of the conspiracy and with the intent to aid, abet, and assist them in the execution thereof, and in escaping from justice after the murder of the President in pursuance of said conspiracy.[64]

All the accused pleaded not guilty to both the charge and the specifications involving them. Afterwards all the accused moved for a severance, which was properly denied,[65] since it is fundamental law that a single individual cannot be guilty of being a conspirator. As Mr. Justice Cardozo said for the Supreme Court in a later case, "It is impossible in the nature of things for a man to conspire for himself. ... In California as elsewhere conspiracy imports a corrupt agreement between not less than two with guilty knowledge on the part of each."[66]

In the end, Mudd was convicted — except for the allegation of receiving, entertaining, harboring and concealing Payne, John Surratt, Mrs. Surratt, O'Laughlin, Atzenrodt, and Arnold. He was sentenced to life imprisonment.[67]

B. Mudd's Earlier Relations with Booth and the Surratts
Dr. Mudd first met Booth in November 1864 through one

Thompson, when Booth was in Charles County ostensibly to buy land and a horse. He did purchase a horse.[68] Actually, Booth was touring both to familiarize himself with escape routes and to find a suitable mount, in connection with his plan to kidnap President Lincoln.

Mudd and Booth met again, this time in Washington, in the spring of 1865, although the precise date was disputed. It was then that, at Booth's request, Mudd introduced him to John H. Surratt, the professional spy. Booth and Surratt had many private conversations afterwards.[69] Surratt had frequently visited the Mudds in the summer of 1864, and Confederate soldiers in gray uniforms had frequently been seen on the Mudd property.[70]

As mentioned above, John's mother, Mrs. Mary E. Surratt, owned a tavern in Surrattsville. After her husband died, she established a boarding house at H Street, N.W., in Washington and leased the tavern to John M. Lloyd. Five or six weeks before the assassination, Herold, Atzerodt, and John Surratt visited the tavern and left two carbines, which Lloyd concealed under the joists of the main building's second floor.[71]

On the Tuesday before the assassination, Mrs. Surratt came to the tavern and asked about the "shooting irons." When Lloyd replied that they were hidden, she told him to get them ready, that they would be needed soon. On April 14, she returned to tell Lloyd:

> [T]o get those shooting irons ready that night, there would be some parties who would call for them. She gave [him] something wrapped in a piece of paper, which ... [he] found to be a field glass. She told [him] to get two bottles of whiskey ready, and that those things were to be called for that night.[72]

About midnight on April 14, Herold came to the tavern and said, "Lloyd, for God's sake, make haste and get those things."[73] Lloyd then gave Herold the carbines, whiskey, and field glass.

Herold arrived at the tavern that night with a man Lloyd did not know, who remained mounted on a large horse. The man accepted a bottle of whiskey from Herold but declined one of the carbines, saying he could not carry it because his leg was broken. As they were leaving Herold told Lloyd, "I am pretty certain that we have assassinated the President and Secretary Seward."[74] Herold gave Lloyd a single dollar bill "which just about paid for the bottle of liquor they had just pretty nearly drank."[75]

C. Mudd's Knowledge of Booth's Identity on April 15

When questioned later about the identity of the man whose leg he had treated on April 15, Dr. Mudd's replies were contradictory and evasive. He seemed frightened, anxious, uneasy, worried, and very much excited.[76] At first, Mudd told investigators that his two visitors were strangers. It was only later, after Mrs. Mudd had produced Booth's initialed boot that her husband admitted an acquaintance with Booth, but still he denied recognizing his patient.[77] Other interviews with Dr. Mudd indicated that he was concealing facts in the case.[78]

After trial, on his way to Fort Jefferson to serve his life sentence, Dr. Mudd finally admitted

> that he knew Booth when he came to his house with Herold, on the morning after the assassination of the President; that he had known Booth for some time, but he was afraid to tell of his having been at his house on the 15th of April, fearing that his own and the lives of his family would be endangered thereby.[79]

Not a single witness before the Army Board for Correction of Military Records in 1991, one of whom specifically said that he was familiar with the Pitman edition of the trial proceedings,[80] ever mentioned that confession.

D. The Irrelevance of Mudd's Duty as a Physician

Much has been made of the assertion that all Mudd did was perform his duty as a physician when faced with an injured patient who came for help. The record of trial sets out the scope of the assistance that Mudd gave Booth. The doctor set Booth's leg, supplied him with a razor to shave off his moustache[81] (Booth on arrival had also worn a false beard[82]), supplied him with food, lodging[83] and a pair of crutches,[84] tried to get him a carriage,[85] showed Booth how to cross the swamp, and gave him a map of the Northern Neck of Virginia.[86]

The normal measure of a medical doctor's duty is of course the Hippocratic Oath.[87] But the text of that commitment does not justify all the steps that Mudd took for Booth's benefit. Setting his leg, providing him with crutches, and even seeking to provide a carriage to ease matters for one whose further travel on horseback would necessarily be painful, can all be deemed medical obligations. But assisting his caller to disguise his normal appearance, providing the fugitive with directions on how to avoid the roads by passing through the Zekiah swamp, and giving him a map suitable for an illegal crossing into hostile Virginia, can only be characterized as aiding and abetting, as being an accessory after the fact, and as tending to prove participation in the earlier conspiracy to harm the President.

Moreover, Mudd had, at Booth's request, already introduced him to John Surratt,[88] who was known to be a Confederate spy,[89] and who had frequently been a guest at Mudd's home,[90] in an area much frequented by Confederate deserters.[91]

Consequently, Mudd's conduct, far from justified by the Hippocratic Oath, shows he had actually forsworn it. Indeed, that solemn pledge directs the new physician to "practice your art in uprightness and honor ... holding yourselves far aloof from wrong, from corruption."[92]

Mudd and his partisans have long insisted the doctor did no more than his profession required for any injured stranger. That might be true if Mudd had never before seen the man whose leg was broken; it might also be true if the doctor had recognized his patient only as John Wilkes Booth, the well-known actor and not John Wilkes Booth, the hunted assassin. But why did Mudd lie to questioners, saying that he never recognized the supplicant? What was there about Booth on the early morning of April 15 that induced Mudd to prevaricate? The only logical inference is that Mudd lied because he knew Booth had just assassinated the President. Only Booth's admission of his acts could have led to Mudd's fear that, if he admitted knowing Booth's identity, his own and his family's lives would be in danger.

Mudd's repeated denials prove Mudd knowingly shielded

the assassin Booth and his henchman Herold from capture. The only conflict with a physician's oath came therefore from the physician's own criminal conduct, and the Hippocratic Oath cannot — even morally — justify Dr. Samuel A. Mudd, the prevaricator, the accessory, the co-conspirator.[93]

III. CREATION, DEVELOPMENT, AND JURISDICTION OF THE MILITARY COMMISSION

A. Original Creation During the Mexican War

Shortly after arriving in Mexico as commander of all American troops then engaged in the war with that country, Major General Winfield Scott (as he then was) issued his "Martial Law" order, which had two objectives. First, he found it necessary to punish the ill-behaved volunteers who were actually completely out of control once they crossed the Rio Grande. Second, he recognized the need for protecting his own forces against offenses committed by the local population. Accordingly, first at Tampico and later at other places, he created the military commission to deal with both classes of incidents.[94]

Scott had been educated as a lawyer, and practiced his profession for a few years.[95] But as hostilities with Britain over the impressment of American seamen loomed ever nearer, Scott became more interested in a military career, and after a meeting with President Jefferson, he was commissioned as a captain of light artillery.[96]

It is therefore safe to conclude that Scott's creation of the military commission[97] reflected, not what he had read and learned from Professor St. George Tucker at the College of William and Mary nor in the law office of David Robertson at Petersburg, but from his experiences and from his wide reading on military matters in his nearly forty years of service as a commissioned officer in the United States Army.[98]

B. Reappearance of the Commission in the Civil War

When the Civil War began, the Army's senior officers looked for guidance back to their Mexican War experiences and procedures. Accordingly, on January 1, 1862, Major General Henry W. Halleck, commanding the Department of Missouri, declared in General Orders No. 1 of that headquarters that the many offenses which, in time of peace, are civil offenses, became, in time of war, military offenses, and were to be tried by a military tribunal, even in places where civil tribunals existed.[99]

General Halleck had been Secretary of State in the military government established for the Mexican territories that eventually became California. Thus, he was thoroughly familiar with General Scott's practice, pursuant to which numerous offenders had been tried by military commissions. Finding civilians in Missouri quite as obstreperous as the former Mexican civilians had been, Halleck also concluded that the courts of Missouri were equally ineffective. Accordingly, he ordered trial by military commission for any person suspected of aiding the Confederacy.[100]

But, when the record of trial by military commission at General Halleck's direction of Colonel Ebenezer Magoffin, C.S.A., reached the War Department, it came to the desk of the Judge Advocate of the Army, Brevet Major John Fitzgerald Lee, who had been appointed to the office created by Congress in 1849,[101] and he held that military commissions were without authority and illegal.[102]

Obviously this would not do. By July 1862, General Halleck was ordered to Washington as General-in-Chief, *vice* the overly timorous McClellan. Shortly thereafter, Congress legislated Major J.F. Lee out of office by substituting for his position as Judge Advocate of the Army that of Judge Advocate General of the Army, with rank, pay and allowances of a colonel of cavalry.[103]

C. Judge Advocate General Holt and the Development of the Military Commission

To the new post the President appointed Joseph Holt of Kentucky, effective September 3, 1862, and on September 4, Major John Fitzgerald Lee, a Virginian and 1834 graduate of the United States Military Academy, resigned from the Army.[104]

Holt, a Democrat, was sufficiently prominent in his profession and in his party to be thrice appointed to high office by President Buchanan, first as Commissioner of Patents, next as Postmaster General, and finally, from January 18 to March 5, 1861, as Secretary of War. Once South Carolina's Ordinance of Secession was passed, he became a firm Unionist of inflexible belief in the righteousness of the Union cause. Thus he was then an all too rare specimen, a convinced War Democrat, and one who contributed substantially to persuading Kentucky to shift from neutrality to support of the Union.[105]

It was Holt who truly developed the military commission into an instrumentality that enabled military authorities to arrest, try, convict, and keep confined many persons who would otherwise have been released by the civil courts.

In the War Department's General Orders No. 100, published on April 23, 1863, "Instructions for the Government of Armies of the United States in the Field" (which were primarily composed by Dr. Francis Lieber), the military commission was formally recognized as the proper tribunal under the laws of war to deal with cases that were not covered by the Articles of War but that were derived from the common law of war.[106]

Holt was legislatively promoted to brigadier general and to head of the newly established Bureau of Military Justice in mid-1864 and eventually, on "the bloody 13th of March, 1865," brevetted major general "for faithful, meritorious and distinguished service in the Bureau of Military Justice during the war."[107]

General Holt not only headed the Bureau of Military Justice during the Civil War, but also presided at the trial of Major General Fitz-John Porter, charged with disobedience of orders at the second Battle of Bull Run, in consequence of which the accused was cashiered (sentenced never again to serve in any military capacity).[108] Likewise, Holt was judge advocate of the military commission that tried the eight conspirators in the Lincoln Assassination, while helped in that task by two assistant judge advocates.[109]

D. Conflicting Contemporary Opinions on the Power of a Military Commission to try the Lincoln Assassination Conspirators[110]

The military commission's trial of the Lincoln assassination conspirators began on May 9, 1865, and concluded on June 30 of the same year with the announcement of its findings and sentences.[111] On July 5, President Johnson approved all of them, directing that the four sentenced to hang —

Atzerodt, Herold, Payne and Mrs. Surratt — be executed on July 7.[112]

Earlier on that last day, there was filed on behalf of Mrs. Surratt a petition for a writ of *habeas corpus*, an application that was denied by a judge of the Supreme Court of the District of Columbia because of the President's suspension of the writ.[113] Accordingly, the executions were duly carried out as ordered.[114]

On April 3, 1866, the United States Supreme Court announced the result in *Ex parte Milligan*,[115] after which, on December 14, 1866, both the opinions of the Court and that of the four concurring justices were delivered.[116]

After Booth's co-conspirators had been rounded up, Attorney General James Speed on April 28, 1865, sent this one sentence opinion to President Johnson: "I am of opinion that the persons charged with the murder of the President of the United States can rightfully be tried by a military court."[117]

Although containing no reasoning whatever, and the shortest formal opinion ever written by any Attorney General,[118] this sufficed for President Johnson to direct the trial of the eight conspirators by military commission.[119]

Of course the jurisdiction of the military commission was questioned at the trial, and, needless to state, was sustained by that tribunal.[120] Senator Reverdy Johnson of Maryland, representing Mrs. Surratt at the trial, made one of the arguments attacking jurisdiction,[121] while Thomas Ewing, Jr., representing Dr. Mudd,[122] made another.[123]

Inasmuch as Ewing had, while serving as a brigadier general in the Union Army, issued the notorious General Orders No. 11, under which some 20,000 refugees were expelled from four Missouri counties which were said to have sustained the notorious Confederate guerrilla band commanded by William C. Quantrill,[124] it was indeed an ironic touch for him to attack military jurisdiction. This point was made to the commission by the special judge advocate, John A. Bingham, Esquire, who delivered the closing argument for the prosecution.[125]

After the four conspirators sentenced to death had been hanged on July 7, Attorney General Speed produced a second opinion, dated July 1865 (without mention of any particular day).[126] In that essentially *ex post facto* expression he said:

At the time of the assassination the Civil War was flagrant, the city of Washington was defended by fortifications regularly and constantly manned, the principal police of the city was by Federal soldiers, public offices and property in the city were all guarded by soldiers, and the President's House and person were, or should have been, under the guard of soldiers. Martial law had been declared in the District of Columbia, but the civil courts were open and transacted business as in times of peace.[127]

Ben Perley Poore wrote, in the introduction to his own edition of the evidence as given at the trial, words that reflected the bitter community feelings against the conspirators in language only slightly paraphrasing the Attorney General's second opinion:

The assassination of Abraham Lincoln was a military crime. While actually in command of the national forces, he was killed in a city which was his headquarters, strongly fortified and garrisoned, with a military governor, and a provost-marshal whose patrols were abroad day and night arresting all persons found violating the rules and articles of war. Not only was the murdered commander-in-chief, to use the words of the Constitution, 'in actual service in time of war,' but it was a time of 'public danger,' in which the assassins were excluded from any right to trial in the civil courts.[128]

There was nothing at all imaginary about the city of Washington's closeness to the war. Only nine months prior to the assassination, in mid-July of 1864, a substantial Confederate force under Lieutenant General Jubal A. Early had left the Shenandoah Valley in Virginia, captured Frederick, Maryland, and reached Fort Stevens, near the Soldiers' Home and so far inside the District of Columbia that the Capitol's dome was visible.[129]

But Washington in July of 1864 was vastly different from the same community in May of 1865. While rebel troops had penetrated the defenses of the Union capital the year before, a Union army now occupied Richmond. Lee had surrendered at Appomattox, Johnston in North Carolina was about to do the same, and the end of the Confederate forces west of the Mississippi was simply a matter of mopping up.

In those changed circumstances the most serious criticisms of Speed's opinions and of the military trial of the assassin-conspirators came from Speed's predecessor as Attorney General of the United States, Edward Bates. Here are excerpts from his wartime diary: "[My] successor ... has been wheedled out of an opinion to the effect that such a trial [by military commission] is lawful. ... [He] must have known better. Such a trial is not only unlawful, but it is a great blunder of policy."[130] And when Mr. Bates saw Speed's July 1865 opinion, he used five and one half pages of print, dated August 21, for a point-by-point rebuttal of what his predecessor had written.[131]

Edward Bates was not alone in entertaining an unfavorable view of Speed's legal talents. Mr. Justice Miller of the Supreme Court, on the day before the arguments in the *Milligan* case (in which Speed was to participate) had begun, wrote in a private letter about Speed: "[T]he session of the Court has developed his utter want of ability as a lawyer — [h]e is certainly one of the feeblest men who has addressed the Court this term."[132]

Senator Thomas Ewing, Sr. advised President Johnson to the same effect on March 15, 1866:

> It is of the utmost importance that you have a stronger man in that place — It is due to yourself and also to the Court, for Mr. Speed is not a competent legal adviser especially on the present critical condition of affairs — I know that the Court does not rely on him.[133]

The precise number of trials by military commissions during the Civil War remains unclear. Winthrop, whose service as a judge advocate commenced on July 28, 1864,[134] estimated there had been upwards of 2,000 such trials during that period; a later author, writing nearly a century afterwards, fixed the figure at 4,271, more than half of which took place in the strife-torn border states of Missouri, Kentucky, and Maryland.[135] There the matter must rest for the moment.

IV. THE *MILLIGAN* CASE

Shortly after the Hunter Commission's trial of the Lincoln assassination co-conspirators, the United States Supreme Court was presented an opportunity to pass on the legality of another well-publicized case in which civilian citizens of a free state were convicted and condemned to death by a military commission. The Court's stinging rebuke of this use of military tribunals, coming so quickly on the heels of the Hunter Commission's verdicts, was, then and since, brandished as another sign of the illegality of Dr. Mudd's trial. However, a careful look at the Court's opinion in *Ex parte Milligan*[136] shows that its bombast outweighs its persuasion.

A. Who Were the Copperheads?

Copperheads were almost exclusively Democrats who were willing to let the Confederate States leave the Union and hence sought the end of hostilities. "The stealthiest, most venomous serpent of the prairies ... lay in hiding, struck without warning, and his sting was death. The anti-slavery men and other ardent Unionists employed the title of the reptile to denounce the enemies they deemed traitors."[137] But the men so designated "regarded themselves as lovers of liberty. They were determined to cut the Liberty head out of the penny, affix a pin to it, and wear the copper Liberty head on lapel or shirt as a badge of true respect for the Constitution and the Union."[138]

The military portion of the Copperheads was known as the Order of American Knights. Its members wished to form a Northwest Confederacy, to ally itself with that of the South. They planned to attack all Union installations that held Confederate prisoners of war, and collected arms for that purpose. They were particularly strong in the area of the old Northwest Territory: Ohio, Illinois, and Indiana. But in that latter state they encountered Governor Oliver P. Morton, who was truly the dictator of Indiana.[139]

The critical year, according to George Fort Milton, was 1864, and his narrative makes it easy to follow the Northwest Conspiracy and the means that the pro-Union forces used, first to infiltrate the O.A.K. ranks, and then to nullify their planned attacks. What Union agents discovered led to the Indiana treason trials and, ultimately, to *Ex parte Milligan* which freed the three conspirators whom the military commission had sentenced to hang. Those three were Lambdin P. Milligan, Dr. William A. Bowles, and Stephen Horsey.

B. Trial of Milligan et al. by Military Commission

The full text of their trial by military commission was published in 1865 by Benn Pitman,[140] the same who later reported the trial of the Lincoln Conspirators, and was afterwards reprinted verbatim in Samuel Klaus' *The Milligan Case* in 1929.[141]   As has been seen, Mr. Milton condensed the proceedings into narrative form, with considerable emphasis on the reactions of the accused when a number of their closest associates, who were actually secret Union agents, suddenly appeared as vital prosecution witnesses against them. There were five charges against Milligan *et al.*: (1) conspiracy against the government of the United States, four specifications; (2) affording aid and comfort to rebels against the authority of the United States, three specifications; (3) inciting insurrection, two specifications; (4) disloyal practices, five specifications; and (5) violations of the laws of war, two specifications.[142]

After examining the testimony, Mr. Klaus concluded that "the men were guilty of the charges made there can be little room for dispute, nor that there was in fact ground for a civil indictment for treason."[143]

True enough, but the fact that Indiana was up to its neck in Copperheads meant that, if the accused had been tried in a civil court, a single individual on a jury could block conviction. And, if any one troubles to read the 1864 case of *Griffin v. Wilcox*,[144] an opinion emanating from Indiana's Supreme Court, he will find that Copperhead sentiments were well reflected among the members of that state's highest judicial tribunal.

In Indiana, therefore, only a military tribunal, from which Copperheads were certain to be excluded, would be able to ascertain objectively the guilt or innocence of this collection of accused individuals.

Appeals for clemency were discussed with President Lincoln even before any sentences had been adjudged, but after his assassination, President Johnson approved the three death sentences and ordered them executed on May 11, 1865.[145]

Meanwhile, counsel for Milligan *et al.* sought a writ of *habeas corpus* from the United States Circuit Court in Indianapolis and pressed further appeals for clemency to President Johnson. He was persuaded to commute all three sentences to life imprisonment.[146]

In the circuit court, action on the petitions for the writ went forward. After the close of the hearing, Justice Davis and District Judge McDonald certified that they differed in opinion, and this under the law then in force automatically brought the case to the Supreme Court on writ of error.[147] Here were the questions presented: First, on the facts set out, viz., the entire record before the military trial, should the writ be issued? Second, ought Milligan et al. be discharged? Third, did the military commission have jurisdiction legally to try Milligan and his fellows?

C. The Supreme Court Decision

Here we come to the Supreme Court's ultimate determination, and we see once again the mischief that can result from wholly unnecessary dicta, some of which were still in every lawyer's recollection when the *Milligan* case was filed in the Supreme Court on December 27, 1865.[148]

Every lawyer recollected the notorious *Dred Scott* case,[149] which could have been decided solely on the footing that, since Dred Scott as a Negro could not become a citizen, his suit was not within the diversity jurisdiction of the circuit court. Instead, the Supreme Court undertook in that case to settle the slavery question judicially, affirming the liberty of a slave-owning citizen to bring his slave into any territory of the United States.[150]

The *Milligan* case, likewise, could also have been disposed of without unwarranted excursions into hypothetical areas had the Court rested its determination on a statute of which all of its members were fully aware, and which clearly pointed the way to a result identical with the one actually reached.

Sections two and three of the Habeas Corpus Act of March 3, 1863,[151] provided in substance that, when a citizen of a state where the courts are open is arrested or confined by order of the President or of the Secretaries of State or War, those officers are directed to furnish the United States courts in such states with lists of the persons held as prisoners because of the commission of crimes against the United States, and when the grand juries in such districts have terminated their sessions without finding an indictment, such persons shall within twenty days be released from custody upon taking an oath of allegiance to the government of the United States, and to support the Constitution thereof, and that he or she will not hereafter in any way encourage or give aid and comfort to the present rebellion or to the supporters thereof.[152]

Accordingly, deference to the Habeas Corpus Act would have sufficed to dispose of the cases of Milligan, Bowles, and Horsey; all else that was said on both sides of the 5-4 decision was dictum elaborated into emotional stump speeches. That conclusion is not in any sense a revisionist evaluation formulated a century and a quarter after the event; it represented contemporary professional opinion of the most thoughtful character. Indeed, that was the view of the new *American Law Review*, edited by John Chipman Gray and John C. Ropes of Boston.[153]

Where the two Supreme Court opinions in the *Milligan* case differed was on the issue of whether Congress could ever authorize trial of crime by military commission. But, as Professor Fairman wrote, "[I]t was Executive action against which Milligan sought relief: yet the opinion managed to rule against Congress in respect of pending matters about which Congress felt most concerned and most sensitive,"[154] namely the need to protect freedmen against homicide or other violence in the former Confederate state courts and whether the only foreseeable remedy for the existing situation would be the enactment of legislation to authorize a full-blown Reconstruction regime.

Justice Davis had consistently opposed military trial of civilians by military tribunals and their military arrest and the suppression of newspapers, making those views available to President Lincoln.[155] Now, however, he had an unlimited audience, and was able to speak from the very highest seat of authority:

> During the late wicked Rebellion, the temper of the times did not allow that calmness in deliberation and discussion so necessary to a correct conclusion of a purely judicial question. *Then*, considerations of safety

were mingled with the exercise of power; such feelings and interests prevailed which are happily terminated. *Now* that the public safety is assured, this question, as well as all others, can be discussed and decided without passion or the admixture of any element not required to form a legal judgment. We approach the investigation of this case, fully sensible of the magnitude of the inquiry and the necessity of full and cautious deliberation.[156]

In due course, Justice Davis warmed up to his subject, in language that has been regularly repeated ever since:

The Constitution of the United States is a law for rulers and people, equally in war and in peace, and covers with the shield of its protection all classes of men, at all times, and under all circumstances. No doctrine, involving more pernicious consequences, was ever intended by the wit of man than that any of its provisions can be suspended during any of the great exigencies of government. Such a doctrine leads directly to anarchy or despotism, but the theory of necessity on which it based is false; for the government, within the Constitution, has all the powers granted to it, which are necessary to preserve its existence; as has been happily proved by the result of the great effort to throw off its just authority.[157]

Chief Justice Chase for the minority agreed with the result, but disagreed that Congress lacked power ever to authorize trial by military commission. He said:

We cannot doubt that, in such a time of public danger, Congress had power, under the Constitution, to provide for the organization of a military commission, and for the trial by that commission of persons engaged in this conspiracy. The fact that the Federal courts were open was regarded by Congress as a sufficient reason for not exercising the power; but that fact could not deprive Congress of the right to exercise it. Those courts might be open and undisturbed in the execution

of their functions, and yet wholly incompetent to avert threatened danger, or to punish, with adequate promptitude and certainty, the guilty conspirators.[158]
***
We have no apprehension that this power, under our American system of government, in which all official authority is derived from the people, and exercised under direct responsibility to the people, is more likely to be abused than the power to regulate commerce, or the power to borrow money. And we are unwilling to give our assent by silence to expressions of opinion which seem to us calculated, though not intended, to cripple the constitutional powers of the government, and to augment the public dangers in times of invasion and rebellion.[159]

From 1866 to 1940, military-legal opinion differed sharply on which of the two conflicting sets of dicta correctly expressed the state of the law. Colonel Winthrop was certain that the better reason lay with the minority.[160] His chief, Judge Advocate General G. Norman Lieber (son of the Dr. Francis Lieber who framed General Orders No. 100),[161] was equally positive that only the majority had expressed sound constitutional doctrine.[162] Chief Justice Hughes, in the interim between his two terms of service on the Court, said in 1917, "Certainly the test should not be a mere physical one, nor should substance be sacrificed to form."[163] And back in 1940, the present author published a work that, it is believed, correctly set out the state of the law at that time.[164]

Seventy years ago, Charles Warren, an earlier historian of the Supreme Court, called Davis' words an "immortal opinion," "one of the bulwarks of American history," and "the palladium of the rights of the individual."[165]

Fairman himself calls Davis' statement "as fine a sentence as can be found anywhere in the United States Reports."[166]

D. *Milligan* Does Not Accurately Portray Today's Law
Unhappily Justice Davis' emotional stem-winder about the Constitution being always the same in war and peace is demonstrably not the law in the 1990s — nor has it been for more than three-quarters of a century. It seems appropriate to

append a list.

1. In the fall of 1916, Congress hastily passed a railroad eight-hour work law to avert a nationwide railroad strike. This was at a time when trucks and planes were not yet available to transport people or products. The Court sustained the act as being within the congressional power to regulate commerce in *Wilson v. New*.[167] What is notable about the decision is that the dissenters quoted David Davis' dithyramb about the irrelevance of emergencies.

2. The year 1934 brought up the Minnesota mortgage moratorium law in *Home Building and Loan Ass'n v. Blaisdell*.[168] That legislation was upheld five to four, on the footing that, "while emergency does not create power, emergency may furnish the occasion for the exercise of power."[169] The minority of four who believed that Minnesota lacked the power to relieve mortgagors quoted the immortal passage from Justice Davis' *Milligan* opinion — immortal but quite unavailing.

Indeed, once wartime cases are examined, some from the First World War but most of them from the Second, it will be found that much is authorized in time of war that is wholly impermissible in time of peace, notably in the area of economic regulation.

Here are a baker's dozen of cases that wholly contradict "as fine a sentence that can be found anywhere in the United States Reports."[170]

(a) Rent and price control. *Block v. Hirsh*, 256 U.S. 135 (1921); *Chastleton Corp. v. Sinclair*, 264 U.S. 543 (1924); *Yakus v. United States*, 321 U.S. 414 (1944); *Bowles v. Willingham*, 321 U.S. 503 (1944); *Woods v. Cloyd W. Miller Co.*, 333 U.S. 138 (1948).

(b) Renegotiation of contracts. *Lichter v. United States*, 334 U.S. 742 (1948).

(c) Wartime prohibition. *Hamilton v. Kentucky Distilleries & Warehouse Co.*, 251 U.S. 146 (1919); *Ruppert v. Caffey*, 251 U.S. 264 (1920).

(d) Seizure of enemy property. *Miller v. United States*, 78 U.S. (11 Wall.) 268 (1870); *Stoehr v. Wallace*, 255 U.S. 239 (1921); *Central Union Trust Co. v. Garvan*, 254 U.S. 554 (1921); *Silesian American Corp. v. Clark*, 332 U.S. 469 (1947).

(e) Suppression of houses of ill-fame within the States. *McKinley v. United States*, 249 U.S. 397 (1919) (although this would impinge on what would otherwise be exclusively the subject of state police power. *Keller v. United States*, 213 U.S. 138 (1909)).

Mention has already been made of the German saboteurs' case, *Ex parte Quirin*, decided in 1942.[171] There, it should be noted, what they did was not in violation of any United States statute for which they could have been indicted by a federal grand jury. In *Quirin*, the Supreme Court held *Milligan* "inapplicable to the case presented by the present record," and specifically overruled a passage therein that it deemed too exuberant.[172]

All of the foregoing decisions antedate Mr. King's biography of Justice Davis, which was published in 1960, and which actually cites *Ex parte Quirin*.[173]

Instead, Mr. King continues his erroneous hagiography of *Ex parte Milligan*:

> In subsequent wars, the administration has again and again urged the Supreme Court to repudiate the *Milligan* case, but it still stands in all the grandeur of its original utterance.[174]
> ***
> Davis' great contribution to constitutional law was the *Milligan* decision that ended military trials of civilians in the North. He maneuvered to get the case before the Supreme Court and then delivered the opinion that forever put an end to such trials. 'The Constitution of the United States is a law for rulers and people, equally in war and in peace.' Those nineteen words and the eternal place in history of the friend he made President must remain the Judge's monument.[175]

At this point it should also be noted that even Chief Justice Chase's minority opinion now requires amendment.[176] He recited three recognized heads of military jurisdiction:

(a) Military law, the code governing the armed forces (e.g., *Toth v. Quarles*, 350 U.S. 11 (1955); *Reid v. Covert*, 354 U.S. 1 (1957); *O'Callahan v. Parker*, 395 U.S. 258 (1969); *Solorio v. United States*, 483 U.S. 435 (1987)).

(b) Military government, where the military occupant in time of war supersedes the local government (e.g., *United*

States v. Rice, 4 Wheat. 246 (1819), through a host of decisions arising out of the Mexican, Civil, and Spanish Wars, down to *Madsen v. Kinsella*, 343 U.S. 341 (1952), involving occupied Germany after World War II).

(c) Martial law (or, more accurately, martial rule), involving the temporary suspension of civil rule by military authority when required by necessity (e.g., *Ex parte Milligan*, 71 U.S. (4 Wall.) 2 (1866); *Duncan v. Kahanamoku*, 327 U.S. 304 (1946)).

Now there must be added a fourth head of military jurisdiction — the international law of war — long recognized, but never considered by American civil courts until during and after World War Two (e.g., *Ex parte Quirin*, 317 U.S. 1 (1942); *Yamashita v. Styer*, 327 U.S. 1 (1946); *Homma v. Patterson*, 327 U.S. 759 (1946); *Johnson v. Eisentrager*, 339 U.S. 763 (1950)).

Contemporaneously, however, Lambdin P. Milligan did recover when he sued for damages the officer who had appointed the military commission that tried him and sentenced him to be hanged. He was ultimately successful, but hardly satisfied: the jury only awarded him five dollars.[177]

Perhaps a note should be included here, simply for the sake of completeness, about the post-*Milligan* trials by military commission under the Reconstruction Acts. It is estimated that, from the end of April 1866 to January 1, 1869, another 1,435 trials by military commission took place, tapering off as time passed; in 1869 and 1870, they occurred only in Texas and Mississippi.[178]

When the legality of such military trials under the Reconstruction Acts[179] might have come again before the Supreme Court for decision,[180] adjudication was forestalled, in one instance by a legislative withdrawal of appellate jurisdiction,[181] in the other by a release of the petitioner from the challenged custody. In effect, the second case was settled after the readmission of Mississippi to representation in Congress.[182]

E. Deciding Wartime Cases After Cessation of Hostilities

By 1866, when *Ex parte Milligan* reached the Supreme Court, the Civil War was over. At least some of the bitterness associated with four years of all-out war had diminished, and the way seemed clear for the highest court in the land to determine once and for all the powers of military tribunals to try and to punish persons who were not members of the armed forces or individuals accused of spying.

As we have seen, much that was said in both *Milligan* opinions has not withstood the test of time. But in *Milligan* the government had no choice but to defend what had been done. It was otherwise in *Duncan v. Kahanamoku* and its companion case, *White v. Steer*, argued on Pearl Harbor Day in 1945, and decided on February 25, 1946.[183] Both cases involved trials of civilians by military courts in the territory of Hawaii, which was under martial law pursuant to the Hawaiian Organic Act of 1900.[184]

White was a civilian stockbroker found guilty of that occupational disease, embezzling a client's funds. He was tried and convicted by a military provost court on August 25, 1942, and sentenced to five years' imprisonment. Duncan was a civilian ship-fitter who quarreled with two armed marine sentries at the gate of the Pearl Harbor Navy Yard. On March 3, 1944, he was brought before a provost court and sentenced to six months' confinement in the Honolulu County jail for the offense of assault and battery against military personnel.

The writ of *habeas corpus* had been suspended on December 7, 1941, by the Territorial governor acting with authority delegated by Congress in the Organic Act.[185] Believing the suspension to have been lifted by the governor on February 8, 1943, the district court entertained petitions for the Great Writ filed on behalf of both White and Duncan. The court went on to order both released on the ground that military jurisdiction over civilians was no longer warranted by the provost court by the time of their trials.[186] The U.S. Court of Appeals for the Ninth Circuit reversed, en banc,[187] assuming without deciding that the writ suspension had been lifted, but disagreeing with the court below over the propriety of military jurisdiction over civilians at the time White and Duncan were brought to trial.

Before V-J Day could come, marking the end of hostilities, the Supreme Court granted both White's and Duncan's petitions for writ of certiorari. At this point, the government had a five judge Ninth Circuit decision in its favor. Had it then remitted the remaining sentences of the two petitioners, their contentions would have been moot, as had been Yerger's contention in 1870.[188] Unhappily, however, the Government's position was, "We've got to back up the theater commander."[189]

Result? They backed him right into the rapidly revolving buzz-saw of a stunning reversal, written by Justice Black for the Court. Chief Justice Stone concurred in the result, being of the opinion that, on the facts presented, there was no adequate showing of necessity to support a military trial. Justices Burton and Frankfurter dissented.[190] Their reasons were that the result would have been wholly different if on the days that the two petitioners had been tried, in 1942 and 1944, the Supreme Court had been asked on proper pleadings to oust the two military courts of their claimed jurisdiction.[191]

V. EFFORTS AFTER 1865 TO SET ASIDE MUDD'S CONVICTION

A. Habeas Corpus Proceedings

Four of the Lincoln assassination conspirators — Mrs. Surratt, Atzerodt, Herold, and Payne — were hanged. The other four — Mudd, O'Laughlin, Spangler and Arnold — were sentenced to imprisonment at hard labor: Arnold for six years, the other three for life, ultimately in the military prison at Fort Jefferson in the Dry Tortugas, Florida.[192] Those four were advised of their destination on July 22, 1865.[193]

A few days before December 19, 1866, after the announcement of the *Milligan* decision, but before the opinions had been made public, Mudd, represented by Reverdy Johnson and the latter's son-in-law, made application for a writ of *habeas corpus* to Mr. Justice Wayne, whose circuit included Florida, the place of confinement. Failing there,[194] counsel turned to Chief Justice Chase, whose circuit did not cover that state. Argument was heard, whereupon the Chief Justice denied the application, on the view that "he had no power himself to issue such a writ to be executed outside his own circuit."[195]

Dr. Mudd accordingly stayed at Fort Jefferson, where presently he rendered heroic service during an epidemic of yellow fever that carried off many soldiers and also O'Laughlin, a co-conspirator, who died on September 23, 1867.[196]

On July 4, 1868, President Johnson extended amnesty to all those who had participated in the late rebellion, whereupon Mudd applied to District Judge Thomas J. Boynton of the

Southern District of Florida for a writ of *habeas corpus*. So did his remaining co-conspirators, Arnold and Spangler.[197]

Judge Boynton's opinion, dated September 1868, makes three substantive points. First, he held Mudd's offense to be a military one for these reasons:

> I do not think that *Ex parte Milligan* is a case in point here. There is nothing in the opinion of the Court in that case, nor in the third article of the Constitution, nor in the Habeas Corpus Act of 1863, to lead to the conclusion that if an army had been encamped in the State of Indiana, (whether in the immediate presence of the enemy or not), and any person, a resident of Indiana or any other state (enlisted Soldier or not) had, not from any private animosity, but from public reasons, made his way within the Army lines and assassinated the Commanding General, such a person could not have been legally tried for his military offense by a military tribunal and legally convicted and sentenced.
> ***
> The President was assassinated not from private animosity nor any other reason than a desire to impair the effectiveness of military operations and enable the rebellion to establish itself into a Government; the act was committed in a fortified city, which had been invaded during the war, and to the northward as well as the southward of which battles had many times been fought, which was the headquarters of all the armies of the United States, from which daily and hourly went military orders. The President is the Commander in Chief of the Army, and the President who was killed had many times made distinct military orders under his own hand, without the formality of employing the Secretary of War or Commanding General. It was not Mr. Lincoln who was assassinated but the Commander in Chief of the Army, for military reasons. I find no difficulty, therefore, in classing the offense as a military one and with this opinion arrive at the necessary conclusion that the proper tribunal for the trial of those engaged in it was a military one.[198]

Actually, the foregoing rationale is far more convincing than anything ever written by Attorney General Speed.[199]

Secondly, Judge Boynton held that the three petitioners were not comprehended within the President's amnesty and pardon of July 4, 1868:

> [T]hat proclamation plainly excludes all persons standing in the position of these petitioners, whether they have been convicted or not. It pardons the crime of treason; that is, it pardons persons who have levied war against the United States, or given aid and comfort to their enemies, within the laws and usages of war; but it pardons no person who has transgressed the laws of war, no spy, no assassin, no person who has been guilty of barbarous treatment of prisoners. Let us bring out the point by a supposed case. Two soldiers or officers fight side by side in the same battle; their forces remain masters of the field. After the battle, one conducts himself in an unimportant manner, and the other sabres the wounded or prisoners. They are both guilty of treason, but one is guilty of treason with an important plus-sign added. It is the opinion of the Court that the proclamation of the President reaches one of these cases and not the other.
> ***
> I think it is clear that the President, wishing no longer to make other than necessary exceptions, and to pardon all who were only guilty of participating in the rebellion, purposely chose this language to effect his purpose, and no other one. I do not see that under it a person who transgressed the laws of war, who was guilty not only of treason but of additional military crimes, may not still be tried for additional crimes.[200]

And, finally, Judge Boynton found that the petitioners' contentions based on insufficiency of evidence were beyond the scope of any relief available in a *habeas corpus* proceeding.[201]

Later, on February 9 and 12, 1869, counsel for the three unsuccessful petitioners before Judge Boynton sought and obtained leave to file petitions for *habeas corpus* on the Su-

preme Court. The Court's order invited argument on the
question whether its jurisdiction in respect of the writ of
habeas corpus was original or appellate.[202]

We may pass by both the latter procedural questions fairly
presented when the cases were argued on February 26, 1869,
as well as the substantive question of the military commission's
jurisdiction in the trial of the assassination conspirators, because, in actuality, no decision was ever reached. On March
1, 1869, just before leaving office, President Johnson pardoned all of the petitioners then before the Court. When their
counsel brought this fact to the Court's attention, their petitions were dismissed, as none of them still remained in custody.[203]

B. Application to the Army Board for the Correction of Military Records

After the Judge Advocate General of the Army and the
Army's General Counsel had both ruled that the Army Board
for Correction of Military Records could entertain an application to correct Dr. Mudd's record by setting aside his conviction, such an application (No. AC91-05511), asking that Dr.
Mudd be declared innocent, was filed in 1991 by a grandson,
Dr. Richard Dyer Mudd, himself a nonagenarian.[204]

A hearing before the Board was held on January 22,
1992.[205] In the course of that hearing, the applicant said:

> I always think that Dr. Mudd had three strikes against
> him, and I might have to be really excused for saying
> this. He was first a slave owner. Secondly he was a
> Catholic at a time when the Pope was accused of
> causing the Lincoln assassination, and three of the
> conspirators had attended Georgetown University, a
> Catholic school including my grandfather; and of
> course, Mrs. Surratt was a Catholic. And the third
> thing is, his name was Mudd. That was the worst.[206]

Six months after the conclusion of the hearing, the board
held that, while it was not authorized to consider the guilt or
innocence of Dr. Mudd, it could, looking to *Ex parte Milligan*,
determine whether the military commission that tried Dr.
Mudd had jurisdiction to do so.

Nothing in the Board's conclusions indicated the slightest awareness on its part that the actual *Milligan* opinion rested on sections 2 and 3 of the Habeas Corpus Act of March 3, 1863;[207] or that what was said about the jurisdiction *vel non* of the tribunal was purest dictum;[208] or that what the Court's opinion had announced in its flowing language was no longer law in 1992.[209]

Again, there is nothing in what counsel told the Board or in anything that the Board wrote to reflect the slightest familiarity with Judge Boynton's opinion in *Ex parte Mudd*, the only judicial opinion directly on point.[210] Nonetheless, the Board concluded that Dr. Mudd's trial by military commission "constituted such a gross infringement of his constitutionally protected rights that his conviction should be set aside" — and that was its recommendation.[211]

Six months later, on July 22, 1992, the Acting Assistant Secretary of the Army rejected that recommendation, and denied the application for relief. Said the Secretary:

> I note at the outset that the ABCMR did not consider the guilt or innocence of Dr. Mudd, and that its recommendation does not speak to the question of his guilt or innocence.

> The ABCMR concluded that the military commission which tried Dr. Mudd did not have jurisdiction over civilians and recommended that Dr. Mudd's conviction be set aside on that basis.

> Accordingly, my denial of that recommendation should not be taken as a determination of either the guilt or the innocence of Dr. Mudd. It is not the role of ABCMR to attempt to settle historical disputes. Neither is the ABCMR an appellate court. The precise issue which the ABCMR proposes to decide, the jurisdiction of the military commission over Dr.Mudd, was specifically addressed at the time in two separate *habeas corpus* proceedings, one before the Chief Justice of the United States, the other before a U.S. District Court.[212] There also was an opinion by the Attorney General of the United States.

The effect of the action recommended by the ABCMR would be to overrule all those determinations. Even if the issue might be decided differently today, it is inappropriate for a nonjudicial body, such as the ABCMR, to declare that the law 127 years ago was contrary to what was determined contemporaneously by prominent legal authorities. [213]

It should be remembered that, on March 1, 1869, Dr. Mudd received a full and unconditional presidential pardon.[214] Does not that act adequately set aside Dr. Mudd's conviction?[215] Or, to ask the same question in somewhat altered phraseology, if an individual has been pardoned during his lifetime, is he also further entitled as a matter of right to a second, posthumous pardon more than a century after his death?[216]

It was not until 1938 that Congress granted any remedy to persons erroneously convicted in courts of the United States, and that enactment provided that a subsequent pardon was proof of innocence only if the stated ground for the pardon was innocence and unjust conviction, and even then recovery was limited to $5,000. Obviously Mudd's pardon did not meet the statutory condition, and, equally obvious, the 1938 statute cannot be deemed retroactive so as to reach a conviction that took place in 1865.[217]

VI. CONCLUSIONS

A. Preservation of the Union

The struggle between Federalists and Anti-Federalists that marked the debates from 1787 to 1789 over the ratification of the Constitution did not end on April 30, 1789, when Washington was inaugurated as our first President; indeed, those differences led to the Civil War and did not wholly terminate with Appomattox.

And, although it is surely heresy even to think as much in the Commonwealth of Virginia, it is a fact that Thomas Jefferson, a much revered son of the Commonwealth, has never been a truly qualified guide to the meaning of the document composed at Independence Hall in Philadelphia during the summer of 1787.

To begin, he was not there; he was in Paris, serving as

American Minister to France.[218] And within the first decade of
the new nation's existence under its Constitution, he authored
and/or influenced the Kentucky and Virginia Resolutions
that supported the power of individual states to override
measures of the general government.[219] Soon afterwards,
elected President himself, Thomas Jefferson declared the following in his first Inaugural on March 4, 1801:

> If there be any among us who would wish to dissolve
> the Union or to change its republican form, let them
> stand undisturbed as monuments of the safety with
> which error of opinion may be tolerated where reason
> is left free to combat it.[220]

It is therefore completely accurate to conclude that the
spiritual godfather of both nullification and secession was the
presently greatly revered Thomas Jefferson.

Indeed, it was not in the South that the first serious
advocacy of secession appeared. That was a consequence of
Jefferson's Louisiana Purchase, a step that led extremist Federalists to propose the secession of the northeastern portion of
the nation, because the acquisition of that vast tract of trans-
Mississippi territory was certain to diminish the national
influence that New England wielded prior to 1803 — and also
because the War of 1812 was violently unpopular there. The
high-water mark of this New England secessionist surge was
the infamous Hartford Convention; that sentiment died suddenly, however, when Andrew Jackson overwhelmingly de-
feated the British at New Orleans on January 8, 1815, and
when, simultaneously, news of the December 24, 1814 Peace
of Ghent reached the United States.[221] At that point there also
died the Federalist Party.

There was relative quiet thereafter until, in the 1830s,
South Carolina undertook to nullify federal revenue legislation. Then the moving spirit was John C. Calhoun. But when
this happened, Andrew Jackson was President. The victor of
New Orleans thundered forth, "The Federal Union shall and
will be preserved," took appropriate steps to that end, and the
result was that South Carolina, Jackson's state of birth, backed
down as best it could.[222]

A generation or so later, in 1860, the new Republican Party

had become home to New England's abolitionists, and the Democratic Party, supporting slavery, was split only over the degree of its support of the "peculiar institution." Stephen A. Douglas led the moderates; Jefferson Davis insisted on the more extreme view. A third group — the National Constitutional Union — sought a compromise that got nowhere, and in the end Abraham Lincoln led the Republicans to both popular and electoral victory.[223]

South Carolina reacted by formally seceding from the Union on December 20, 1860, and six other states followed before March 4, 1861.[224]

President James Buchanan, whose timidity was accurately reflected on his countenance, inquired whether he could legally use force to return the seceded states to the Union. A technically competent but equally irresolute Attorney General, Jeremiah S. Black, advised in the negative.[225] Matters rocked along for six weeks without much except discussion until April 15, 1861, when South Carolina opened fire on Fort Sumter, forcing the fairly prompt surrender of that unrelieved and unsupplied Union post. When President Lincoln then called for troops to oppose the rebellion, four more states seceded, and the Civil War, or the War of the Rebellion, or the War Between the States, was on.[226]

For Lincoln, the sole object of the conflict at its outset was the restoration of the Union, regardless of what happened to slavery. It was only later that emancipation became an additional and equally vital objective.[227]

Nothing whatsoever was permitted to stand in the way of the primary objective. Arbitrary arrests became commonplace early in the war; anti-administration newspapers were suppressed and their editors were imprisoned; thousands of offenders were tried by military commissions; and the Bill of Rights was jettisoned. Opposition was minimal, as the bulk of those dissatisfied with these measures were opposed to continuation of the war and perfectly satisfied to let the seceding States depart in peace.

Lincoln deeply regretted the hardships that such a program necessarily imposed, and he ameliorated them to the greatest extent possible consistent with his primary objective. Accordingly, in mid-February 1862, he issued Executive Order No. 1, which declared a general amnesty for political prisoners and brought the deliberate policy of repression to a halt.[228] Thus, as a careful historian has noted, "the North was spared the omnipresent shadow of Fort Lafayette,"[229] that formidable structure on Governor's Island in New York Harbor, which had housed so many of the disloyal.

Once the war was over, the struggle turned to the need for a Fourteenth Amendment to effectuate the Thirteenth, and to the regime of Reconstruction where the opposing viewpoints were fought out. But secession was dead.[230]

Today we are still struggling with the problem of where to draw the line between violence on the one hand and free speech on the other, the identical problem with which Abraham Lincoln had to deal throughout the Civil War. Zeroing in on that precise issue, we find, just forty-five years back, this expression in the United States Reports. Unhappily, that quotation comes from a dissent in a five-to-four case:

> This Court has gone far toward accepting the doctrine that civil liberty means the removal of all restraints from these crowds and that all local attempts to maintain order are impairments of the liberty of the citizen. The choice is not between order and liberty. It is between liberty with order and anarchy without either. There is danger that, if the Court does not temper its doctrinaire logic with a little practical wisdom, it will convert the constitutional Bill of Rights into a suicide pact.[231]

B. Was the Tribunal that Tried the Assassin Conspirators Lawfully Constituted?

Judge Advocate General Enoch H. Crowder,[232] whom Justice Frankfurter deemed "one of the best professional brains I've encountered in life,"[233] characterized Colonel William Winthrop as "the Blackstone of military law."[234]

Colonel Winthrop quite properly deserves such an honorific, and his views on the legality of trying the Lincoln assassination conspirators ought to be considered with a deference withheld from less luminous commentators. The virtue of applying Winthrop's views on the constitutionality of military trial of civilians in this case is best demonstrated by recounting the history of two closely related jurisdictional issues: military trial of civilians for crimes committed in previous military service and military trial of civilians accompanying the army abroad in peacetime. In both instances, Winthrop's position that such jurisdiction was unconstitutional was repeatedly rejected. But, while the Solicitor General of the United States said in April 1956 that "the world about which Colonel Winthrop wrote no longer exists,"[235] the nation would ultimately learn, within a short few years, that the Blackstone of military law had correctly discerned the limits that the Constitution of the United States laid down respecting military jurisdiction.

If Winthrop was right about military jurisdiction over former service members and civilians with the army overseas, then he was very likely right about jurisdiction over civilian fifth columnists in wartime. Having argued against the tide of popular and legal opinion that jurisdiction could not attach to the first two classes, no matter what Congress legislated at the Army's behest, he nevertheless declined, when presented the opportunity, to fault the assertion of military jurisdiction by the Hunter Commission.

When Winthrop in 1895 published both volumes of the second edition of his ultimately classic *Military Law and Precedents*, he did not believe that any general revision of the Articles of War, then in force as R.S. § 1342, was either necessary or desirable. But he did recommend that the last clause of the Sixtieth Article, making officers and soldiers amenable to military trial after they had become civilians, should be deleted.[236]

Trials of former military personnel were supported as constitutional, however, by Professor Edmund M. Morgan,[237] later draftsman of the Uniform Code of Military Justice; by Colonel L.K. Underhill of the U.S. Army;[238] and, following the reasoning of his erstwhile teacher and of his subsequent military superior, by the present author[239] — this on the view that the "cases arising in the land and naval forces" clause of the Fifth Amendment authorized military jurisdiction over all such cases regardless of the accused's personal status.

The Articles for the Government of the Navy included no such continuing jurisdiction clause, with the result that in the case of a U.S. Naval prisoner of war who had been convicted of mistreating fellow prisoners during a previous enlistment, the Supreme Court held that he could not be tried by court-martial after re-enlisting: an honorable discharge terminated all criminal liability for anything done in the prior enlistment.[240]

In order to plug this loophole, Congress provided in Article 3(a) of the new Uniform Code of Military Justice that, subject to the applicable statute of limitations,

> [A]ny person charged with having committed, while in a status in which he was subject to this Code, punishable by confinement of five years or more, and for which the person cannot be tried in the courts of the United States or any State or Territory thereof or of the District of Columbia, shall not be relieved from amenability to trial by court-martial by reason of the termination of said status.[241]

This new provision would soon be tested in *Toth v. Quarles*.[242] Toth, an airman, received an honorable discharge after service in Korea. Afterward, evidence came to light that he had participated in the premeditated murder of a Korean civilian, a murder for which both of his accomplices had already been tried and punished.[243] The first question in Toth's case was whether he could be returned to Korea for trial by a U.S military court.

Undoubtedly, Toth's case was one "arising in the land and naval forces" within the exception written into the Fifth Amendment. But it was Winthrop's view that this "Amendment, in the particular indicated, is rather a *declaratory recognition and sanction* of an existing military jurisdiction rather than an original proposition initiating such a jurisdiction."[244] (After all, the purpose of the Bill of Rights was to limit the powers of the newly created general government, not to enhance them.) Accordingly, Winthrop deemed such a recapture clause "necessarily ... unconstitutional."[245]

The Supreme Court disagreed with Professor Morgan and agreed with Colonel Winthrop, holding that Article 3(a) of the Uniform Code was indeed unconstitutional.[246]

At this point it is necessary to backtrack and to re-examine the 1919 controversy over the Army's court-martial system,

which unfortunately degenerated into an ugly personal dispute between former Brigadier General Samuel T. Ansell,
Acting Judge Advocate General during most of World War I
and that officer's sponsor and benefactor, Major General
Crowder, who as Provost Marshal General operated the draft,
and whose characterization of Colonel Winthrop has already
been quoted.[247] Full details appear in a 1,400-page booklet,
about a third of it in fine print, which the present author has
read in full on four separate occasions.[248] As a matter of
contemporary psychiatry, former General Ansell's conduct
can be expertly diagnosed as an adjustment disorder; in
Victorian terms of disesteemed behavior, as unforgivable
disloyalty.[249]

The issue significant here is that, throughout the World
War I court-martial dispute, Professor Morgan was fully on
General Ansell's side, and, with the tenacity of a mountaineer
feudist who has outlived all of his earlier opponents, adhered
for thirty years more to the views he had then formulated.[250]

Accordingly, Professor Morgan agreed with General
Ansell's statement that "Colonel Winthrop was first a military man, and he accepted easily and advocated the view that
courts-martial are not courts, but are simply the right hand of
the military commander,"[251] a view fully concurred in by
Professor Morgan.[252] Yet Morgan, following Ansell, entirely
overlooked Winthrop's insistence, just seven pages further
along in his treatise, that a court-martial was indeed "a court
of law and justice."[253] In this unjustifiable omission, Morgan
was simply repeating Ansell's earlier inaccuracy.[254] Still believing that the constitutional basis for military jurisdiction
lay in the "cases arising in the land and naval forces" clause of
the Fifth Amendment, Professor Morgan carried into the
Uniform Code in Articles 2 (11) and 2 (12) the provision in the
Second Article of the 1916, 1920, and 1948 Articles of War that
granted military jurisdiction over all persons serving with,
employed by, or accompanying the armed forces without the
United States.

It was Colonel Winthrop's view that *"a statute cannot be
framed by which a civilian can lawfully be made amenable to
military jurisdiction in time of peace."*[255]

Who was correct, Professor Morgan or Colonel Winthrop?
The bitterly fought issue was before the Supreme Court in six

cases over a period extending from February 17, 1956, when the first case was filed,[256] to January 18, 1960, when the last four cases were decided.[257]

At first that tribunal sustained the right of the armed forces to try by court-martial an Air Force sergeant's wife who had accompanied her husband to an airbase in England (*Reid v. Covert*)[258] and an Army colonel's wife staying with her husband in Japan (*Kinsella v. Krueger*).[259] But, on rehearing both appeals, the Court diametrically altered its holdings; on further reflection, it held that there could be no military jurisdiction in time of peace over military dependent wives charged with capital offenses and ordered its earlier opinions, rendered just 364 days earlier, "withdrawn."[260] According to the Court, such jurisdiction could be sustained only in time of war, as provided in Article 2(10) of the Uniform Code.[261]

Two and a half years later, these new restrictions were widened. Military jurisdiction over civilians in time of peace was denied in the case of a dependent wife charged with a non-capital offense,[262] over a civilian employee of the Army charged with a capital offense,[263] and over civilian employees of the armed forces charged with non-capital crimes.[264]

Accordingly, in both areas of military jurisdiction — ex-servicemen and accompanying dependents or employees —

the crowning paradox was that, whereas Professor Morgan had mordantly decried Colonel Winthrop's concept of a court-martial as intolerable, an author whom he had earlier denigrated as 'first a military man,' in the end it was that career officer's perception of the Constitution's limitations on military power that ultimately prevailed over the rejection of those limitations by the lifetime professor of law.[265]

The world about which Colonel Winthrop had written, far from being moribund, was authoritatively shown to be leading a very healthy and active existence.

We now turn, in the light of the foregoing modern decisions, to our ultimate legal question: Was the tribunal that tried Mudd *et al.* legally constituted?

At this point we can, for two reasons, overlook the infirmities of *Ex parte Milligan*,[266] first because Winthrop disagreed with the dicta in the majority opinion, deeming the views of the dissenters more sound;[267] and, second, because Judge Boynton of the Southern District of Florida, whose opinion denied Dr. Mudd a writ of *habeas corpus*, distinguished *Milligan* on the ground that Mudd's crime was indeed a war offense.[268]

Richmond, the Confederacy's capital, had fallen on April 3, 1865, and Lee had surrendered at Appomattox on April 9. President Lincoln was shot on April 14 and died the next day. It was only after this that Johnston offered his surrender to Sherman on April 18, but that offer lay unaccepted until April 26, because the assassination had so greatly curdled Northern sensibilities. All other Confederate forces laid down their arms by May 26. And it was not until May 29 that President Johnson's proclamation of amnesty officially ended the Civil War.[269]

Thus Lincoln's assassination took place more than a full month before all the shooting stopped. True, no one can be tried by a military tribunal for spying once a war has ended,[270] but those charged with other war crimes are still subject to both trial and punishment once hostilities cease and before peace is formally declared. That proposition is demonstrated by the trial of Captain Henry Wirz, commandant of the infamous Andersonville prison where so many Union prisoners of war died of mistreatment and neglect,[271] and by post-World War II war criminal trials held at Nuremberg and Tokyo.

How then does Winthrop treat what in his treatise he designates as "the Assassination Conspirators Trial?" He mentions it on seven occasions to illustrate procedural details.[272] But nowhere in all 1,596 pages of the second and last edition of his *Military Law and Precedents* does Winthrop say a single word about the legality of that proceeding; on that central issue the silence of the Blackstone of military law is positively deafening. The only inference possible is that Colonel Winthrop, like all contemporary military lawyers a century later, deemed utterly illegal the trial of the Assassination Conspirators by military commission.[273]

What then did Winthrop think of Judge Boynton's decision? We know that, on occasion, he cited unreported decisions in his treatise.[274] But it can easily be established that Winthrop never saw what Judge Boynton had written in the only judicial opinion considering (and upholding) the jurisdiction of the tribunal that had tried Mudd and the others.

We know that the Winthrop treatise does not cite *Ex parte Mudd*; it is not in his table of cases and trials. We also know that the reference to Mudd's case in the Federal Cases states, "Nowhere reported; opinion not now accessible." Finally, we know that one copy of that opinion was printed in a Washington daily newspaper, and that another can be seen in a Library of Congress scrapbook.[275]

Broadening our search, we find in 1895 four significant dates, three of them dealing directly with Winthrop. On January 3, he was promoted to Colonel and Assistant Judge Advocate General.[276] On August 3, he was retired for age by operation of law.[277] And, on November 1, he signed the Preface to the second edition of his treatise.[278] Finally, during the same year, without the exact date anywhere shown, there was published Volume 17 of the Federal Cases series, at page 954 of which there appears the reference to *Ex parte Mudd*, Fed. Case No. 9899.

On the basis of using and relying on Winthrop's *Military Law and Precedents* for almost 50 years, often on a daily basis, the present author firmly believes that, even if the Assistant Judge Advocate General of the Army had ever seen the Boynton opinion — which, it clearly appears, he never in fact did — it would not have changed his views. He did so inferentially, no doubt because he did not wish to declare publicly his disagreement with his erstwhile chief, General Holt. But his silence on the merits of the trial make it crystal clear that, in his opinion, the military trial of the assassination conspirators was a precedent that should never be followed.

This necessarily leads to the conclusion that what the Acting Assistant Secretary of the Army ultimately determined in 1992, namely, that the legality of the trial was, by those in authority in the late 1860s, regarded differently than it would be regarded in the 1990s, more than a century and a quarter later. Or, otherwise stated, the aim of Dr. Mudd's descendants before the Army Board for the Correction of Records was not only a request to set aside a conviction for which their ancestor had already been pardoned, but also one to rewrite history. Therefore the Army Secretariat correctly disposed of Dr. Mudd's case.

We are however left with the inquiry whether, in the light

of all the facts and circumstances, Samuel A. Mudd, M.D. was done an injustice.

Bear in mind that Mudd lied about his not recognizing Booth throughout his being questioned on that point, and that he was afraid to tell of [Booth's] having been at his house on the 15th of April, "fearing that his own and the lives of his family would be endangered thereby."[279]

Thus, Mudd was not innocent; he knew that Booth was a fugitive from justice who had shot the President — why else the fear for his and his family's lives? — and yet he aided Booth in several non-medical ways, and took significant steps to facilitate Booth's escape. Mudd was, at the very least, an accessory after the fact, conduct for which his actual confinement for somewhat less than four years was surely not excessive punishment.

The Secretary of the Army was in consequence fully correct, 127 years afterward in 1992, in refusing to alter, and thus refusing to falsify, the record of Dr. Mudd's conviction for substantially assisting the murderer of Abraham Lincoln to elude capture, even if only for an additional eleven days.

Intensive study of the record of trial and of every relevant background factor inevitably lead to this clear conclusion: Dr. Samuel A. Mudd was, beyond any reasonable doubt, guilty of the charge against him, and suffered no injustice whatever in the ultimately attenuated sentence that he so deservedly served.

Notes

¹ Samuel A. Mudd, M.D., ABCMR Docket No. AC91-0511 (Jan. 22, 1992) [hereinafter cited simply as ABCMR]. *See* Appendix B *infra* pp. 259-71.

² *See* Appendix C *infra* pp. 273-75. Here are the basic sources relied upon in what follows. First, there is Benn Pitman's *The Assassination of President Lincoln and the Trial of the Conspirators*, which sets forth all the testimony taken during the trial, together with all official documents relating thereto. This was first published in 1865. A facsimile edition, to which was affixed a lengthy introduction by Philip Van Doren Stern, appeared in 1954. Pitman's verbatim record is cited as PITMAN, followed by page numbers in arabic numerals. Stern's summary is cited as STERN, followed by page references in lower case roman numerals.

A modern summary by Gene Smith, *The Booth Obsession*, appeared in *American Heritage*'s issue for September 1992; the author added his contemporary observations of the terrain followed by Booth from Ford's Theater to the Garrett tobacco barn in which he died. It is cited as *Booth Obsession*. The map accompanying that article is, with the permission of the cartographer, reproduced above at 127.

³ ABCMR, *supra* note 1, Finding 15 at 6, Appendix B *infra* p. 264.

⁴ Act of March 16, 1878, ch. 37, 20 Stat. 30, 31; 2 WIGMORE ON EVIDENCE § 579 (4th ed. 1979); Act of Aug. 12, 1898, 61 & 62 Vict., ch. 36 (England).

⁵ Twining v. New Jersey, 211 U.S. 78 (1908); Adamson v. California, 332 U.S. 46 (1947).

⁶ 378 U.S. 1 (1964).

⁷ That ultimate result makes both bad law as well as bad sense. It is bad law because the holding that the Due Process Clause of the Fourteenth Amendment incorporates the provisions of the first eight so as to make all of them binding on the States is unsupported by anything in the legislative history of the Fourteenth Amendment. Charles Fairman, *Does the Fourteenth Amendment Incorporate the Bill of Rights? The Original Understanding*, 2 STAN. L. REV. 5 (1949); Felix Frankfurter, *Memorandum on the "Incorporation" of the Bill of Rights into the Due Process Clause of the Fourteenth Amendment*, 73 HARV. L. REV. 746 (1965).

Chief Justice John Marshall, who had been a prominent member of the Virginia convention that ratified the Constitution, held in Barron v. Baltimore, 32 U.S.(7 Pet.) 243 (1833), that the Fifth Amendment did not apply to the States, and that holding was adhered to repeatedly as long as Adamson v. California, 332 U.S. 46 (1947), was law. Stanley Morrison, *Does the Fourteenth Amendment Incorporate the Bill of Rights? The Judicial Interpretation*, 2 STAN. L. REV. 140 (1949).

The 1964 result also runs counter to normal human nature, for which this author can vouch personal experience. Back in 1940, while sitting in the Second Circuit waiting for my case to be reached, Judge Learned Hand (then presiding) asked appellant's counsel in the criminal appeal being heard just ahead of me,

"Did the defendant testify?"

And, in World War II during the years before military justice had become completely lawyerized, I was regularly engaged in teaching and explaining military law to the lay officers whose duty it was to administer it. They could understand that the burden of proof was on the prosecution, and that the accused was under no obligation to establish his innocence. But it was never really possible to convince them that they were never permitted to infer that the accused's failure to take the stand could not be held against him.

Apart from law, and simply as a matter of realism, every counsel representing a commissioned accused knows perfectly well that, in order to have any genuine possibility of obtaining an acquittal, his officer-client *must* testify.

[8] Von Moltke v. Gillies, 332 U.S. 708, 727, 730 (1948) (Frankfurter and Jackson, JJ., concurring).

[9] PITMAN, *supra* note 2, at 90 (Testimony of Willie S. Jett).

[10] *Id.* at 94 (Testimony of Sgt. Boston Corbett).

[11] STERN, *supra* note 2, at viii.

[12] United States v. Broce, 388 U.S. 563, 570-71 (1989) ("A single agreement to commit several crimes constitutes one conspiracy.")

[13] DEAN SPRAGUE, FREEDOM UNDER LINCOLN 14 (1965).

[14] SAMUEL ELIOT MORISON, THE OXFORD HISTORY OF THE AMERICAN PEOPLE 603-05 (1st ed. 1965) [hereinafter cited simply as OXFORD HISTORY].

[15] SPRAGUE, *supra* note 13, at 9.

[16] James R. Randall, a Marylander teaching English and Latin at Poydras College in Louisiana, heard of the wounding of one of his classmates in Baltimore as the Massachusetts troops fired on the rioters, and, deeply stirred, was unable to sleep. Rising at midnight, he jotted down these lines:

> The despot's heel is on thy shore,
>   Maryland!
> His torch is at thy temple-door,
>   Maryland!
> Avenge the patriotic gore
> That flecked the streets of Baltimore,
> And be the battle-queen of yore,
>   Maryland, my Maryland!

BARTLETT'S FAMILIAR QUOTATIONS 813 (Nathan Haskell Dole ed., 10th ed. 1914); THE OXFORD DICTIONARY OF QUOTATIONS 405:19 (2d ed. 1955).

Set to the tune of an old German song, it became the battle song of the South, and even today remains the best known of all state songs. 16 DICTIONARY OF AM. BIOGRAPHY 349 (Allen Johnson et al. eds., 1958).

[17] SPRAGUE, *supra* note 13, at 9.

[18] *Id.* at 18-27.

[19] *Id.* at 27.

[20] *Id.* at 30; *see generally*, *id.* at 28-39.

[21] THE WAR OF THE REBELLION: A COMPILATION OF THE OFFICIAL RECORDS OF THE UNION AND CONFEDERATE ARMIES, ser. II, vol. II, 19 (Washington, GPO 1897) [hereinafter cited simply as WAR OF THE REBELLION].

[22] 60 U.S. (19 How.) 393 (1857).

23 CHARLES FAIRMAN, MR. JUSTICE MILLER AND THE SUPREME COURT, 1862-1890, at 74 (1939) [hereinafter cited simply as FAIRMAN, MILLER]

24 *Ex parte* Merryman, 17 F. Cas. 144 (C.C.D. Md. 1861) (No. 9,487).

25 *Id.* at 153; *see* LAMBDIN P. MILLIGAN, THE MILLIGAN CASE 459-73 (Samuel Klaus ed., 1929) [hereinafter cited simply as KLAUS].

26 U.S. CONST. art. I, § 9, cl. 2 ("The privilege of the writ of *habeas corpus* shall not be suspended, unless when in cases of rebellion or invasion the public safety may require it.")

27 CHARLES FAIRMAN, THE LAW OF MARTIAL RULE 165 (1930); F.B. WIENER, A PRACTICAL MANUAL OF MARTIAL LAW § 76 (1940); WILLIAM WINTHROP, MILITARY LAW AND PRECEDENTS 1293 (Washington, GPO, 2d ed. 1895).

28 FAIRMAN, MILLER, *supra* note 23, at 74.

29 WALKER LEWIS, WITHOUT FEAR OR FAVOR: A BIOGRAPHY OF CHIEF JUSTICE ROGER BROOKE TANEY ch. 33 (1965).

30 JOEL PARKER, HABEAS CORPUS AND MARTIAL LAW 47 (2d ed. 1862). Moreover, we learn from Taney's opinion in Luther v. Borden, 40 U.S. (7 How.) 1 (1849), how he had understood the basic national law at a time when his thinking was not distorted by emotional pressure, as Professor Fairman also showed. FAIRMAN, MILLER, *supra* note 23, at 75. What was there said describes much more fittingly the situation in Maryland in 1861 than that in Rhode Island during the Dorr war. *See generally*, *id.* at 69-90; F.B. Wiener, *Helping to Cool the Long Hot Summers*, 53 A.B.A. J. 713 (1967) (for a study of domestic violence written a generation later in the light of the *Merryman* case).

31 10 Op. Att'y Gen. 74 (1861).

32 CHARLES FAIRMAN, RECONSTRUCTION AND REUNION 1864-68, PART ONE, 6 OLIVER WENDELL HOLMES DEVISE HISTORY OF THE SUPREME COURT OF THE UNITED STATES 55 n.94 (Paul A. Freund ed., 1971) [hereinafter cited simply as FAIRMAN, RECONSTRUCTION].

33 SPRAGUE, *supra* note 13, chs. 13, 14.

34 *Id.* at ch. 15.

35 *Id.*

36 *Id.*

37 *Id.* at 203.

38 *Id.* at ch. 17.

39 *Id.* at 206.

40 *Id.* at ch. 18.

41 The doings in Kentucky and in Missouri are also dealt with in SPRAGUE.

42 MARGARET BROWN KLAPTHOR & PAUL DENNIS BROWN, THE HISTORY OF CHARLES COUNTY, MARYLAND frontispiece (1958).

43 *Id.* at 121.

44 *Id.* at 124-26. Thomas A. Jones appeared again nearly thirty years later when the Columbian Exposition opened in Chicago in 1893, which brought the entire country a vision of the future. *See* P. Patton, *Sell the Cookstove if Necessary, but Come to the Fair*, 24 SMITHSONIAN 28 (June 1993). Jones thought he could profit by selling a book there entitled *J. Wilkes Booth, An Account of His Sojourn in Southern Maryland After the Assassination of Abraham Lincoln, His Passage Across the Potomac and His Death*. KLAPTHOR, *supra* note 42, at 165 n.6. But this was a substantial miscalculation, particularly when word spread that the man

who hid Booth would deliver a talk, "and gangs of graying Yankee veterans gathered with unpleasant designs in mind. Jones was spirited away. That concluded his publicity tour for the book, which is quite rare in its original form." *Booth Obsession, supra* note 2, at 112.

[45] STERN, *supra* note 2, at viii.

[46] *Id.* at xiv-xvi.

[47] *Booth Obsession, supra* note 2, at 110. Mrs. Surratt's son, John H., was a professional spy for the Confederacy, intimately acquainted with southern Maryland and all routes to the South. At the time of the assassination, he was in Canada. STERN, *supra* note 2, at xxi.

[48] PITMAN, *supra* note 2, at 144 (Testimony of Robert R. Jones).

[49] *Booth Obsession, supra* note 2, at 104.

[50] KLAPTHOR, *supra* note 42, at 131.

[51] *Id.*

[52] For an illustration of a flyer actually offering that amount, see 4 CARL SANDBURG, ABRAHAM LINCOLN: THE WAR YEARS 303 (1939).

> [I]nto that insulated world of southern Maryland the news leaked slowly and obscurely, the bare facts untouched with comment or public reaction. There was little of horror in the first reports, especially to those who had hated Lincoln for five long years and whose world had been filled with little but hate. The old habits and attitudes of the war years lingered. The Union was the enemy, the southern states the friend. ... [I]t might be concluded that, much as the Potomac had changed the course of war, the war itself had little changed the Potomac.

FREDERICK GUTHEIM, THE POTOMAC 321, 322 (1949).

[53] KLAPTHOR, *supra* note 42, at 132. As Stern very astutely points out, no effort was made to trace Booth's movements between Mudd's house and Port Conway on the Rappahannock River, where he arrived nine days later. Cox and his brother-in-law Jones got off easily and were never tried. STERN, *supra* note 2, at xiv.

[54] *Booth Obsession, supra* note 2, at 114.

[55] *Id.*

[56] *Id.*

[57] *Id.* at 115.

[58] *Id.*

[59] *Id.*

[60] STERN, *supra* note 2, at xv-xviii; PITMAN, *supra* note 2, at 90-95; *Booth Obsession, supra* note 2, at 115-19.

[61] STERN, *supra* note 2, at xviii-xix. The charge also included as co-conspirators President Jefferson Davis of the Confederacy and numerous Confederate agents in Canada. *Id.* at xix. Inclusion of the Confederate President was essentially a reflection of the hysteria of the time, and the prosecution unsuccessfully went to considerable length to prove that the Confederate government was implicated in President Lincoln's assassination. While Confederate guerrilla warfare was real enough (witness the raid by Confederate irregulars on St. Albans, Vermont, on October 19, 1864, involving a robbery of three banks and

the killing of one inhabitant), there was no credible evidence linking established Confederate misdeeds (i.e., the shocking mistreatment of Union prisoners of war at Andersonville, Georgia) with the assassination plot. *Id.* at xx-xxi.

Unhappily, the effort to link Jefferson Davis to Abraham Lincoln's murder left uninvestigated the activities of Booth and John H. Surratt in Canada during the winter of 1864-1865. Indeed, Stern points out that no proper attention has ever been paid to the Confederate agents who were stationed in Canada. *Id.* at xxi.

[62] *Id.* at xx-xxi.

[63] Those on trial plus John H. Surratt, Mrs. Surratt's son. who, as we have seen, was a professional Confederate spy, intimately acquainted with Southern Maryland and the various underground routes to the South, but who left Washington on April 3 to go to Canada. *Id.* at vii, ix.

[64] *Id.* at xx-xxi.

[65] *Id.* at xxi, xiii.

[66] Morrison v. California, 291 U.S. 82, 92 (1934).

[67] PITMAN, *supra* note 2, at 249 (President Andrew Johnson's approval of the findings and sentences).

[68] *Id.* at 88 (Testimony of Lt. Alexander Lovett), 90 (Testimony of Joshua Lloyd), 114 (Testimony of Louis Wiechmann), 169 (Testimony of Col. H.H. Wells).

[69] *Id.* at 114 (Testimony of Louis Wiechmann).

[70] *Id.* at 170 (Testimony of Mary Simms).

[71] *Id.* at 85 (Testimony of John M. Lloyd).

[72] *Id.* at 85-86 (Testimony of John M. Lloyd).

[73] *Id.*

[74] *Id.* at 86 (Testimony of John M. Lloyd).

[75] *Id.* at 86-87 (Testimony of John M. Lloyd).

[76] *Id.* at 88 (Testimony of Lt. Alexander Lovett), 89-90 (Testimony of Simon Gavacan), 169 (Testimony of Col. H.H. Wells).

[77] *Id.* at 87-88 (Testimony of Lt. Alexander Lovett), 89 (Testimony of Simon Gavacan).

[78] *Id.* at 169 (Testimony of Col. H.H. Wells).

[79] *Id.* at 421 (Affidavit of Capt. G.W. Dunton).

[80] ABCMR, *supra* note 1, Hr'g Tr. at 74 (Testimony of Jack McHale).

[81] PITMAN, *supra* note 2, at 87 (Testimony of Lt. Alexander Lovett), 89 (Testimony of William Williams).

[82] *Id.* at 87 (Testimony of Lt. Alexander Lovett), 169 (Testimony of Col. H.H. Wells).

[83] *Id.*

[84] *Id.* at 89 (Testimony of William Williams), 169 (Testimony of Col. H.H. Wells).

[85] *Id.* at 89 (Testimony of William Williams), 169 (Testimony of Col. H.H. Wells).

[86] *Id.* at 89 (Testimony of William Williams), 95 (Testimony of Capt. Edward Doherty), 169 (Testimony of Col. H.H. Wells).

[87] The traditional oath of physicians reads:

You do solemnly swear, each man by whatever he holds most sacred, that you will be loyal to the profession of medicine and just and generous to its members; that you will lead your lives and practice your art in uprightness and honor; that into whatsoever house you shall enter, it shall be for the good of the sick to the utmost of your power, you holding yourselves far aloof from wrong, from corruption, from the tempting of others to vice; that you will exercise your art solely for the cure of your patients and will give no drug, perform no operation, for a criminal purpose, even if solicited, far less suggest it; that whatsoever you shall see or hear of the lives of men which is not fitting to be spoken, you will keep inviolably secret. These things do you swear. Let each man bow his head in sign of acquiescence. And now, if you will be true to this, your oath, may prosperity and great repute be ever yours; the opposite, if you shall prove yourselves forsworn.

THE NEW COLUMBIA ENCYCLOPEDIA 1246 (William H. Harris & Judith S. Levey eds., 1975).

[88] PITMAN, *supra* note 2, at 119 (Testimony of Louis Wiechmann).

[89] STERN, *supra* note 2, at vii.

[90] PITMAN, *supra* note 2, at 160 (Testimony of Margaret Branson).

[91] *Id.* at 170 (Testimony of Col. H.H Wells).

[92] THE NEW COLUMBIA ENCYCLOPEDIA, *supra* note 87.

[93] Another factor rendering untenable the consistent and insistent argument of Mudd's relatives and supporters that he was innocent of any offense because he was only doing what any doctor should have done reappeared almost eighty years later.

In mid-1942, early in the United States' participation in World War II, eight German saboteurs seeking to disable American war production plants were apprehended in Florida and on Long Island, New York. They were tried and convicted by a military commission appointed by the President for violations of the laws of war. Their convictions were sustained by the Supreme Court, *Ex parte Quirin*, 317 U.S. 1 (1942), and six of them were executed, among them Herbert Max Haupt, an American citizen.

Subsequently, the latter's father, Hans Max Haupt, was tried for treason in a U.S. District Court for having given his son shelter and sustenance between the time of his arrival at the parental home in Chicago and his subsequent apprehension. Father Haupt's conviction was duly affirmed, Haupt v. United States, 331 U.S. 631 (1947), because what he had done came squarely within the constitutional definition of treason: "Treason against the United States, shall consist only in levying war against them, or in adhering to their enemies, giving them aid and comfort." The United States Supreme Court affirmed with only a single dissent on the less than tenable ground that what a father does for a son cannot add up to treason. Said the dissenter:

> But the act of providing shelter was of the type that might naturally arise out of petitioner's relationship to his son, as the Court recognizes. By its very nature, therefore, it is a non-treasonous act. That is true even when the act is viewed in light of all the surrounding circumstances. All that can be said is that the problem of whether it was motivated by treasonous or non-treasonous factors is left in doubt. It is therefore not an overt act of treason, regardless of how

unlawful it might otherwise be.

331 U.S. at 649. That dissent was written by Mr. Justice Frank Murphy, who, it may fairly be said, stands as the least qualified individual ever appointed to the Supreme Court so far in the present century.

Or, by way of conclusion, neither the duty of a parent to a child nor that of a physician to a patient overcomes the infinitely stronger duty of every American citizen to refrain from treason against his own country.

[94] 2 WINFIELD SCOTT, MEMOIRS OF LIEUT. GENERAL SCOTT, LL.D 392-96, 540-49 (New York, Sheldon and Co. 1864); CHARLES WINSLOW ELLIOTT, WINFIELD SCOTT: THE SOLDIER AND THE MAN 460-61 (1937); WINTHROP, *supra* note 27, at 1298-99. General Scott also created a Council of War to deal specifically with violations of the laws of war by guerrillas and the like, but that body never reappeared. *Id.* at 1299 n.118.

At this time (1846-1848), the existing Articles of War, enacted in 1806, did not make punishable a number of serious crimes that constituted common law felonies when committed by military personnel in time of war or rebellion. Accordingly, such cases were also brought before military commissions. That gap was not filled until 1863 (Act of March 3, 1863, ch. 75, 12 Stat. 731, 735-36), after which that provision became AW 58 of R.S. § 1342, 18 Stat. 229, 235 and in that form it became the familiar AW 93 of the 1916, 1920, and 1948 Articles of War that governed the U. S. Army in World War I, World War II, and during the first half of the Korean conflict. Act of August 29, 1916, ch. 418, 39 Stat. 619, 664; National Defense Act Amendments, Act of June 4, 1920, ch. 227, 41 Stat. 759, 805; Act of June 24, 1948, ch. 625, 62 Stat. 604, 640.

[95] 1 SCOTT'S MEMOIRS, *supra* note 94, at chs. 2-3; ELLIOTT, *supra* note 94, at 4-6, 8-13, 18-25.

[96] 1 FRANCIS BERNARD HEITMAN, HISTORICAL REGISTER AND DICTIONARY OF THE UNITED STATES ARMY 870 (1903).

[97] While a military commission differs from a court-martial convened under the Articles of War, the procedure followed by those two tribunals is essentially similar. The basic differences are jurisdiction, scope of authorized sentences, and method of post-trial procedure. Details are available in the pages of Winthrop's classic treatise and of the Digest of Opinions of the Judge Advocate General that Winthrop himself compiled in 1868. *See* DIGEST OF OPINIONS OF THE JUDGE ADVOCATE GENERAL OF THE ARMY 225-32 (Major W. Winthrop ed., 3d ed., Washington, GPO 1868) [hereinafter cited simply as DIGEST OF OPINIONS].

[98] Perhaps it should be noted that there was no provision for any legal officers during the Mexican War. The judge advocates provided for by the Act of April 14, 1818, ch. 61, 3 Stat. 426, were dropped in the military reorganization effected three years later in the Act of March 2, 1821, ch. 13, 3 Stat. 615, and the office of Judge Advocate for the Army was not again established for twenty-eight more years. It reappeared in the Act of Mar. 2, 1849, ch. 83, 9 Stat. 351.

[99] DIGEST OF OPINIONS, *supra* note 97, at 229 n.30.

[100] THE ARMY LAWYER: A HISTORY OF THE JUDGE ADVOCATE GENERAL'S CORPS, 1775-1975, at 46 (U.S. Army, Judge Advocate General's Corps ed., 1976) [hereinafter cited simply as THE ARMY LAWYER].

[101] Act of Mar. 2, 1849, ch. 83, 9 Stat. 351.

[102] THE ARMY LAWYER, *supra* note 100, at 46.

[103] *Id.* at 47; Act of July 17, 1862, ch. 201, 12 Stat. 597, 598. The advantage of being a colonel of cavalry over colonel of infantry was that the former received an allowance for the upkeep of a horse.

[104] THE ARMY LAWYER, *supra* note 100, at 47; HEITMAN, *supra* note 96, at 539, 625.

[105] 5 DICTIONARY OF AMERICAN BIOGRAPHY 181 (Allen Johnson et al. eds., 1958).

[106] General Orders No. 100, War Dep't (Apr. 24, 1863) *in* WAR OF THE REBELLION, *supra* note 21, at ser. III, vol. III, 148 (1899); PITMAN, *supra* note 2, at 410-11. Lieber's Code, as it was known in the service, was actually the first phase of the booklets that were later entitled *Rules of Land Warfare*, an exposition of the laws of war that were generally recognized as a part of international law. *See Ex parte* Quirin, 317 U.S. 1 (1942).

[107] HEITMAN, *supra* note 96, at 539. Unhappily I have not been able to obtain a copy of Major General J.B. Fry's pamphlet *Brevets*, which I had in my hands fifty years ago, and on which I drew freely for my 1943 two-installment article in the old *Infantry Journal* on "Mex Rank Through the Ages." That pamphlet noted that, when it was published, every officer in the Bureau of Military Justice except two had been honored by higher brevet rank.

The adjective "bloody" was a sarcastic reference to the fact that virtually all Civil War brevets awarded officers of the Regular Army were given this identical date, March 13, 1865. Subsequently, brevets for volunteer officers, awarded by General Orders No. 67, July 16, 1867, were similarly back-dated to March 13, 1865. Thus Captain Oliver Wendell Holmes Jr., of the 20th Massachusetts Volunteers, received successive brevets to Major, Lieutenant Colonel, and Colonel for each of the engagements in which he had been wounded. General Orders No. 67 at 21, 35, 56.

[108] THE ARMY LAWYER, *supra* note 100, at 72; WINTHROP, *supra* note 27, at 617-19.

[109] In 1942, at the trial of the saboteurs considered in *Ex parte* Quirin, 317 U.S. 1, the Judge Advocate General of the Army, Major General Myron C. Cramer, was appointed one of the prosecutors.

The photograph of all three prosecutors in the Lincoln Assassination case shows Holt in civilian attire, from which one can fairly assume that he never wore uniform from 1862, when he was first appointed, until 1875, when he retired. *See* HEITMAN, *supra* note 96, at 539; *see also* THE ARMY LAWYER, *supra* note 100, at 51. He died in August 1894, leaving an alleged will the validity of which was contested in what is doubtless the leading Supreme Court decision on the rules of evidence in probate cases. Throckmorton v. Holt, 180 U.S. 552 (1901).

[110] Contemporary opinions, in this context, mean views expressed prior to December 14, 1866.

[111] PITMAN, *supra* note 2, at 18, 247-49.

[112] *Id.* at 249.

[113] *Id.* at 250.

[114] STERN, *supra* note 2, at xxii; *Booth Obsession, supra* note 2, at 109.

[115] 18 L.Ed. 281.

[116] 71 U.S. (4 Wall.) 2 (1866).

[117] 11 Op. Att'y Gen. 215 (1865).

[118] HOMER CUMMINGS & CARL MCFARLAND, FEDERAL JUSTICE: CHAP-

TERS IN THE HISTORY OF JUSTICE AND THE FEDERAL EXECUTIVE 515 (1937).

[119] PITMAN, *supra* note 2, at 17.

[120] *Id.*

[121] *Id.* at 251-63. Curiously enough, the account of Reverdy Johnson's life in the Dictionary of American Biography never mentions his participation in Mrs. Surratt's defense. 5 DICTIONARY OF AMERICAN BIOGRAPHY, *supra* note 105, at 112.

[122] PITMAN, *supra* note 2, at 22.

[123] *Id.* at 264-67. He also presented an argument on the facts on behalf of Edward Spangler. *Id.* at 276-88.

[124] MARK E. NEELY JR., THE FATE OF LIBERTY: ABRAHAM LINCOLN AND CIVIL LIBERTIES 46-69 (1991). The article on Thomas Ewing, Jr. at 3 DICTIO-NARY OF AMERICAN BIOGRAPHY, *supra* note 105, at 238-39, states that he depopulated those counties.

[125] PITMAN, *supra* note 2, at 354 (Argument of John A. Bingham). A consecutive reading of the jurisdictional arguments of Senator Johnson and of Mr. Bingham leaves the distinct impression that the latter is far more convincing, and that the former failed even to touch on numerous significant topics. It may however be doubted whether, in sustaining their own jurisdiction, the members of the military commission were making any evaluation whatever of these two lawyers' powers of forensic persuasion.

[126] 11 Op. Att'y Gen. 297 (1865); PITMAN, *supra* note 2, at 403-09.

[127] Opinion of the Attorney General on the constitutional power of the military to try and execute the assassins of the President. PITMAN, *supra* note 2, at 403.

[128] STERN, *supra* note 2, at xviii. For comments on the three volume Poore edition, see *id.* at xx.

[129] 3 DOUGLAS SOUTHALL FREEMAN, LEE'S LIEUTENANTS, A STUDY IN COMMAND 564-68 (1944). Early's raid was stopped by the Union Army's VI Corps, Major General H. G. Wright commanding, which Grant had sent from Virginia for just that purpose. As Early approached Fort Stevens, the President and Mrs. Lincoln drove out in a carriage to see the war at first hand. At one point the President climbed up the parapet so that his tall form made him an easy target for Confederate sharpshooters. A young captain on General Wright's staff with three years' experience of actual combat, yelled at him, though probably unaware of his actual identity: "Get down, you damned fool, before you get shot!" That young captain was Oliver Wendell Holmes Jr., ultimately Chief Justice of Massachusetts and an Associate Justice of the Supreme Court of the United States. MARK DEWOLFE HOWE, JUSTICE OLIVER WENDELL HOLMES: THE SHAPING YEARS 1841-1870, at 167-69 (1957).

[130] EDWARD BATES, THE DIARY OF EDWARD BATES 1859-1866 (Howard K. Beale ed., 1933); 4 ANNUAL REPORT OF THE AMERICAN HISTORICAL ASSOCIATIONN (1939); H.R. DOC. 818, 71st Cong., 3d Sess.

[131] BATES, *supra* note 130, at 483, 498-503.

[132] FAIRMAN, MILLER, *supra* note 23, at 118.

[133] FAIRMAN, RECONSTRUCTION, *supra* note 32, at 204.

[134] HEITMAN, *supra* note 96, at 1051.

[135] NEELY, *supra* note 124, at 168.

[136] 71 U.S. (4 Wall.) 2 (1866).

[137] GEORGE FORT MILTON, ABRAHAM LINCOLN AND THE FIFTH COLUMN

192 (1942).

[138] *Id.*

[139] *Id.* at 191.

[140] THE TRIALS FOR TREASON AT INDIANAPOLIS, DISCLOSING THE PLANS FOR ESTABLISHING A NORTH-WESTERN CONFEDERACY (Benn Pitman ed., Cincinnati, Moore, Wilstach & Baldwin 1865).

[141] KLAUS, *supra* note 25, at 251-458.

[142] *Id.* at 67-75.

[143] *Id.* at 36.

[144] 21 Ind. 320 (1864).

[145] FAIRMAN, RECONSTRUCTION, *supra* note 32, at 196-97.

[146] *Id.* at 197-99.

[147] Inasmuch as District Judge McDonald's appointment had been recommended to President Lincoln by Justice Davis, and had expressed views similar to those of his patron, the asserted difference between the two jurists was fictitious, although it sufficed to get the case into the Supreme Court. WILLARD L. KING, LINCOLN'S MANAGER: DAVID DAVIS 224, 250 (1960). Both concurred in asking President Johnson to commute the death sentences of Milligan et al. to life imprisonment. *Id.* at 250-51.

[148] FAIRMAN, RECONSTRUCTION, *supra* note 32, at 202.

[149] Dred Scott v. Sanford, 60 U.S. (19 How.) 393 (1857).

[150] *Id.*; *see* FAIRMAN, RECONSTRUCTION, *supra* note 32, at 216-17. Professor Fairman rightly comments, "This attempt, by a gratuitous judicial pronouncement, to settle the slavery question, was surely the worst mistake the Justices ever made." *Id.* at 216 n.102.

[151] 12 Stat. 755.

[152] *Id.* at 755-56.

[153] FAIRMAN, RECONSTRUCTION, *supra* note 32, at 74, 224-25.

[154] *Id.* at 229.

[155] KING, *supra* note 147, at 204, 211-12, 247.

[156] 71 U.S. at 109 (emphasis in original).

[157] *Id.* at 120-21.

[158] *Id.* at 140-41.

[159] *Id.* at 142.

[160] WINTHROP, supra note 27, at 1275.

[161] *See* discussion *supra* part III C, pp. 134-35.

[162] G. NORMAN LIEBER, THE JUSTIFICATION OF MARTIAL LAW 5 passim (Washington, GPO 1898).

[163] Hughes, *War Powers Under the Constitution*, 42 A.B.A. Rep. 232, 245; SEN. DOC. NO. 145, 65th Cong., 1st Sess., 12 (1917).

[164] WIENER, *supra* note 27, §§ 107-10.

[165] CHARLES WARREN, THE SUPREME COURT IN UNITED STATES HISTORY, ch. 22 (2d ed. 1928) *quoted in* FAIRMAN, RECONSTRUCTION, *supra* note 32, at 211-212.

[166] FAIRMAN, RECONSTRUCTION, *supra* note 32, at 212.

[167] 243 U.S. 332 (1917).

[168] 290 U.S. 398 (1934).

[169] *Id.*

[170] *See supra* note 165.

[171] *See* discussion *supra* part II D, pp. 131-33.

[172] 317 U.S. at 45, 46.

[173] KING, *supra* note 147, at 362 n.32.

[174] *Id.* at 258.

[175] *Id.* at 312.

[176] 71 U.S. at 132.

[177] Milligan v. Hovey, 17 F. Cas. 380 (C.C.D. Ind. 1871) (No. 9,605).

[178] NEELY, *supra* note 124, at 176-80.

[179] WINTHROP, *supra* note 27, at 1331-36.

[180] *Ex parte* McCardle, 73 U.S. (6 Wall.) 318 (1867); *Ex parte* Yerger, 75 U.S. (8 Wall.) 85 (1868).

[181] *Ex parte* McCardle, 74 U.S. (7 Wall.) 506 (1868).

[182] FAIRMAN, RECONSTRUCTION, *supra* note 32, at 589-91. Anyone seeking a complete account of the legal aspects of the Reconstruction regime in the South is strongly urged to examine carefully Chapters VI through XII of the late Professor Fairman's work. That account is definitive.

[183] 327 U.S. 304 (1946).

[184] Act of Apr. 30, 1900, ch. 339, § 67, 31 Stat. 141, 153.

[185] *Id.*; *see Ex parte* Zimmerman, 132 F.2d 442 (9th Cir. 1944), *cert. denied,* 319 U.S. 744. The suspension was subsequently lifted by Presidential Proclamation on October 24, 1944.

[186] *Ex parte* Duncan, 66 F. Supp. 982 (D. Haw. 1944); *Ex parte* White, 66 F. Supp. 976 (D. Haw. 1944).

[187] *Ex parte* Duncan, 146 F.2d 576 (9th Cir. 1944). It was reported that Judge Stephens did not participate in the decision of these cases. *Id.* at 591.

[188] FAIRMAN, RECONSTRUCTION, *supra* note 32, at 589-90.

[189] Author's personal knowledge.

[190] 327 U.S. 337, 357-58 (1946).

[191] But this was not the last of the *Duncan* and *White* cases. The Supreme Court opinions came down on February 25, 1946. Six days afterward, on March 1, 1946, Circuit Judge Stephens, who as indicated, had been reported as then not participating in the 1944 Ninth Circuit decision, belatedly filed a dissent, "Nunc pro tunc as of November 1, 1944." *Ex parte* Duncan, 153 F.2d 943 (9th Cir. 1946). As counsel for petitioners in *Duncan* later reported:

> In a preliminary statement, Judge Stephens explained that he had reached the conclusion that the judgment should be affirmed and had distributed an opinion to his colleagues on the circuit court of appeals, but because the war was still in progress he had concluded that a dissenting opinion held more possibility of harm than of good and had accordingly withheld it.

J. Garner Anthony, *Hawaiian Martial Law in the Supreme Court,* 57 YALE L.J. 27, 53 (1947). How can one fairly characterize such a performance?

Reports of judicial proceedings in England and in the United States extend back to the Eleventh Century. The earliest of which this author is aware was the lawsuit in King William the Conqueror's court between the Bishop of Worcester and the Archbishop of York in 1070 or 1071. 106 ENGLISH LAWSUITS FROM WILLIAM I TO RICHARD I, at 3 (R.C. Van Caenegem ed., 1990). But he seriously doubts whether, in the more than nine hundred years that have passed since that dispute was heard and determined there can anywhere be found an instance of judicial gutlessness — no other word is even partially appropriate — as disgraceful as the doings of Circuit Judge Stephens of the Ninth Judicial Circuit in the *Duncan* and *White* cases in 1944 and again in 1946!

[192] PITMAN, *supra* note 2, at 247-50.

[193] *Id.* at 421 (Affidavit of Capt. George W. Dutton).

[194] FAIRMAN, RECONSTRUCTION, *supra* note 32, at 237.

[195] *Id.* at 237-39.

[196] *Id.* at 239, 488.

[197] *Ex parte* Mudd, 17 F. Cas. 954 (S.D. Fla. 1868) (No. 9,899), where it is stated, "opinion not now accessible." The opinion was actually published in the National Intelligencer on October 5, 1868. FAIRMAN, RECONSTRUCTION, *supra* note 32, at 488 n.191; *see* Appendix A *infra* pp. 253-57.

[198] *See* Appendix A *infra* pp. 253-57.

[199] 11 Op. Att'y Gen. 215 (1865) (one sentence opinion); *see also* 11 Op. Att'y Gen. 297 (1865), *reprinted in* PITMAN, *supra* note 2, at 403-09.

[200] *See* Appendix A *infra* pp. 253-57.

[201] *Id.*

[202] FAIRMAN, RECONSTRUCTION, *supra* note 32, at 488-89.

[203] *Id.* at 490-92.

[204] ABCMR, *supra* note 1, Finding 29 at 10, Appendix B *infra* pp. 268-69; *id.* Hr'g Tr. at 125 (Testimony of Richard Dyer Mudd).

[205] *Id.*

[206] *Id.* Hr'g Tr. at 128 (Testimony of Richard Dyer Mudd). The author acknowledges his indebtedness to Dr. Richard Dyer Mudd for supplying the title for the present study.

[207] *See* discussion *supra* part III C, pp. 134-35.

[208] *Id.*

[209] *See* discussion *supra* part III D, pp. 135-38.

[210] *See* discussion *supra* part V A, pp. 149-52.

[211] ABCMR, *supra* note 1, Findings 11-13 at 5, Appendix B *infra* pp. 263-64.

[212] *See* discussion *supra* part V A, pp. 149-52.

[213] Action of the Acting Assistant Secretary of the Army.

[214] FAIRMAN, RECONSTRUCTION, *supra* note 32, at 491-92.

[215] *See* Samuel Williston, *Does a Pardon Blot Out Guilt?* 28 HARV. L. REV. 647 (1915).

[216] Mudd died in 1883.

[217] The 1938 provision is the Act of May 24, 1938, ch. 266, 52 Stat. 438, now to be found in 28 U.S.C. §§ 1495, 2513 (Supp. IV 1992).

(a) The court in which such an action can be maintained has changed titles and functions over the years: (i) before 1948, it was the Court of Claims of the United States; (ii) in 1948, revision of Title 28 of the United States Code brought the name to the United States Court of Claims; (iii) in 1982, it became the United States Claims Court; and (iv) in 1992 the United States Court of Federal Claims.

(b) In the only reported case under the basic provision, a sailor whose enlistment had expired and whose reenlistment was still ineffective was held entitled to recover damages when imprisoned after a trial by court-martial which took place while he was still a civilian. Roberson v. United States, 124 F. Supp.

857 (1954). Roberson died before this result was reached, but when the United States then moved to vacate the judgment, the court ruled that such an action did not abate with the death of the claimant. Roberson v. United States, 130 Ct. Cl. 813 (1955). *Cf.* Howley v. United States, 133 Ct. Cl. 967 (1955) (settlement of similar claim for $4,000).

The author acknowledges the assistance of Iris Lee of the University of Richmond's Law Library staff for supplying the foregoing references.

(c) For non-retroactive effect, see Landgraf v. USI Film Products, 62 U.S.L.W. 4255 (No. 92-757), Apr. 26, 1994; Rivers v. Roadway Express Inc., 62 U.S.L.W. 4271 (No. 92-938), Apr. 26, 1994.

[218] 2 DUMAS MALONE, JEFFERSON AND HIS TIME xxv-xxvi (1951).

[219] OXFORD HISTORY, *supra* note 14, at 354-55.

[220] 1 MESSAGES AND PAPERS OF THE PRESIDENTS 310 (James D. Richardson ed., Washington, GPO 1898).

[221] OXFORD HISTORY, *supra* note 14, at 364-68, 396-97; 1 HENRY ADAMS, HISTORY OF THE UNITED STATES OF AMERICA 1801-1817, at 23-134, 391-92 (New York, C. Scribner's Sons 1889-1891); *see* HENRY ADAMS, DOCUMENTS RELATING TO NEW ENGLAND FEDERALISM (Boston, Little, Brown & Co. 1877).

[222] OXFORD HISTORY, *supra* note 14, at 435-37; 2 ROBERT V. REMINI, ANDREW JACKSON 233-37 (1981).

[223] OXFORD HISTORY, *supra* note 14, at 602-06.

[224] *Id.* at 607; CONCISE DICTIONARY OF AMERICAN HISTORY 861 (W. Andrews ed., 1962).

[225] 9 Op. Att'y Gen. 516 (1860).

[226] OXFORD HISTORY, *supra* note 14, at 608-14.

[227] *Id.* at 651-55.

[228] SPRAGUE, *supra* note 13, at ch. 26.

[229] *Id.* at 302.

[230] In Texas v. White, 74 U.S. (7 Wall.) 700 (1869), Chief Justice Chase declared in a resounding phrase that "The Constitution, in all its provisions, looks to an indestructible Union, composed of indestructible States." *Id.* at 725. That question is therefore no longer in issue, even though, ironically enough, on the substantive question that it decided, Texas v. White has long since been overruled. Morgan v. United States, 113 U.S. 476 (1885).

[231] Terminiello v. Chicago, 337 U.S. 1, 37 (1949) (Jackson, J., dissenting).

[232] THE ARMY LAWYER, *supra* note 100, at 104, 106.

[233] FELIX FRANKFURTER, FELIX FRANKFURTER REMINISCES: RECORDED IN TALKS WITH DR. HARLAN B. PHILLIPS 99 (Harlan B. Phillips ed., 1960).

[234] *Establishment of Military Justice, 1919: Hearings on S.64 before a Subcomm. of the Senate Comm. on Military Affairs*, 66th Cong., 1st Sess. 1171 (1919), *quoted without in* Reid v. Covert II, 354 U.S. 1, 19 n.38 (1957) (without attribution) [hereinafter cited simply as *Establishment*].

[235] Brief for the Appellant at 44, Reid v. Covert, 351 U.S. 487 (1956) (No. 703).

[236] WINTHROP, *supra* note 27, § 1201. The Sixtieth Article of War, R.S. § 1342, 18 Stat. 229, 236, became the Ninety-Fourth Article of War in 1916, 39 Stat. 619, 665. It remained so in the 1920 version of the Articles of War, National Defense Act Amendments, Act of June 4, 1920, ch. 227, 41 Stat. 759, 805-07, and the 1948 version, Selective Service Act of 1948, Act of June 24, 1948, ch. 625, 62

Stat. 604, 641. In 1950, the Ninety-Fourth Article of War became Art. 3(a) of the Uniform Code of Military Justice, ch. 169, 64 Stat. 107, 109-10. As amended in 1992, Art. 3(a) appears at 10 U.S.C. § 803(a) (Supp. V 1993).

[237] Edmund M. Morgan, *Court-Martial Jurisdiction over Non-Military Persons Under the Articles of War*, 4 MINN. L. REV. 79 (1920).

[238] L.K. Underhill, *Jurisdiction of Military Tribunals in the United States over Civilians*, 12 CAL. L. REV. 75 (1924).

[239] WIENER, *supra* note 27, §§ 128-29.

[240] Hirshberg v. Cooke, 336 U.S. 210 (1949).

[241] Uniform Code of Military Justice, ch. 169, 64 Stat. 107, 109-10; *see* H.R. REP. NO. 491, 81st Cong., 1st Sess. 11 (1949) and SEN. REP. NO. 486, 81st Cong., 1st Sess. 8 (1949).

[242] 350 U.S. 11 (1950).

[243] F.B. Wiener, *American Military Law in the Light of the First Mutiny Act's Tricentennial*, 126 MIL. L. REV. 1, 50 n.284 (1984) [hereafter cited simply as *Mutiny Act Tricentennial*].

[244] WINTHROP, *supra* note 27, at 52-53 (emphasis in original).

[245] *Id.* at 144-46.

[246] Toth v. Quarles, 350 U.S. 11 (1950).

[247] F.B. Wiener, *The Seamy Side of the World War I Court-Martial Controversy*, 123 MIL. L.REV. 109 (1989) [hereinafter cited simply as *Seamy Side*].

[248] *Establishment, supra* note 234.

[249] *Seamy Side, supra* note 247, at 124-28.

[250] *Mutiny Act Tricentennial, supra* note 243, at 33.

[251] *Establishment, supra* note 234, at 123.

[252] Edmund D. Morgan, *The Existing Court-Martial System and the Ansell Army Articles*, 29 YALE L.J. 52, 66 n.48 (1919).

[253] WINTHROP, *supra* note 27, at 54, 61-62.

[254] Morgan overlooked other matters also, and capped these omissions by making a demonstrable error of law in asserting that "there is an appeal from the general court-martial to the civil courts in England." *Mutiny Act Tricentennial, supra* note 243, at 33-35. Dead wrong in 1919; it did not come true until 1952. *Id.* at 34-35.

[255] WINTHROP, *supra* note 27, at 146 (emphasis in original).

[256] Cover on Transcript of Record, Reid v. Covert, 351 U.S. 487 (1956) (No. 701).

[257] 361 U.S. 234 (1960).

[258] 351 U.S. 487 (1956).

[259] 351 U.S. 470 (1956).

[260] Reid v. Covert (II) and Kinsella v. Krueger (II), 354 U.S. 1 (1957) (headnote).

[261] *Id.* at 33-35.

[262] Kinsella v. Singleton, 361 U.S. 234 (1960).

[263] Grisham v. Hagan, 361 U.S. 278 (1960).

[264] McElroy v. Guagliardo and Wilson v. Bohlender, 361 U.S. 281 (1960).

[265] *Mutiny Act Tricentennial, supra* note 243, at 36 (footnotes omitted).

[266] 70 U.S. (4 Wall.) 2 (1866).

[267] WINTHROP, *supra* note 27, at 1275.

[268] *See* discussion *supra* part V A, pp. 149-52.

[269] R. ERNEST DUPUY & TREVOR N. DUPUY, THE ENCYCLOPEDIA OF MILITARY HISTORY: FROM 3500 B.C. TO THE PRESENT 904 (1st ed. 1970).

[270] WINTHROP, *supra* note 27, at 1199.

[271] For a detailed account of the charges brought against and the conviction and subsequent hanging of Captain Henry Wirz, see WAR OF THE REBELLION, *supra* note 21, at ser. II, vol. VIII, 773-94 (1899); WAR OF THE REBELLION, *supra* note 21, at ser. III, vol. V, 491-93 (1900).

[272] In view of the renumbering of all footnotes in the 1920 reprint of Winthrop's treatise, the references that follow are to that text: (1) 167 n.44; (2) 169 n.57 and text; (3) 185 n.37; (4) 334 n.40 (5) 834 n.77 (6) 836 n.90; (7) 839 n.5.

[273] If it is permissible to obtrude a personal experience, the author received his first Reserve commission as Captain, Judge Advocate General's Department, early in 1936. The first training session he thereafter attended, in The Judge Advocate General's Office, then located in the Otis Building in the 800 block of 18th Street, N.W., in Washington, D.C., was conducted by the then Lt. Col. Harry A. Auer. In the course of that session, Col. Auer told the class that no one currently regarded the military tribunal of the Assassination Conspirators as a precedent that would or should be followed.

[274] *E.g.*, United States v. Plenty Horses, (D.S.D.), cited at 1212 of his text, and listed as "Plenty Horses — Case of in his list of "Cases and Trials Cited;" and the trial of John Thomas, an Army paymaster's civilian clerk, cited at 137 of his text, and listed in his table as "Thomas, John — Case of."

[275] *See* discussion *supra* part V A, pp. 149-52.

[276] HEITMAN, *supra* note 96, at 1051.

[277] *Id.*

[278] WINTHROP, *supra* note 27, 1920 reprint at 7.

[279] PITMAN, *supra* note 2, at 421.

The Curious Case of Dr. Mudd

Forest J. Bowman*

It was about 4:00 on the morning of April 15, 1865, when John Wilkes Booth and David E. Herold turned their horses onto the narrow, rutted lane which led to the home of Dr. Samuel A. Mudd, a quarter of a mile off the main road to Bryantown, in southern Maryland's Charles County. After a few minutes the riders could make out the doctor's plain, two-story clapboard house silhouetted against the sky at the top of a long rise. They stopped at the edge of the lawn and Herold, who had ridden ahead of Booth, dismounted and pounded on the door while Booth sat hunched on his horse, the very image of misery and discomfort.

The doctor and his wife were asleep in a back room on the first floor of the house and they were startled by the heavy pounding on their door. Dr. Mudd had not been feeling well so he asked his wife to answer the door. But the loud banging frightened Mrs. Mudd and she told her husband, "I would rather you would go and see for yourself."[1] So the 31-year-old doctor rose and trudged wearily to the door in his nightshirt, curious who should be knocking so loudly at that hour. Without opening the door he asked who was there and was told — or so he always insisted — that his callers were two

---

* The Hale J. Posten Professor of Law, West Virginia University, Morgantown, West Virginia 26506.

"strangers" on their way to Washington. One of their horses had fallen, the voice said, and the rider believed his leg had been sprained or fractured.[2] Dr. Mudd opened the door and helped the dismounted rider bring the injured man into the parlor where they laid him on a sofa. Trouble — big trouble — had descended on the little household of Dr. Samuel A. Mudd.

With the possible exception of Mrs. Surratt, no other person punished for complicity in the Lincoln plot has been so steadfastly and vociferously defended as an innocent victim of the federal government's thirst for vengeance as has Dr. Mudd. He has had a school named after him, historical pageants have been presented in honor of his memory, and his plight has been publicized in radio and television programs.

In 1936, Twentieth Century-Fox released a film, *Prisoner of Shark Island*, which portrayed the doctor's imprisonment.[3] That same year, Congressman Jennings Randolph, Democrat of West Virginia, introduced a resolution to place a tablet in the ruins of Fort Jefferson in recognition of Dr. Mudd's "innocence of a crime for which he was held prisoner for four years."[4] In 1973, the Michigan Legislature, at the urging of Dr. Richard Mudd, who has spent a lifetime trying to clear his grandfather's name, adopted a resolution stating that Dr. Samuel A. Mudd "was innocent of any complicity in the assassination of President Abraham Lincoln," that "[h]istory has subsequently revealed that Dr. Samuel A. Mudd acted only as a physician and not as a conspirator," and that he had been unjustly convicted.[5] In 1979, President Jimmy Carter declared his personal belief in Dr. Mudd's innocence.[6]

He is remembered as a kind and gentle country doctor who was sucked into the whirlwind of violence by his innocent ministrations to an injured nighttime visitor who, unbeknownst to him, had shot the President of the United States a few hours earlier. Dr. Mudd, his supporters maintain, was the American Dreyfus, an innocent man convicted and sent to prison for a crime he did not commit, by an unconstitutional military commission comprised of second-rate officers who were on a government-sanctioned blood quest. Even his place of confinement — Fort Jefferson in the Dry Tortugas — smacks of Devil's Island.

I. JURISDICTION OF THE MILITARY COMMISSION

Dr. Mudd's conviction by a military tribunal, instead of a trial before a civil court, has been one of the most persistent complaints of his supporters. And, since a civil jury failed to convict John H. Surratt Jr. in 1867, this view has strongly reinforced the doctor's supporters in their belief that the military commission was a "hanging court." F. Lee Bailey, co-counsel for Dr. Mudd in the Mudd appeal, "predicted" that Surratt would not be convicted by civil jury and used that possibility to attack the military tribunal.[7]

However, to argue that the same evidence was brought out in the military commission and John Surratt's civil trial and use this circumstance to criticize the military tribunal is unreasonable. Given the inflamed conditions of 1865 it appears that a civil trial would have dealt with the conspirators in a similar manner.[8] By 1867, the interest of the public had moved on from the Lincoln murder to Reconstruction policy, the power struggle in President Johnson's cabinet, and the possible impeachment of the President. The trial of Dr. Mudd and the other conspirators before a military commission in 1867 may well have resulted in a different outcome than before the 1865 military commission.

Before Dr. Mudd could be convicted by the military commission he first had to be tried before that body. As with the grand jury process by means of which defendants are brought to trial before civil courts on criminal charges, it took more than just being a Southern-leaning doctor who had treated the President's assassin to be named a defendant before the military commission. The government's list of defendants who were ultimately brought to trial for the murder of Abraham Lincoln was a curious one, not so much because innocent citizens were dragged before this military body as for the fact that so many individuals who might reasonably have been indicted were not.

The government decided not to prosecute Samuel Cox, Thomas Jones,[9] John Lloyd,[10] and James Maddox,[11] all known to have aided Booth's escape or to have obstructed justice. There were others who almost certainly knew about the conspiracy, but against whom no hard evidence had been gathered. Booth's brother, Junius Brutus Jr., was the author of, and recipient of, some suspicious correspondence with

Wilkes Booth, and their sister, Blanch Booth DeBar, clearly knew of the plot.[12] Anna Surratt, the daughter of Mrs. Mary Surratt and younger sister of John Surratt Jr., cannot seriously be considered to have been unaware of the plotting going on around her at her mother's boarding house and some papers that were confiscated at the Surratt house support this suggestion.[13] Sara Antoinette Slater, a Rebel spy and dispatch carrier who sometimes traveled with John Surratt Jr., and who had stayed at the Surratt boarding house at the height of the plotting, hovered somewhere on the periphery of the plotting against Lincoln.[14] Yet none of these was indicted.

The government settled on nine conspirators: David E. Herold, Lewis Payne,[15] George A. Atzerodt, Mary E. Surratt, Edman Spangler,[16] Samuel B. Arnold, Michael O'Laughlin,[17] and Dr. Samuel A. Mudd, all of whom were in custody, and John H. Surratt Jr., who was hiding in Canada. The inclusion of Dr. Mudd among the conspirators to be tried reflected the government's sense of the strength of the evidence that had been gathered against him, not some sinister plot to punish an innocent physician.

However, a major question loomed: Before what tribunal should the conspirators be tried? President Andrew Johnson turned to Attorney General James Speed,[18] who, on April 28, at what one writer calls "the prodding of the War Department,"[19] advised the President that trial before a military commission, rather than before a civil court, was proper.[20]

This was not a universally-accepted opinion. Gideon Welles, Secretary of the Navy, was of the opinion that Secretary of War Stanton had pressured Speed into this opinion, perhaps even converting the Attorney General from an earlier inclination. Welles wrote in his diary on May 9, 1865: "[T]he rash, impulsive, and arbitrary measures of Stanton are exceedingly repugnant to my notions, and I am pained to witness the acquiescence they receive. He carries others with him, sometimes against their convictions as expressed to me."[21]

Former Attorney General Bates shared the view that Stanton was behind Speed's opinion. He wrote in his diary on May 25, 1865: "I am pained to be led to believe that my successor, Atty Genl. Speed, has been wheedled out of an *opinion*, to the effect that such a trial is lawful. If he be, in the

lowest degree, qualified for his office, he must know better ...
. I do not doubt that that unwise determination was the work
of Mr. Stanton. He believes in mere force, so long as he wields
it, but cowers before it, when wielded by any other hand."[22]
Bates then summed up the problem with a remarkable proph-
esy: "[I]f the offenders be done to death by that tribunal,
however truly guilty, they will pass for martyrs with half the
world."[23]

Bates exhibited a incredible sense of clairvoyance. While
he was imprisoned, not executed, the martyrdom of Dr. Samuel
A. Mudd began with the difficult question of the jurisdiction
of the military commission.

A great deal of the difficulty stems from the fact that no
real precedent existed for what the government faced — the
trial of civilians engaged in paramilitary actions at the close of
a civil war. Military commissions were created during the
Mexican War to try civilians who committed crimes normally
cognizable by a civil court, and they had limited jurisdiction
to try civilians for crimes not cognizable by a court martial,
but committed during a period of martial law; and for violations of the laws of war.[24]

The two major arguments raised against the commission
which tried Dr. Mudd were that the laws of war did not apply
with respect to the American Civil War and, even if they did,
the Civil War was over and the civil courts were open, so no
necessity required trial before a military commission.

The first of these arguments was grounded on the contention that the United States had not formally recognized the
Confederacy as a belligerent,[25] a condition deemed necessary
for the application of the laws of war. But this argument was,
at best, a weak reed. Three years before the President's
murder the Supreme Court, speaking through Justice Grier in
The Prize Cases,[26] said that:

> Insurrection against a government may or may not
> culminate in an organized rebellion, but a civil war
> always begins by insurrection against the lawful authority
> of the government. A civil war is never solemnly declared;
> it becomes such by its accidents — the number, power
> and organization of the persons who originate and carry
> it on. When the party in rebellion occupy and hold in a

hostile manner a certain portion of territory; have declared
their independence; have cast off their allegiance; have
organized armies; have commenced hostilities against
their former sovereign, the world acknowledges them as
belligerents, and the contest is *war*. *They* claim to be in
arms to establish their liberty and independence in order
to become a sovereign state, while the sovereign party
treats them as insurgents and rebels who owe allegiance,
and who should be punished with death for their treason
.... As a civil war is never publicly proclaimed, *eo nomine*
against its insurgents, its actual existence is a fact in our
domestic history which the court is bound to notice and
to know.[27]

Moreover, the Confederate Congress had formally recognized the existence of war on May 6, 1861.[28] The Act declared
that "war exists between the Confederate States and the
Government of the United States and the States and territories
thereof except the States of *Maryland*, North Carolina, Tennessee, Kentucky, Arkansas, Missouri, and Delaware, and the
territories of Arizona and New Mexico, and the Indian Territory south of Kansas," thus suggesting the Confederate Congress' conception of where the authority of the Confederacy
extended (and placing Dr. Mudd's home State of Maryland
squarely within the Confederacy).[29]

General Orders No. 100, which was issued after the Supreme Court's decision in the *Prize Cases*, recognized that the
rebellion was "civil war."[30] And the mere fact that the Union
did not document its recognition of the Confederacy's status
as a belligerent did not alter the fact that both sides accorded
the other belligerent rights.[31]

The central issue, however, in the trying of the conspirators before a military commission was whether a military
commission was the proper body to try the conspirators since
(1) the civil courts were open in the District of Columbia at the
time the commission was convened, and (2) with the surrender of Lee's Army of Northern Virginia on April 9, 1865, and
of Joseph E. Johnston's army on April 26, 1865, the Civil War
had ended in the East, and, thus, there was no "military
necessity" such as to justify trying the conspirators before a
military commission.

In 1867, the Supreme Court held, in *Ex parte Milligan*,[32] that military commissions organized during the Civil War, in a state not invaded and not engaged in rebellion and in which the federal courts were open and exercising their judicial functions, had no jurisdiction to try a civilian[33] for any criminal offense. Supporters of Dr. Mudd and other conspirators have long sought to apply this decision to the trial of the Lincoln conspirators in an effort to demonstrate the trial's illegality. Fitting *Milligan* into the case of the Lincoln conspirators is a more difficult exercise than it first appears.

The *Milligan* case arose out of Indiana, where federal authority had never been seriously challenged during the Civil War.[34] In Washington, however, the threat to federal authority had been, and remained, very real. Despite the surrender of the armies of Lee and Johnston, the "war" had not yet ended. The government argued in the Mudd appeal that the United States and the Confederate States had fought a battle near the Rio Grande on May 12 and that Confederate warships continued to wage war against Union vessels until November 6, 1865. But the danger from Confederate "wartime" activity was even more real to Union authorities in Washington, D.C. in early May, 1865, than the Government's argument suggested.

John Singleton Mosby, the noted Confederate guerrilla leader, had disbanded his command, but still remained in hiding, a potential threat. Mosby had been Lewis Payne's commander and had, in 1863, captured General Edwin H. Stoughton from the midst of his army at Fairfax Court House, Virginia.[35] On February 22, 1865, Lieutenant Jesse C. McNeill had led the McNeill Rangers[36] from near Moorefield, West Virginia, into Cumberland, Maryland, and there, from the midst of the Army of West Virginia a command of over 10,000, had spirited away Generals George Crook and Benjamin F. Kelly along with the command's adjutant and a passel of headquarters flags.

A few days later, as Lieutenant Isaac Welton, McNeill's second-in-command, was escorting the prisoners to Richmond by train, he encountered Colonel Mosby. In an obvious reference to his earlier capture of General Stoughton, Mosby told Lt. Welton, "You boys have beaten me badly. The only way I can equal this is to go into Washington and bring out

Lincoln."[37] The threat posed by a man like Mosby could not be lightly dismissed. Lincoln might be dead, but Washington, D.C. contained other tempting targets.

On May 8, 1865, Jesse McNeill and his Rangers had met with Union authorities on the Northwest Turnpike a mile west of Romney, West Virginia, deposited a pile of "arms" on the road, signed parole documents, and disbanded. But the "arms" they left on the road consisted of little more than ancient shotguns and nonfunctioning weapons of dubious ancestry.[38] These hard-riding, hard-hitting cavalrymen were still armed and could be called into action. Undoubtedly, many of them would have relished taking to the hills and continuing the guerrilla war against the Yankees, as would many of Mosby's men and others who were not anxious to accept the fact of Southern defeat.

Hindsight is always "20/20." We now know that, with Lee's surrender of the Army of Northern Virginia, the soldiers of the Confederacy marched off the battlefield into the peaceful glory of the "Legend of the Lost Cause." But in late April and early May of 1865 the direction of the rebel soldiers' march was not nearly so certain. Had Lee or some other charismatic Southern leader issued the call to guerrilla warfare, Mosby and McNeill and other still-armed and still-angry Southern soldiers may well have taken up the call, on the very outskirts of the nation's capital. The history of civil wars is that they end in this fashion far more commonly than as did the American Civil War.[39] At the time of Attorney General Speed's opinion that trial before a military commission was proper and President Johnson's order establishing the military commission, the idea that a "state of war" existed in Washington, D.C. was not a mere fanciful notion.

One of the myths that surrounds the assassination of President Lincoln is that his death was uniformly mourned throughout the South, where it was seen as a catastrophe, at least by all but the most ardent firebrands.

In truth, Southerners reacted to Lincoln's death much the same as Americans reacted to the news of the death of Mussolini.[40] They saw it as the fitting end for a tyrant.[41] As the government brief in the appeal stated:

Washington, D.C. remained a fortified city and

headquarters for directing military operations against the rebels during Mudd's trial. Sentries manned and controlled the flow of people into and out of the city. The city was fully guarded by national forces. Washington was a city policed by soldiers with the army as the protector as well as the defender of the Capitol ... . The war was still in effect and President Andrew Johnson did not declare martial law over and peace within the United States until 20 August 1866.[42]

Whether it was politically astute to try the conspirators before a military commission or whether the conspirators received fair trials before the commission are not the issues here. The question is whether the United States had the *legal right* to try the conspirators before a military commission. It is clear that it did.

II. THE QUESTION OF DR. MUDD'S GUILT

Dr. Mudd's defense clearly rested on the argument that his treatment of Booth's leg had merely been the act of mercy of a medical doctor, performed on a man he had not recognized, having met him briefly only once before. That position underlies the appeal of Dr. Mudd before the Special Court of Military Review. In the brief on behalf of Dr. Mudd,[43] as well as in counsels' argument before the Special Court, there is virtually no reference to the *evidence* on which Dr. Mudd was convicted, except to argue that the testimony of the witnesses against Dr. Mudd had been discredited.[44]

That Dr. Mudd recognized Booth and knew at some time before Booth left his home that he had murdered President Lincoln, that Dr. Mudd might have been involved in the Confederate underground in Charles County, that Dr. Mudd was well acquainted with two of the main characters in the plot against Lincoln and had met with them on several occasions, or that Dr. Mudd deliberately misled government officials in an effort to assist Booth and Herold in avoiding capture, are all matters that supporters of the doctor would prefer to pass over quickly.

But it is not that simple. The facts are these. In November 1864, Booth had gone into lower Maryland, armed with letters of introduction to Dr. William Queen and Dr. Mudd.[45] He was

introduced to Dr. Mudd following church services on November 20. Later that afternoon, Dr. Mudd called for Booth at
Montgomery's Hotel in Bryantown and brought him back to
the Mudd farm.[46]   Booth spent the night with the Mudds.[47]
During this visit Booth bought a horse from a George Gardiner,
coming to Gardiner's place in the company of Dr. Mudd.[48]

On December 23, 1864, Dr. Mudd was in Washington — in
the company of John Wilkes Booth! That evening the doctor
introduced Booth to Louis J. Weichmann, a friend of John H.
Surratt Jr., and a clerk in the Office of the Commissary General
of Prisoners, a bureau of the War Department.[49] As Weichmann
described the meeting, he and Surratt were walking down 7th
Street when Dr. Mudd hailed them, calling out, "Surratt,
Surratt!" Weichmann and Surratt turned and saw Dr. Mudd
with John Wilkes Booth. Surratt introduced Dr. Mudd to
Weichmann and then the doctor introduced Booth to
Weichmann.[50] The four men went to Booth's room at the
National Hotel where Mudd, Booth, and Surratt, all seated
around a table, discussed what appeared to be a map Booth
was sketching.[51] While Weichmann claimed to have stayed in
the room the whole time, he testified that at times the others
went out into the hall for a while, with Booth and Dr. Mudd
going out first, staying "not more than five or eight minutes."[52]

At the conspiracy trial Dr. Mudd's former slave, Mary
Simms, testified that John Surratt had visited with the Mudds
during the summer of 1864. He visited there "often," she said
in response to the Judge Advocate's leading question. "He
was there from almost every Saturday night to Monday night.
When he would go to Virginia, or come back from there, he
would stop."[53] Ms. Simms said he slept in the woods with
others (most of whom were Confederate soldiers), and they
took their meals in the house while the Mudds "put us all out
to watch." The Mudds provided the bedclothes for the rebel
soldiers to sleep on in the woods.[54] Three other witnesses,
Elzee Eglent, Melvina Washington, and Milo Simms, corroborated Ms. Simms' testimony.[55] Bennett F. Gwynn, a neighbor
of Dr. Mudd, testified that he and his brothers, who were
trying to avoid arrest by General Dan Sickles, had slept in the
woods behind the Mudd home, on bedclothes provided by
the Mudds, and were fed by the Mudds. Gwynn testified he

feared arrest because he was a captain in the home guard, a militia unit organized "to stand by the State in any disloyal position it might take against the [United States] Government," and that Dr. Mudd, knowing of his concern over being arrested (and being aware of why Gwynn was concerned, i.e., aware that Gwynn was a member of the Rebel militia), sheltered him.[56] Then Gwynn, under cross-examination, revealed a bit of information that serves to take Dr. Mudd out of the "civilian" class and into the class of "enemy soldier," so far as the United States government was concerned. He admitted that Dr. Mudd was a member of one of these militia companies.[57] If Bennett Gwynn's testimony is to be believed, and there is no reason not to believe it, Dr. Mudd was a member of the Confederate underground in Charles County and a member of the organized Confederate militia.

In another damaging, if not wholly credible bit of testimony, one witness at the conspiracy trial, William A. Evans, a minister of the Presbyterian Church, swore he saw the doctor enter Mrs. Surratt's boarding house on H Street a day or two before Lincoln's second inauguration.[58] In truth, Dr. Mudd's involvement in the rebel militia and his dealings with Booth and Surratt is less a condemnation of Dr. Mudd than a recognition that all of lower Maryland was rebel territory and that the men who lived in the area were very likely to be rebel sympathizers. In *Maryland and the Confederacy*, a book privately published in 1976 by Harry W. Newman, an author who describes himself as a "one-time member of the Sons of Confederate Veterans," and which is exceedingly sympathetic to the Confederate cause, the author writes:

> If any portion of Maryland was the heart and soul of the Confederacy, Southern Maryland definitely possessed that quality, especially Prince Georges, Charles and St. Mary's Counties ... . This portion of Maryland furnished more men to the Confederate Army and Navy than any other section and thus sustained the heaviest casualties and sorrows.[59]

But the important thing to understand here is that, while Dr. Mudd's behavior may well have been understandable, and certainly in line with that of his neighbors, it is nonetheless a fact that he was involved in the pro-rebel underground in lower Maryland, that he was rather well acquainted with Booth and Surratt, two prime plotters against President Lincoln, and that he lied about all this. Understandable this may be (including his lying about it to save his neck), but that does not alter the evidence.

To this decidedly suspicious portrait of Dr. Mudd must be added his curious behavior after taking Booth into his parlor shortly before dawn on April 15, 1865. After placing his visitor on the sofa in the parlor, the doctor went into the back bedroom to dress and to tell his wife who had barged in upon them at that hour. He explained that one of the men appeared to have broken his leg and asked his wife to tear some bandages for him. After dressing he returned to the parlor with a light and he and Herold helped Booth into the same upstairs bedroom where the actor had slept the previous fall. With Booth stretched out on an ornate Victorian bed in the corner of the room, the doctor cut a 12-inch slit in the actor's long riding boot and pulled the boot from the swollen ankle. On examination he found a straight fracture of the left tibia about two inches above the ankle, an injury he did not regard as particularly painful though Booth appeared to be suffering intensely. The doctor had no proper pasteboard for making splints so he took wood from an old bandbox and put together a homemade splint. Then, with his patient as comfortable as possible, he and Herold left Booth to rest as the faint light of dawn appeared across the sky.[60]

Dr. Mudd then either returned to bed (Mrs. Mudd's statement)[61] or went out into the barnyard to do his chores (Dr. Mudd's statement).[62] When breakfast was ready, he called Herold to the table and they ate.

For the rest of the morning the doctor worked about his farm pretty much as usual. After the noon meal he took Herold and rode over to his father's place to see about a carriage for the wounded man, a rather strange accommodation for two men he later described as total strangers. Finding no carriage available, the two went into Bryantown to look for a conveyance. Dr. Mudd said later that only Herold went into Bryantown and gave the impression, though he did not clearly say so, that he had called on a neighbor instead of going to town. And, so he implied, he had missed learning of the

President's death, the news of which had all of Bryantown abuzz.

However, a number of witnesses at the conspiracy trial recalled seeing Dr. Mudd and Herold riding into town together and several remembered seeing the doctor alone in town that afternoon.[63] Both prosecution and defense witnesses agreed that word of the President's murder reached Bryantown by the time the doctor arrived and that Lincoln's assassin had been identified as a man named "Booth."[64]

On his return from Bryantown the doctor stopped at the farm of a neighbor, John F. Hardy. At the conspiracy trial Hardy was called as a defense witness for Dr. Mudd but, curiously, was not questioned about this visit. Later, however, he was called to the stand for the prosecution and testified that Dr. Mudd had told him during the visit that he had learned in Bryantown that "the President and Mr. Seward and his son had been assassinated the evening before."[65] The assassin was John Wilkes Booth, Dr. Mudd said, and Hardy asked if Booth had not visited the doctor the previous autumn. Dr. Mudd replied that he didn't know whether his visitor was the same man or one of his brothers. He said nothing, however, about the two horsemen who had called at his home before dawn. Francis R. Farrell, Hardy's hired hand, corroborated this testimony.[66]

While Hardy and Farrell were both called by the prosecution, neither man could be called a hostile witness. Both witnesses seemed genuinely sympathetic to Dr. Mudd and said that he had expressed his sorrow at the death of the President and that this expression of sorrow seemed genuine.[67]

Dr. Mudd returned home an hour or so before dark, just as Booth and Herold were leaving, he later testified. Herold asked for directions but the doctor claimed he did not see them leave. "I do not know where they went" he told a federal officer the day after his arrest.[68]

Doctor and Mrs. Mudd put together a fanciful tale about the visit of Booth and Herold which has been universally accepted by the doctor's supporters and repeated as if it were Holy Writ. Yet this story is so incredible as to nearly collapse of its own weight, and it came very close to sending Dr. Mudd to the gallows. Studied carefully, the Mudds' story was a

classic case of the use of the magician's favorite tool —
misdirection. Much was made of the doctor's "duty" to assist
the injured Booth, while the crux of the case against Dr. Mudd
was not that he had given medical aid to an injured nighttime
visitor, but that he had delayed telling authorities of the visit
of the President's assassin long enough to permit him to
escape.

The Mudds always claimed that the doctor became suspicious about his visitors about an hour after he returned home
on Saturday afternoon (after his guests had already left) and
decided he had best go into Bryantown and notify the authorities.[69] Mrs. Mudd agreed that the men were suspicious all
right but said that she begged the doctor not to leave her alone
because she was afraid there might be guerrillas about.

So it was not until the following morning at church that
Dr. Mudd sought out his second cousin, Dr. George Mudd, an
older man with a reputation as a staunch Union loyalist and
a resident of Bryantown. Dr. George Mudd was close to Sam
and had served as his preceptor in the study of medicine.[70]
Sam told George that two strangers had come to his home a
little before daybreak on Saturday; that they were very excited; that one of the men had a broken leg; that he had set the
leg and improvised some crutches for him; that the man had
shaved his mustache; and that the pair had left in the direction
of Parson Wilmers' place.[71]

At least that is what George Mudd later testified under
oath that his cousin had told him. And considering George's
reputation and the candid nature of his testimony, it seems
likely that this was precisely what Sam had related to his
cousin. In any event, the two doctors parted with the understanding that the elder Mudd would pass this information on
to the military authorities in Bryantown. And the following
morning, Monday, April 17, George reported to Lieutenant
David D. Dana the story Sam had told him of the strangers'
visit to his farm.

On Tuesday Lt. Dana sent Lieutenant Alexander Lovett
along with Dr. George Mudd and three "special officers" to
the Samuel Mudd farm to question the doctor. The doctor's
statements to Lt. Lovett and his men that day are of scant
comfort to those who insist that the doctor tried to be helpful
to the federal authorities.

Dr. Mudd told Lt. Lovett: (1) His visitors had remained at the farm for "a short time" (from which the lieutenant reasonably inferred that they had left Dr. Mudd's on Saturday *morning*, instead of Saturday *evening*, as was actually the case); (2) He had learned of the President's assassination at church on Sunday (which, if the pair had left his home on Saturday morning, would have placed Dr. Mudd's knowledge of the crime at twenty-four hours *after* the departure of his visitors, a circumstance which argued strongly for the doctor's innocence); and (3) The lame man walked away on crutches (a disclosure which would have encouraged the federal troopers to look for "a man on crutches" instead of two men on horseback).[72] Understandably, Lt. Lovett left the Mudd farm with more questions than answers.[73]

Three days later, on Friday, April 21, Lt. Lovett and his men returned to Dr. Mudd's and questioned him again. When the lieutenant announced that he would have to search the place, Dr. Mudd suddenly "remembered" that, since the soldiers' last visit, he had "found" the boot he had cut off the injured man. The doctor said something to his wife and Mrs. Mudd went upstairs and returned with the boot. She handed it to Lt. Lovett who turned the top of the boot down and spied the name "J. Wilkes" written in it. Dr. Mudd said he had not noticed the name before but that it now appeared that his injured guest had indeed been John Wilkes Booth.[74]

The atmosphere in the room changed immediately. Lt. Lovett had stumbled over the assassin's trail and Mudd was in deep trouble. Both men sensed it. The lieutenant asked the doctor if either of his visitors had been armed. Dr. Mudd replied that the "injured man" — he still could not bring himself to call him "Booth" — "had a pair of revolvers." He did not mention Herold's carbine, a more effective defense to pursuing cavalry.[75]

Lt. Lovett had heard enough. He placed the doctor under arrest and they took off for Washington. The next day, Dr. Mudd was brought before Colonel H.H. Wells and interrogated at length. At the conclusion of that interview he signed a sworn statement for Wells in which he continued his game of playing the loyal Southerner for his neighbors and the cooperating witness for the federal officials.[76]

Dr. Mudd said that Booth, his former house guest and

sometime companion in Washington — a man he surely should have recognized — did not show his face at all. He "had his cloak thrown about his head," said Dr. Mudd, strange and mysterious behavior for one whose injury was at the other end of his body. Yet the doctor professed not to have been curious. He merely set the man's leg, presumably without asking him the sorts of professional questions one would expect of a doctor treating an injured patient, and went about his daily business.

At breakfast, the doctor's statement continued, the injured man's companion was talkative. He gave his name as "Henston" and said that his injured companion's name was "Tyson." The only thing he thought suspicious, Dr. Mudd said, was that after breakfast the wounded man asked for a razor and he later noticed that "Tyson" had shaved his mustache but that he still had his beard. Mrs. Mudd said she noticed his whiskers had become partially detached as the stranger was coming downstairs and concluded that the whiskers were false.[77]

Covered up head, face to the wall, shaved mustache, false whiskers, and fictitious name. On this slender thread hung Dr. Mudd's story that he did not recognize his nighttime visitor. Viewed in the cold light of hindsight, Dr. Mudd's statement to Colonel Wells raises more questions than it answers.

First, the doctor said, "I have never seen Booth since that time to my knowledge" (i.e., since Booth's first visit to Charles County in November 1864).[78] He later admitted, however, that he had seen Booth in Washington on December 23, 1864.[79] Why would Dr. Mudd lie about this relationship with Booth if the relationship were innocent?

Second, the doctor said he did not recognize Booth as the injured man who called at the house on April 15 because: (1) he had his head covered; (2) he kept his face turned to the wall; (3) he shaved his mustache; (4) he wore false whiskers; and (5) he and Herold gave fictitious names.

In 1877 Dr. Mudd and Samuel Cox Jr. were Democratic candidates of the Maryland Legislature from Charles County. Cox told O.H. Oldroyd in 1901 that when he and the doctor were alone during that campaign Mudd talked often of the assassination. He told him, Cox related, that Booth came to him early in the morning of April 15, 1865, without any effort at concealment of his identity but without telling him of his deed. The doctor treated his injury and made him as comfortable as possible and that afternoon went into Bryantown where he learned of the murder and of Booth's involvement. He went home and upbraided Booth angrily for involving him and his family, and Booth pleaded pitifully, in the name of his mother, not to deliver him up to the authorities. Dr. Mudd yielded, he said, but he made Booth and Herold leave his home immediately.[80]

Cox's story has a ring of truth to it and is not altogether unflattering to the doctor. Even with his admission that he recognized Booth, however, the story doesn't fit. Dr. Mudd also told Cox he had met Booth only once before, on the weekend of November 12, 1864, when the actor spent the night at his farm. Since we know that Dr. Mudd also saw Booth in Washington on December 23, it is obvious the doctor still felt constrained to lie about his role in the kidnap conspiracy as late as 1877.

Yet, aside from Cox's story, a mass of circumstantial evidence suggests that Dr. Mudd was lying about not knowing Booth when he set the assassin's leg that morning.

The doctor's story that Booth kept his cloak over his head, for example, is discredited by his detailed description of his patient's forehead — "He had a pretty full forehead and his skin was fair." — and his hair — " ... black and seemed to be inclined to curl."[81]

That he kept his face turned to the wall, as Dr. Mudd swore, is also highly unlikely, particularly since the doctor noted later that he had shaved off his mustache. How could he have known Booth had shaved his mustache if he had not seen the mustache earlier and how could he have seen it if Booth had kept his head covered and his face to the wall? Admittedly this argument runs to the ridiculous but only because Dr. Mudd's story leads it there.

The shaved mustache is yet another story. Dr. Mudd's apologists use this fact as a central argument in support of the doctor's claim that he did not know who his visitors were. There is, however, substantial evidence that Booth did not shave his mustache at Dr. Mudd's. In Thomas A. Jones' little book, *John Wilkes Booth*, Jones described his introduction to

Booth on April 16, the morning after the pair had left Mudd's place. "Though he was exceedingly pale and his features bore the evident traces of suffering, I have seldom, if ever, seen a more strikingly handsome man," Jones wrote. *"He wore a mustache* and his beard had been trimmed about two or three days before."[82]

Lieutenant A.R. Bainbridge, one of three young Confederates who came upon Booth and Herold at the Rappahannock crossing on April 24, nine days after they had left Dr. Mudd's, described that experience: "His long dark mustache swept over his mouth in a straggling, unkempt manner, though it was evident that he had tried to preserve its shape by frequent handling."[83]

Richard B. Garrett was an eleven-year-old boy when Booth came to his father's farm to die. Garrett, who grew up to be a Baptist minister, wrote his recollection of Booth's brief visit to his father's farm and in the early 1880s often lectured on the subject. In his written account, the Reverend Garrett recalled going into Booth's room early one morning: "The stranger was still sleeping and as I dressed myself his face was turned toward me. I remember vividly the impression made upon me at that time. I had never seen such a face before. Jet black curls clustered about a brow as white as marble and a heavy dark mustache shaded a mouth as beautiful as a babe's."[84]

The conclusion is inescapable — Booth did not shave his mustache at Dr. Mudd's. The Mudds also insisted that Booth wore false whiskers. Since he made no effort to conceal or alter his appearance anywhere else along the escape route, even though his description was being widely broadcast throughout the land, this, too, can be dismissed as another effort to explain away their failure to recognize their "mystery" guest. This conclusion is bolstered by the fact that no one else with whom Booth came into contact during his flight mentioned whiskers, false or otherwise. None were found on his body or discovered along the route. The reason is, of course, because it is highly unlikely that Booth wore such an absurd device.

Dr. Mudd and Mrs. Mudd also insisted that their guests gave fictitious names and did not mention their involvement in the assassination, an exceedingly curious assertion in view of the conduct of the pair elsewhere along their flight. Booth gave his name to Sergeant Cobb at the Navy Yard bridge as he fled the city.[85] At Lloyd's Tavern Herold was acquainted with the proprietor and no introduction was necessary. Booth did, however, volunteer to Lloyd: *"We* have assassinated the President."[86] When the pair finally emerged from Zekiah Swamp and made their way to Colonel Samuel Cox's farm, about seven miles from Bryantown, they told Cox who they were and what they had done.[87] They made no effort to conceal their identities or their deed from Thomas A. Jones who hid them for five days.

Across the Potomac, they appear to have identified themselves to Mrs. Quesenberry who nervously refused to help them. At the Rappahannock River, the pair readily identified themselves, first to Major Ruggles and then to Jett and Bainbridge, as "the assassins of the President." Only at the Garrett farmhouse do they appear to have used aliases and even that is questionable since everything the Garretts told about their mysterious visitors must be balanced against the family's interest in avoiding the gallows for harboring the assassins. Assuming, however, that the Garretts' story is true, Booth's alias of "John William Boyd" makes a great deal more sense, in view of the initials "JWB" which Booth had tattooed on his hand, than the name "Tyson."

Thus if Booth and Herold so readily identified themselves and talked openly of their accomplishment to almost everyone they encountered along the escape route, how can we believe the Mudds' incredible story that the pair identified themselves only by the names of "Tyson" and "Henston?"

Third, the final absurdity in Dr. Mudd's statement to Colonel Wells was his story that, though he gave the pair directions, he did not know where they went when they left his home. From other sources we know, however, that the pair departed, not by the main road but by a path through Zekiah Swamp since the country was crawling with soldiers searching for them. Not even Herold, whose intimate knowledge of the lower Maryland countryside had brought him into the plot, was acquainted with the interior of the Zekiah Swamp. No, Dr. Mudd, though he wanted very much to keep it a secret, had sent his visitors on a hidden route to Colonel Cox's plantation. As accessory before the fact to the kidnap conspiracy, Dr. Mudd became an accessory after the fact to the murder of the President by aiding his killer's escape.

The Mudds always insisted that the doctor did not return to Bryantown on Saturday night to inform the authorities about his visitors because Mrs. Mudd was afraid to be left alone. Her fear appeared to be centered in a Confederate guerrilla, John H. Boyle, a desperate character who had assassinated Captain Thomas H. Watkins of Anne Arundel County, near the Prince Georges County line, on March 25, and who was still at large. This fear of Boyle would have been perfectly justified. At the time of the general election of 1864, Boyle — who knew of Dr. George Mudd's Union sympathies — sent word to him that he would kill him and steal his horses. Mrs. Mudd surely heard of this threat to her husband's cousin. Moreover, about ten days before the President's murder, Boyle was allegedly involved in a robbery and murder near Nottingham in Prince Georges County and federal authorities were on the lookout for Boyle even as the search for Booth was taking place.[88]

By Saturday morning, April 15, Lt. Dana was sent into Southern Maryland to search for the two suspicious characters who had crossed the Navy Yard bridge late the night before. He became convinced that the "person who murdered Secretary Seward is Boyce or Boyd, the man who killed Captain Watkins in Maryland."[89] That afternoon someone put Dana straight as to the names and the feared desperado John H. Boyle was identified as Seward's "assassin." When the doctor told Mrs. Mudd that Boyle was supposedly involved, she understandably became frightened and asked him not to leave her that night.

This does not, however, explain Dr. Mudd's roundabout way of sending his suspicions about his visitors to the authorities in Bryantown. He left Mrs. Mudd alone while he rode to church when, if he were truly concerned about informing the authorities, he could as well have ridden to Bryantown and back and been gone from home no longer than he was on his trip to church. And Lt. Dana would have had the word twenty-four hours earlier.

Yet the truth was that Dr. Mudd was trapped. He knew who his visitors were and what they had done, and realized that sooner or later the federal authorities would make the connection to his former association with Booth. Surratt's name was also appearing as a conspirator and the doctor had met with him as well and this association, too, was bound to surface and cause him trouble. On the other hand he could not turn Booth over to the Federals without becoming an outcast among his neighbors, who were largely pro-Southern. Then there was Boyle. Mrs. Mudd later swore that she begged her husband not to leave her alone that Saturday night. "I told him that if he went himself that Boyle was reported to be one of the assassins and who had killed Captain Watkins ... might have him assassinated for it ... ."[90] So the doctor tried to straddle the issue and failed.

Everything considered, however, the most damning evidence against Dr. Mudd is circumstantial. The doctor's defenders have always insisted that Booth and Herold were merely seeking medical attention when they stopped at Dr. Mudd's, and that this gentle country physician was simply obeying his Hippocratic oath when he set Booth's leg that night. But this argument ignores the fact that by 1865 Dr. Mudd was no longer a practicing physician. Charles County had two or three other physicians, all competing for what little medical business there was in a 19th century rural county, and medicine was not a particularly easy way to make a living. Dr. Mudd's father had given him a 500-acre farm and ten slaves, and Sam had sensibly abandoned a medical practice which had earned him little to become a full-time farmer.

He was not, then, the simple country doctor who has become an American folk hero, a kindly follower of Hippocrates who hitched up his buggy night after night and drove across the lower Maryland farmlands to care for the sick. He was a farmer, and Booth's early morning call to his home had less to do with his medical knowledge than his past association with Booth in conspiracy against Lincoln.

Consider. When Booth fled south on the night of April 14, he passed near the dwellings of at least three other physicians whose presence would likely have been known to him or to Herold. Given Davy Herold's intimate knowledge of Southern Maryland and Booth's recent trips to the area, either or both of them must have been aware of the presence of one or more of these doctors. And there were, very likely, other medical practitioners whose presence in 1865 we cannot be certain of today, and of whom Booth and Herold would have been aware. Yet the fugitives raced south, ignoring these medical doctors and abandoning the route which Atzerodt said they intended to follow (straight south to Maryland Point) in their haste to reach Dr. Mudd's house.[91]

They did not make their way to Dr. Mudd's then, simply because Booth was in need of *any* doctor. They arrived there, having ignored the presence of other doctors who could have afforded Booth relief earlier, because they knew Mudd was a fellow conspirator on whom they could rely. The doctor himself indirectly suggested as much in his sworn statement to Colonel Wells. He said Booth "wanted to get back, or get home and have [his leg] done by *a regular physician*."[92] Yet he had already by-passed a number of "regular physicians" on his way to Dr. Samuel A. Mudd, a retired, or inactive, physician. The selection of Dr. Mudd had, it seems, a good deal more to do with the doctor's politics than with his medical reputation.

In August 1865, Captain George W. Dutton of Company C, 10th Regiment of the Veterans' Reserve Corps, who was the commanding officer of the guard which accompanied Dr. Mudd to Fort Jefferson in the Dry Tortugas, made a sworn statement before a notary public in Washington. He swore that Dr. Mudd had told him while under his charge enroute to prison that Mudd knew Booth when he came to his house with Herold, on the morning after the assassination of the President; that he had known Booth some time but was afraid to tell of his having been at his house on the 15th of April fearing that his own and the lives of his family would be endangered thereby; that he was with Booth on the evening referred to by Weichmann in his testimony (December 23, 1864); and that he came to Washington on that occasion to meet Booth by appointment.[93]

From his prison cell at Fort Jefferson, Dr. Mudd denied having made this confession, and there is no way of knowing who was telling the truth on this score. It is difficult to imagine what would have prompted Capt. Dutton to *swear* to such an outrageous lie as Dr. Mudd suggested the "confession" was, particularly since it is in accord with what we know the facts to be. It is equally difficult to imagine why Dr. Mudd would have abandoned the story he had stood by publicly when public belief in his innocence was his one big hope of ever leaving prison a free man.

Dr. Mudd's repudiation of Captain Dutton's statement does confirm to us, however, his position within the Rebel underground. The doctor said that Booth, on his visit to the farm in November 1864, had inquired into the political sentiments of the residents of lower Maryland and the contraband trade that existed between the North and the South. "These and many minor matters spoken of," Mudd wrote, "caused me to suspect him to be a Government detective and *to advise Surratt regarding him.*"[94] So Dr. Mudd would have us believe that he suspected Booth of being a federal detective when he first met him, though the opposite is almost certainly true. The doctor nonetheless admitted that his reaction to the suspected presence of a Union spy was to warn a known Confederate agent. It is a telling commentary on the loyalty of Dr. Samuel Alexander Mudd.

But we should not be surprised. Dr. George Mudd, testifying as a witness *for* Dr. Sam, said of his cousin at the conspiracy trial: "From my association with him, I have to consider him as sympathizing with the South."[95]

That he did. And when the time came he sided with the South in a dangerous game — protecting the assassin of President Lincoln. The wonder is that Dr. Mudd did not hang. Yet, the Special Military Court of Appeals would now set aside Dr. Mudd's conviction, two judges because they believe the military commission lacked jurisdiction and one because he believed Dr. Mudd's guilt was not proven.

CONCLUSION

The effect of this decision cannot be underestimated. It was more than a mere exercise in the moot court process of training lawyers. Because of the prominence of the lawyers and judges involved, the United States Government will now be required to take notice. The decision of this "court" will demand respect, no matter how flawed it might be. It will become an important tool in the Mudd family's struggle to overturn the conviction of the 1865 military commission. Dr. Richard Mudd, the 92-year-old grandson of Dr. Mudd has already declared: "This will be a wonderful help in dealing with the Secretary of Defense and [President] Clinton."[96]

Lincoln, as might be expected, has the last word. On

December 1, 1862, in his Annual Message to the Congress, the President said, "Fellow citizens, we cannot escape history."[97] He was right, of course. We cannot *escape* history. But, as the Special Military Court of Appeal has shown, we can try to *alter* it.

Notes

1 THE LIFE OF DR. SAMUEL A. MUDD 30 (Nettie Mudd ed., 1906) (privately published by Richard D. Mudd, Saginaw 1962) [hereinafter cited simply as THE LIFE OF DR. MUDD].

2 OTTO EISENSCHIML, WHY WAS LINCOLN MURDERED? 254 (1939).

3 Nettie Mudd Monroe, Dr. Mudd's daughter, received $2,000 from Twentieth Century-Fox for rights to the motion picture. The contract provided that Ms. Monroe was to see and edit the film before it was shown. Ms. Monroe later claimed the company violated the contract. ROY Z. CHAMLEE JR., LINCOLN'S ASSASSINS 560 (1990).

4 *Id.*

5 THE LIFE OF DR. MUDD, *supra* note 1, at foldout, back cover.

6 CHAMLEE, *supra* note 3, at 560.

7 Would it not look rather terrible, distinguished judges, if in a civilian court the prosecution is unable to convict John Surratt who certainly has evidence allayed against him far more deadly than that looked at by Dr. Mudd? I predict that that is exactly what will happen and any affirmance of these convictions will hold the military tribunal in even lower esteem in this country — something we do not need.

Record at 11; *see* Oral Arguments *supra* pp. 53-96.

8 THOMAS R. TURNER, BEWARE THE PEOPLE WEEPING 138 (1982). The *New York Times* made a very perceptive comment on the same issue:

When, therefore, the Government, availing itself of the existing state of war, cited the criminals before a Military Commission, which, while respecting their rights refused all delays and brushed aside the fictions and technicalities usual and useful in common cases, letting in every ray of light from any quarter upon motives and persons, and scanning the widest range of circumstances, most candid persons agreed that a case transcending all experience was rightly tried in modes as extraordinary. ... John H. Surratt was called to his account in a calmer state of the public mind, after time had appeased its righteous anger and the passion for retribution had been allayed.

N.Y. TIMES, Aug. 12, 1867, at 4.

9 A wealthy former slaveholder who lived in lower Maryland, Samuel Cox, who was aware of the identities of Booth and Herold and of their crime, arranged for them to be hidden in a secluded spot covered with low pines. Thomas Jones, a Confederate signal agent and the foster brother of Colonel Cox, fed Booth and Herold and kept them secure in their hideout from Saturday night, April 15, until the 21st, a week after the murder, when he set them out on the Potomac in a boat

he owned. CHAMLEE, *supra* note 3, at 129-30.

[10] Lloyd ran the Surratt Tavern at Surrattsville where Booth and Herold stopped on their flight from Washington to have a drink and to pick up guns that had been stashed there for them earlier. Lloyd had run the tavern since the Fall of 1864, when Mrs. Surratt leased it to him and moved to Washington to open a boarding house. Lloyd knew Booth and Booth told him "*We* have assassinated the President," as he waited on his horse before the tavern that Friday night. 1 BEN POORE, THE CONSPIRACY TRIAL 119 (1972) (Testimony of John M. Lloyd). When soldiers searching for the two stopped at the tavern the following day, Lloyd swore that he knew nothing about the assassination and that no one had come by the tavern. CHAMLEE, *supra* note 3, at 47.

[11] Maddox was wardroom custodian at Ford's Theater and a close friend of Booth. Booth had given him a letter, signed by most of the conspirators, that Maddox was to have published in the *National Intelligencer*. CHAMLEE, *supra* note 3, at 169.

[12] *Id.* at 385. Given their brother's penchant toward overdramatization, they can perhaps be forgiven if they failed to take this conspiracy talk seriously.

[13] *Id.* at 408.

[14] *Id.* at 115.

[15] His name was actually Lewis Thornton Powell, but inasmuch as Conspiracy Trial records and most writings on the subject refer to him by his pseudonym "Lewis Payne," he shall be so designated in this article.

[16] Usually referred to as "Edward" Spangler.

[17] His last name was actually spelled "O'Laughlen," but he is almost universally referred to as "O'Laughlin."

[18] Speed and his brother, Joshua, had been longtime friends of President Lincoln. James Speed had helped organize the Unionist sentiment of Kentucky to prevent that state from seceding in 1861. Speed was a man of strong principles, but somewhat legalistic in his thinking. CHAMLEE, *supra* note 3, at 212. Speed's predecessor as Attorney General, Edward Bates, held a low opinion of the man he called "my poor imbecile successor," believing him to be a mere tool of Secretary of War Stanton and Secretary of State Seward. EDWARD BATES, THE DIARY OF EDWARD BATES 1859-1866, at 483 (Howard K. Beale ed., 1933).

[19] CHAMLEE, *supra* note 3, at 212.

[20] 11 Op. Att'y Gen. 297 (1865).

[21] 2 GIDEON WELLES, THE DIARY OF GIDEON WELLES 304 (Howard K. Beale ed., 1911).

[22] BATES, *supra* note 18, at 483 (emphasis added).

[23] *Id.*

[24] Brief on Behalf of Petitioner at 3 [hereinafter cited simply as *Petitioner's Brief*]; *see* Brief on Behalf of Samuel A. Mudd *supra* pp. 3-31.

[25] *Ex parte* Vallandigham, 68 U.S. (1 Wall.) 243 (1864). The United States had not declared war on the Confederacy, the argument goes, because the Confederacy was not a sovereign power, but rather "represented states in insurrection or rebellion as declared by Congress." In the absence of a formal declaration from the United States, notifying the Confederacy that the two parties would be acting as belligerents, the laws of war could not govern. *Petitioner's Brief, supra* note 24, at 10.

[26] 67 U.S. (2 Black) 635 (1863). The Prize Cases had held that the President

had the right, under the law of war, to blockade the Confederacy's ports, a right which neutrals were bound to respect.

²⁷ *Id.* at 667.

²⁸ THE INTERNATIONAL LAW OF CIVIL WAR 43 (Richard A. Falk ed., 1971).

²⁹ *Id.* at 46 (emphasis added).

³⁰ *Id.* at 47.

³¹ Brief on Behalf of Respondent at 14 [hereinafter cited simply as *Respondent's Brief*]; *see* Brief for the United States in Reply *supra* pp. 33-52.

³² 71 U.S. (4 Wall.) 2 (1866).

³³ "[A] citizen who was not a resident of one of the rebellious states, or a prisoner of war ... and never in the military or naval service ... ." *Id.* at 118.

³⁴ The *Milligan* court said that in Indiana, "there was no hostile foot; if once invaded, that invasion was at an end and with it all pretext for martial law." *Id.* at 126-27.

³⁵ On March 8, 1863, Mosby learned of a break in the Federal picket line between Chantilly and Centreville, Virginia. Mosby stole through the break with twenty-nine of his men and, in the midst of thousands of Union troops, he took General Stoughton from his bed in his headquarters and stole out of town with thirty-two other prisoners and fifty-eight horses. Jeb Stuart called it a "feat unparalleled in the war." EZRA B. WARNER, GENERALS IN BLUE 482-83 (1964).

³⁶ Company H, 18th Virginia Cavalry, C.S.A.

³⁷ J.W. Duffey, *Two Generals Kidnapped*, THE MOOREFIELD EXAMINER (W. Va.), Feb. 1944, at 19. Duffey was one of McNeill's Rangers and participated in the Cumberland raid.

³⁸ "The Federal officer in charge then observed that the implements of war before him were museum pieces at best and not the excellent captured Federal rifles that most of the Rangers were known to possess. 'A competent Judge who saw the arms piled on the ground declared they were not worth ten dollars a ton.' The Federals accepted them with reluctance." Simeon M. Bright, *The McNeill Rangers: A Study In Confederate Guerilla Warfare*, 12 W. VA. HIST. 386 (July 1951).

³⁹ The two men met that day in a house at Appomattox Courthouse, a few miles from the station. But before he went to this meeting Lee quietly spoke a few words that were both a judgment on the past and an omen for the future. To him, as he prepared to meet Grant, came a trusted lieutenant who urged him not to surrender but simply to tell his army to disperse, each man taking to the hills with his rifle in his hand: let the Yankees handle guerrilla warfare for a while and see what they could make of that ... The unquenchable guerrilla warfare this officer had been hinting at was perhaps the one thing that would have ruined America forever. It was precisely what Federal soldiers like Grant and Sherman dreaded most — the long, slow-burning, formless uprising that goes on and on after the field armies have been broken up, with desperate men using violence to provoke more violence, harassing the victor and their own people with a sullen fury no dragoons can quite put down.

BRUCE CATTON, NEVER CALL RETREAT 452-53 (1965).
Note also General William T. Sherman's remark in a letter home to Mrs.

Sherman at the time of Lee's surrender: "There is a class of young men who will never live at peace. Long after Lee's and Johnston's armies are beaten and scattered they will band together as highwaymen and keep the country in a fever begetting a guerilla war." *Id.* at 514 n.12.

[40] "The wretched end of Benito Mussolini marks a fitting end to a wretched life." N.Y. TIMES, Apr. 30, 1945, at 18.

Albert Spalding, a noted violinist who worked in Italy for the U.S. Office of War Information, said at a news conference when asked about the killing of the fallen dictator, that it was "the typical reaction of people who have been living in tyranny for many years," and compared Mussolini's death to the summary justice administered by the vigilante groups in the American West. N.Y. TIMES, May 1, 1945, at 3.

[41] Charles Hardee of Georgia wrote that when the news was received at a nearby store, everyone hurrahed and threw his hat in the air. Mrs. Cornelia McDonald said that when she first heard of Lincoln's death, she felt it was just what he deserved; and Robert Park, who personally opposed the assassination, said that one of his comrades had expressed a willingness to share his last crust of bread with Booth. TURNER, *supra* note 8, at 96.

> Historians ... have generally assumed that the South abhorred Lincoln's assassination and treated Booth with scorn and contempt. At a superficial level this was the reaction of many southerners. However, there is much evidence that many acted because of fear of their own helpless position and the belief that Johnson could only be much worse than Lincoln had been. Still others secretly applauded the deed where circumstances permitted. When northerners assumed that the South would exult over the murder and that it might pump new life into the dying Confederacy, they would not have been so far wrong as historians have assumed, if only conditions had been slightly different.

Id. at 99.

[42] *Respondent's Brief, supra* note 31, at 6.

[43] *Petitioner's Brief, supra* note 28, at 37-50.

[44] *Id.* at 49-50.

[45] 1 POORE, *supra* note 10, at 430 (Testimony of Eaton G. Horner).

[46] CHAMLEE, *supra* note 3, at 306; SAMUEL CARTER III, THE RIDDLE OF DR. MUDD 73-75 (1974).

[47] THE LIFE OF DR. MUDD, *supra* note 1, at 29 (Statement of Mrs. Samuel A. Mudd).

[48] *Id.*; 1 POORE, *supra* note 10, at 361 (Testimony of Thomas L. Gardiner).

[49] Weichmann was a leading government witness at the conspiracy trial and undoubtedly was a Confederate agent who had been involved on the periphery of the Lincoln plot. Samuel Arnold swore that Booth had told him that Weichmann had provided him with information on the number of prisoners held by the north, information that would come to Weichmann by reason of his clerkship at the Commissary General of Prisoners. SAMUEL B. ARNOLD, DEFENCE AND PRISON EXPERIENCES OF A LINCOLN CONSPIRATOR, STATEMENTS AND AUTOBIO-GRAPHICAL NOTES 31 (1943).

Augustus "Gus" Howell, a Rebel blockade runner who was caught and imprisoned shortly before the assassination, wrote (in an unpublished holographic statement in the John T. Ford papers), "Weichmann ... gave me information and said it came from his Books in his office ... He obtained his office in the War Department with the express understanding with Surratt that he would furnish Surratt with all information that came under his notice from time to time to be transmitted South ... He received dispatches for Surratt from Booth and took charge of the whole business [of the Lincoln plot] in Surratt's absence ... ." GEORGE S. BRYAN, THE GREAT AMERICAN MYTH 237-38 (1940).

Weichmann has been heavily criticized for his testimony regarding Mrs. Surratt, which undoubtedly helped send her to the gallows. The proof is too long to explore in this note, but as difficult as Weichmann is to like, his testimony holds up under close examination.

[50] Among the difficulties of remaining convinced of Dr. Mudd's innocence in the plotting that led to the assassination of the President is the realization that Dr. Mudd was obviously well acquainted with both John Wilkes Booth and John H. Surratt Jr. Dr. Mudd initially denied meeting with Booth, Surratt, and Weichmann but in a confession given on August 28, 1865, he admitted to the meeting but attempted to cast a very innocent light on the meeting. THE LIFE OF DR. MUDD, *supra* note 1, at 42-44.

[51] 1 POORE, *supra* note 10, at 69-71 (Testimony of Louis J. Weichmann).

[52] 1 *Id.* at 97 (Testimony of Louis J. Weichmann).

[53] 2 *id.* at 151 (Testimony of Mary Simms).

[54] As if this testimony were not suspicious enough, the Judge Advocate pressed for more details:

Q: Who put you out to watch?

A: Dr. Sam. Mudd, to see if anybody would come; and, when we told them anybody was coming, they would run out, and go off to the woods again; and he would make me take the victuals out to them. I would set their victuals down, and I would stand and watch; and the rebels would come out and get the victuals, while I stood behind a tree and watched them.

Ms. Simms also testified that Dr. Mudd and Surratt "never talked very often in the presence of the family; they always went off by themselves to talk ... up stairs in the room." She said that they brought letters from Virginia and that Mudd took these letters and gave them letters to take back to Virginia. 2 *id.* at 151-52 (Testimony of Mary Simms).

[55] 2 *id.* at 157-58 (Testimony of Elzee Eglen), 160-63 (Testimony of Melvina Washington), 163-68 (Testimony of Milo Simms).

Dr. Mudd's counsel tried, without much success, to blunt the effect of this testimony by introducing the testimony of witnesses who raised questions as to the year when the soldiers camped in the woods, whether Surratt had been among them, and whether Mary Simms could be believed. 2 *id.* at 313-22 (Testimony of Frank Washington), 322-25 (Testimony of Baptist Washington), 325-29 (Testimony of Alben J. Brooke).

[56] 2 *id.* at 294-300 (Testimony of Bennett F. Gwynn).

[57] Gwynn tried mightily to protect Dr. Mudd. When asked if the doctor were "a member of any of the volunteer companies," he replied, "I think he was." He

could not recall the name of the company but remembered "It was a company gotten up in Bryantown." Then he added, "I think." When asked, "Are you sure that he was a member of a company?" Gwynn replied, "I think he was. I do not know it to my knowledge for a fact." Obviously Gwynn had not drilled with Dr. Mudd or seen him at a company gathering. Just as obviously, however, he knew who among his neighbors were members of the militia companies. 2 *id.* at 300.

[58] 3 *id.* at 236-68 (Testimony of William A. Evans).

[59] HARRY W. NEWMAN, MARYLAND AND THE CONFEDERACY 212 (1976). The book is dedicated "to the Maryland men and women who supported the Confederate States of America and to the noble work of the United Daughters of the Confederacy."

[60] EISENSCHIML, *supra* note 2, at 254-55; THE LIFE OF DR. MUDD, *supra* note 1, at 30-31; PHILIP V.D. STERN, THE MAN WHO KILLED LINCOLN 179-84 (1939).

[61] THE LIFE OF DR. MUDD, *supra* note 1, at 30.

[62] EISENSCHIML, *supra* note 2, at 256.

[63] Frank Bloyce testified that he saw Dr. Mudd in Bryantown that afternoon. 2 POORE, *supra* note 10, at 61. John H. Ward testified that the news of Lincoln's assassination had all Bryantown excited by one o'clock on Saturday afternoon and that Booth was the name given for the assassin. 2 *id.* at 63. Mrs. Eleanor Bloyce testified that she saw Dr. Mudd riding into Bryantown late Saturday afternoon in the company of another man. 2 *id.* at 47. Mrs. Becky Briscoe testified that she saw Dr. Mudd riding into Bryantown about three o'clock on Saturday afternoon in the company of another man. 2 *id.* at 50. Dr. Mudd never denied going into Bryantown that afternoon. What he did deny was knowing about the assassination until the following morning.

[64] 2 *id.* at 61 (Testimony of Frank Bloyce), 63 (Testimony of John H. Ward).

[65] 3 *id.* at 431 (Testimony of John F. Hardy).

[66] 3 *id.* at 418-23.

[67] 3 *id.* at 431-34 (Testimony of John F. Hardy), 421 (Testimony of Francis R. Ferrell).

[68] EISENSCHIML, *supra* note 2, at 257.

[69] CLARA M. LAUGHLIN, THE DEATH OF LINCOLN 126-27 (1909). Even if the doctor is viewed in a light most positive to him, it is difficult to understand why he did not become suspicious about two strangers who showed up at his door in the middle of the night, wind-blown, saddle-rumpled and haggard. One of them carried pistols, the other a carbine. A carbine is not a hunting rifle, it is a weapon of war. Of course, in his interrogations Dr. Mudd failed to mention that the two men looked like renegades and that Herold carried a carbine. 1 POORE, *supra* note 10, at 268 (Testimony of Lt. Alexander Lovett). He did say, however, that he and Herold went to Dr. Mudd's father's house to see if he could get a carriage for "the wounded man." War Department Archives, Records, File "E," 315, JAO. *See also* THEODORE ROSCOE, THE WEB OF CONSPIRACY 539-42 (1959). This seems a rather strange accommodation for two men Dr. Mudd insists were strangers.

[70] 2 POORE, *supra* note 10, at 386 (Testimony of George D. Mudd).

[71] 2 *id.* at 391.

[72] One of the great mysteries of the Booth flight is that some soldiers searching for Booth and Herold reported catching glimpses of a lame man on crutches and his companion darting into the swamp near the farm. The tracks of

the two led nowhere and the best modern opinion is that Rebel sympathizers in the area were using decoys to keep the Federals off of Booth's trail. ROSCOE, *supra* note 69, at 351.

[73] 1 POORE, *supra* note 10, at 258-72 (Testimony of Lieutenant Alexander Lovett).

[74] 1 *id.*

[75] 1 *id.*

[76] ROSCOE, *supra* note 69, at 539-42 (Statement of Dr. Mudd).

[77] THE LIFE OF DR. MUDD, *supra* note 1, at 32.

[78] EISENSCHIML, *supra* note 2, at 256.

[79] CHAMLEE, *supra* note 3, at 482-83.

[80] O.H. OLDROYD, THE ASSASSINATION OF ABRAHAM LINCOLN 268-69 (1901).

[81] EISENSCHIML, *supra* note 2, at 254-55.

[82] THOMAS A. JONES, J. WILKES BOOTH 78 (Chicago, Laird & Lee 1893) (emphasis supplied).

[83] Prentiss Ingraham, *Pursuit and Death of John Wilkes Booth*, 39 CENTURY MAG. 443 (1890). The same meeting was described in the same issue of the magazine by Major Mortimer B. Ruggles, an operative of Captain Thomas Nelson Conrad of the Confederate Secret Service. Ruggles wrote: " ... *though he had shaved off his mustache*, upon his lip and face was a beard of some ten days' growth." *Id.* at 494 (emphasis supplied).

We cannot have it both ways. If Booth had shaved his mustache at Mudd's there would have been none for Jones to have seen and, even with ten days growth, it would not have been long enough to have swept over his mouth by the time Bainbridge saw Booth. Someone is mistaken or someone is lying. Fortunately for the sake of historical accuracy, we know that other facets of Ruggles' account are false, leaving his recollection of Booth's mustache open to question. Then, too, aside from the Mudds, Ruggles was the only eyewitness to Booth's flight who spoke of his mustache having been shaved. Most witnesses to the flight and those who viewed his body later never mentioned his mustache. This omission would not be unusual if the mustache were still in place but would be very curious if it had been shaved.

[84] Richard B. Garrett, *End of a Manhunt*, 17 AMERICAN HERITAGE 41 (June 1966).

[85] 1 POORE, *supra* note 10, at 252.

[86] 1 *id.* at 119.

[87] JONES, *supra* note 82, at 71-72.

[88] James O. Hall, *The Guerrilla Boyle*, THE MD. INDEPENDENT, May 7, 1975, pt. I, at 1, 3.

[89] James O. Hall, *The Guerrilla Boyle*, THE MD. INDEPENDENT, May 14, 1975, pt. II, at 1.

[90] *Id.* at 3.

[91] EISENSCHIML, *supra* note 2, at 470; *see also* ATLAS OF FIFTEEN MILES AROUND WASHINGTON, INCLUDING THE COUNTY OF PRINCE GEORGE, MARYLAND (Philadelphia, G.M. Hopkins 1878). This atlas reveals the dwellings or offices of no fewer than fourteen physicians along that portion of Booth's escape route that ran through Prince George County. Undoubtedly, some of these physicians were not there in 1865, but no doubt many of them were. And there

were at least two other physicians Charles County in 1865. The physicians in Prince Georges County in 1878 were as follows:

At the little crossroads village of Good Hope, still in the District of Columbia, Booth's route passed, on his right, the home of a Dr. Wadsworth. *Id.* at 36. Just beyond Silver Hill, about two-and-one-half miles out of Washington and barely a mile beyond the District line, the residence of Dr. McKim sat just off the road to the right of Booth's route. *Id.* at 22. Perhaps a mile south of Dr. McKim's by road and no more than half a mile across country, Dr. William Gunton made his home near the gristmill on Hensons Creek. *Id.*

At Surratsville the pair was less than a mile from the home of Dr. John L. Waring, a physician in the Robeystown-Surrattsville area *since 1841. Id.* at 11. Four-fifths of a mile out of Surrattsville the road branched to the right southwest toward the Potomac. About a mile down this road, in the spring of 1865 (and since 1842) lived the country doctor and member of the Doctors' Line (a Confederate underground dispatch route), Dr. Edward H. Wyvill. A mile beyond Dr. Wyvill's, in Piscataway Post Office, lived two physicians, Dr. Hurtt and Dr. Edelin. *Id.* at 19. But Booth and Herold rode on past the two physicians who were undoubtedly there in 1865, bearing to the east toward Dr. Mudd's.

At the same time they declined to turn west to Dr. Wyvill's home for medical care their route passed the home of Dr. P.H. Heiskell, just a mile due east of the Surrattsville-Tee Bee Road. *Id.* at 26. As they raced on toward Tee Bee their route passed by the roadside residence of Dr. Joseph H. Blanford and, to the east, a mile off the main road, sat the home of Dr. Morgan. *Id.* at 27. In Tee Bee the pair ignored the presence of Dr. Joseph S. Latimer, a physician since 1825, and made an abrupt turn to the southeast, heading for Dr. Mudd's and abandoning their direct route south to the Potomac. *Id.* at 11.

Their new route took them within two miles of the homes of Dr. Richard Perry and Dr. Lewis Mackall, both nestled along a back road where cavalry was unlikely to look in the first dragnet. *Id.* at 18, 27. Assuming the pair had taken that route and found Doctors Perry and Mackall unavailable, they would have been only a mile's ride from the home of yet another physician of the area, Dr. J.H. Skinner. *Id.* at 10, 18.

Still they rode on toward Dr. Mudd's. At Horse Head their route took them within half a mile of Dr. Skinner's. *Id.* at 18. Just a mile or so southeast of Horse Head sat the home of Dr. M.R. Latimer. *Id.* at 23.

These fourteen physicians are merely some of those scattered along the route followed by Booth and Herold through Prince Georges County, Maryland, in 1878. Three of them, Drs. Waring, Wyvill, and Joseph S. Latimer, the Atlas reveals, were along Booth's route in 1865. Undoubtedly, others from the 1878 Atlas were also there in 1865. Moreover, Drs. Waring, Wyvill and Latimer were better situated for immediate medical care than was Dr. Mudd.

[92] EISENSCHIML, *supra* note 2, at 225.

[93] LOUIS J. WEICHMANN, A TRUE HISTORY OF THE ASSASSINATION OF ABRAHAM LINCOLN AND THE CONSPIRACY OF 1865, at 257-58 (Floyd E. Risvold ed., 1975).

[94] THE LIFE OF DR. MUDD, *supra* note 1, at 44.

[95] 2 POORE, *supra* note 10, at 402.

[96] CIV. WAR TIMES ILLUSTRATED, May/June 1993, at 12, 15.

[97] 5 ABRAHAM LINCOLN, *Annual Message to Congress, in* THE COLLECTED WORKS OF ABRAHAM LINCOLN 518, 537 (1963).

Was the Assassination of Abraham Lincoln a War Crime?

Howard S. Levie*

There does not appear to be any dispute about the following facts concerning the assassination of President Abraham Lincoln: that on 14 April 1965, while sitting in a box at Ford's Theater in Washington, D.C., watching a performance of "Our American Cousin," Lincoln was shot and killed by John Wilkes Booth; that in jumping from the box to the stage (where he delivered the *sic semper tyrannis* pronouncement) one of Booth's spurs caught on a flag decorating Lincoln's box with the result that he fell and broke his leg; that despite this he was able to escape from the theater and from Washington; that he was later joined in his flight by David E. Herold; that Dr. Samuel Mudd, a Booth acquaintance living in Maryland, treated Booth's leg and provided him with a makeshift crutch; and that all this occurred five days after Lee's surrender to Grant at Appomattox.

From that point on there is little agreement on the facts[1] — and even less on the applicable law. However, as to some of the facts which are disputed, there is really no basis for

* A.B., Cornell University, 1928; J.D., Cornell Law School, 1930; LL.M., George Washington University Law School, 1957; Colonel (Ret.), U.S. Army, Judge Advocate General's Corps; Professor Emeritus of Law, St. Louis University Law School; Charles H. Stockton Chair of International Law, U.S. Naval War College, 1971-1972; Adjunct Professor of International Law, U.S. Naval War College, 1991 to Present.

argument. For example, it is sometime argued that with Lee's surrender the Civil War (or the War Between the States) came to an end. That is not so. Lee had merely surrendered the Army of Northern Virginia. The Confederate States of America had other armies in the field, armies which continued to fight, armies which did not surrender until well after the date of the assassination.[2] Moreover, because of the presence of thousands of Confederate sympathizers in Washington, martial law had been declared for that city, which was fortified and heavily guarded by Union troops, and that status still existed on 14 April 1865, when the assassination took place.

The current manual on the law of war of the United States Army defines a war crime as "a violation of the law of war by any person or persons, military or civilian."[3] Adopting this definition, the sole question that this article will attempt to answer is: Was the assassination of Abraham Lincoln by John Wilkes Booth (and any co-conspirators) a violation of the law of war and, hence, a war crime? To refine our discussion even further: Is the murder of an individual committed in wartime by one or more individuals of the same nationality as the victim a war crime?

If the answer to these questions is in the affirmative, under the law of war a military commission would unquestionably have jurisdiction to try the accused persons, including Dr. Samuel Mudd, brought before it charged with such an offense. If the answer to these questions is in the negative, the question of the jurisdiction of a military commission becomes one of constitutional and national law which is beyond the purview of this discussion.[4]

For our purposes we will assume the worst case for the accused: 1) that the evidence established that there was a conspiracy to assassinate President Lincoln; 2) that the eight individuals convicted by the military commission on 30 June 1865, including Dr. Samuel Mudd, as well as others who were not charged, were parties to that conspiracy;[5] 3) that all of the conspirators charged, being residents of the District of Columbia or of the State of Maryland, were nationals of the Union; 4) that, nevertheless, all of the conspirators were strong supporters of the Confederate cause; and 5) that the conspiracy to assassinate Lincoln was motivated by a desire on their part to help that cause.[6]

The charge with respect to which the military commission opened its hearings on 9 May 1865, and to which the eight accused pleaded "Not Guilty" on the following day, alleged that they "maliciously, unlawfully and traitorously" combined, confederated, and conspired to kill and murder Abraham Lincoln and others.[7] There is no allegation that their acts were in violation of the law of war. The wording of the charge itself demonstrates that the prosecution considered the offense charged to be a conspiracy to commit treason by murdering the President and his successors-to-be and that it did not consider this to be a war crime.[8] As the present author has said elsewhere:[9]

There are a number of actions which, while they are wartime criminal offenses and are punishable by the injured belligerent, do not come within any definition of war crimes. Thus, while there is a wide-spread belief that espionage and treason are violations of the laws and customs of war and are, therefore, war crimes,[10] this is not so.[11] International law does not forbid espionage and treason; national laws do.[12]

Presumably, the accused, Union citizens, assumed their acts of assassination would in some manner benefit the Confederate cause, even at that late date in the war. Their acts were, therefore, traitorous — but, as it has just been shown, treason is not a violation of the law of war, and it is not a war crime.

The post-World War II trials in which Germans tried Germans, Austrians tried Austrians, Hungarians tried Hungarians, etc., were not true war crimes trials. For the most part they were collaborationist (treason) cases and, in many cases, prosecuted misuse or abuse of power. Nor were the euthanasia cases or the concentration camp cases (involving actions which took place prior to, and after, 1 September 1939, the official date of the beginning of World War II in Europe), which were tried by the Germans, true war crimes cases. They were violations of German criminal law, which had existed at the time of the offenses, but which, for obvious reasons, had not been enforced by Nazi officials.[13]

In the Nordhausen Concentration Camp case, the review of the case contains the following statement:

For an illegal act to be a war crime certain elements must be present, viz., (1) the act must be a crime in violation of international law; (2) there must be a disparity of nationality between the perpetrator and the victim; and (3) the criminal act must have been committed as an incident of war.[14]

These elements were not present in the trial of those alleged to have been parties to the conspiracy to assassinate Abraham Lincoln. The act charged was not a violation of international law; there was no disparity of nationality between the persons charged as perpetrators and the victim; and it is extremely doubtful that the assassination of Lincoln may be considered to have been an incident of the war. Therefore, it was not a war crime.

Proponents of the argument that the law of war governed the assassination of Abraham Lincoln, a Union citizen, by those who were likewise Union citizens, will find support in the trial of Mariano Uyeki,[15] a case for which the present author can find no justification:

Mariano Uyeki was born in 1924 in Iloilo, Panay, the Philippines, of Japanese parents. When the war broke out in 1941 he apparently suffered at the hands of his Filipino schoolmates because he was pro-Japanese and it was alleged that on 10 May 1942, after the Japanese occupation of Panay, and without any justification, he shot and killed a fellow Filipino teenager. There was some evidence at that period he was acting as an interpreter for the Japanese and that he was wearing at least parts of a Japanese Army uniform. However, he was not conscripted into the Japanese Army until October 1944. He became a prisoner of war on 1 September 1945. Early in 1946 he was tried for the murder by a United States Military Commission. He was convicted and sentenced to death. That conviction was vacated because "the validity of the proceedings is faulty." Unfortunately, there is no explanation of the basis for that statement. He then made an application to the Supreme Court of the Philippines for a writ of habeas corpus, claiming that he was a Filipino citizen and that the United States Military Commission had no jurisdiction to try him. His application was denied on the ground that even if he had originally been a national of the Philippines, he had forfeited that nationality by rendering military service to the Japanese Government. This was not a decision that the military commission had jurisdiction to try him, it was a decision that the Supreme Court of the Philippines had no jurisdiction to rule on the jurisdiction of the United States court because he was not a citizen of the Philippines. He was retried by another United States Military Commission in April 1946 and was again convicted and sentenced to death.[16]

Concerning this case the present author went on to say:

When the offense was committed in 1942, it was a matter of the murder of one (pro-American) Filipino civilian by another (pro-Japanese) Filipino civilian. It was a violation of the criminal law of the Commonwealth of the Philippines. Surely, this was a case for the courts of the Philippines and not a war crime for trial by a United States Military Commission. Even though the accused may have lost his Filipino nationality in 1944, upon entering the Japanese Army, and even though the Philippines were not yet fully independent, it did have its own fully-developed criminal justice system. It is difficult to find a basis for the jurisdiction of the United States military commission for this offense committed in 1942. Regrettably, no application for a writ of habeas corpus was made to the United States Courts.[17]

In other words, it is not believed that motive alone can convert an offense which is a violation of national law into one which is a violation of international law. Had Booth and his fellow conspirators been disappointed office seekers, the as-sassination of President Lincoln would certainly not have been a war crime; and the fact that they acted as they did because of their political motivation, because of their desire to support the Confederacy, does not convert a common law national crime into an international crime.

The conclusion is reached that the assassination of President Abraham Lincoln by John Wilkes Booth and his fellow conspirators was not a violation of the law of war and, therefore, was not a war crime, but was a politically motivated, treasonous act committed by Union citizens in the hope that it would help the Confederate cause. Accordingly, even if we assume that the evidence supported Dr. Mudd's conviction of conspiracy to commit treason and murder under national law, he was properly convicted only if a trial by military commission at that time and place complied with the constitutional and statutory law of the United States.

Notes

[1] *See* OTTO EISENSCHIML, WHY WAS LINCOLN MURDERED? (1937) (discussing one extreme, and perhaps discredited, version of the facts); WILLIAM HANCHETT, THE LINCOLN MURDER CONSPIRACIES (1983) (containing a 15-page bibliography and more scholarly discussion on the subject); *see also* LOUIS J. WEICHMAN, A TRUE HISTORY OF THE ASSASSINATION OF ABRAHAM LINCOLN AND THE CONSPIRACY OF 1865 (Floyd H. Risvold ed., 1975) (setting forth the contents of a number of interesting documents).

[2] For example, Confederate General Joseph E. Johnston did not surrender to Union General William T. Sherman until 18 April 1865. THE WAR OF THE REBELLION: A COMPILATION OF THE OFFICIAL RECORDS OF THE UNION AND CONFEDERATE ARMIES, ser. I, vol. XLVII, pt. III, 243-45 (Washington, GPO 1895). General Sherman was reprimanded for giving General Johnston what were considered to be excessively favorable conditions for his surrender and the Federal Government repudiated the surrender agreement! *Id.* at 301-02, 334-36, 345.

[3] DEPARTMENT OF THE ARMY, FIELD MANUAL FM27-10, The Law of Land Warfare ¶ 499 (1956). Much of this manual was the work of the late Richard R. Baxter, subsequently the United States Judge on the International Court of Justice. In amplification of the foregoing the present author has stated:

> Anyone — military or civilian, man or woman, enemy nationals, allied nationals, and neutral nationals — may commit a war crime and may be tried and punished for the criminal act.

HOWARD S. LEVIE, TERRORISM IN WAR: THE LAW OF WAR CRIMES 431 (1993). No national of the United States was tried by a United States military commission for a war crime during or after World War II although a considerable number were tried by courts-martial for violations of the Articles of War, then the Army's penal code; and many of those trials would have been considered to be war crimes trials if they had been tried by the enemy. For such activities during Vietnam, see W. Hayes Parks, *Crimes in Hostilities* (pt. 1 & conclusion), 60 MARINE CORPS GAZETTE 16 (Aug. 1976), 60 MARINE CORPS GAZETTE 33 (Sept. 1976).

[4] There were a number of trials by military commissions after the Civil War which, unquestionably, involved war crimes, primarily the maltreatment of Union prisoners of war held in the South. The most famous of these was the trial of Captain Henry Wirz, who had commanded the notorious prisoner-of-war camp at Andersonville, Georgia. *See* H.R. EXEC. DOC. No. 23, 40th Cong., 2d Sess. (1867); 8 AMERICAN STATE TRIALS 657 (John Davison Lawson ed., 1918). For a different type of war crime, see T.E. Hogg *et al.*, Gen. Orders No. 52, Dep't of the Pac. (June 27, 1865) *in* THE WAR OF THE REBELLION: A COMPILATION OF THE OFFICIAL RECORDS OF THE UNION AND CONFEDERATE ARMIES, ser. II,

vol. VIII, 674-81 (Washington, GPO 1899).

⁵ Of course, Booth must be added to this group. He was not a defendant at the trial because, while being pursued by the Union authorities, he had been shot and killed in Garrett's barn, near Bowling Green, Virginia. John Surrat, another alleged conspirator, had left the country and, not having been apprehended and returned to the United States until a considerable period thereafter, could not be tried with those whom we are assuming to be his fellow conspirators. He was tried in a civil court in 1867, the trial resulting in a hung jury. He was not retried.

⁶ It has often been charged that the conspiracy to assassinate President Lincoln was approved by Jefferson Davis and members of the Confederate Cabinet. In fact, the charge (or indictment) includes their names and the specification includes a statement to the effect that the conspirators were "incited and encouraged" by Davis and other well known Confederates. However, no substantial evidence of their involvement was adduced at the conspiracy trial. Davis was taken into Union custody on 10 May 1865, after the trial was under way, and he was not brought before the Commission. He was released from custody in May 1867 without having been tried for any offense.

⁷ BENN PITMAN, THE ASSASSINATION OF PRESIDENT LINCOLN AND THE TRIAL OF THE CONSPIRATORS 18-21 (New York, Moore, Wilstach & Baldwin 1865) (*facsimile ed.* 1954). This is the courtroom testimony as recorded by Pitman, the official court reporter.

⁸ In *Ex parte* Quirin, 317 U.S. 1 (1942), where unlawful belligerents, including one individual who claimed to be a citizen of the United States, had entered this country for purposes of espionage and sabotage, the Court stated that "even when committed by a citizen, the offense [entering the country for the purpose of committing sabotage while wearing civilian clothes] is distinct from the crime of treason ... since the absence of uniform essential to one is irrelevant to the other." *Id.* at 38.

In other words, unlawful combatants wearing civilian clothes and bent on sabotage are in violation of the law of war; inasmuch as only citizens can commit treason, their attire at the time of the commission of the act is immaterial, and there is no unlawful combatancy involved.

⁹ LEVIE, *supra* note 3, at 3.

¹⁰ *See, e.g.,* Iu. A. Reshetov, *International Criminal Responsibility of Individuals for International Crimes,* in THE NUREMBERG TRIALS AND INTERNATIONAL LAW 167 (George Ginsburgs & V.N. Kudriavtsev eds., 1990); Jacob Berger, *The Legal Nature of War Crimes and the Problem of Superior Command,* 38 AM. POL. SCI. REV. 1203, 1204 (1944); W.L. Ford, *Resistance Movements in Occupied Territory,* 3 NETH. INT'L L. REV. 355, 372 (1956). Ford appears to take the position that neither spying nor sabotage is a violation of the law of war. Sabotage by legal combatants is not a violation of the law of war. Sabotage by illegal combatants is such a violation. Roling says: "Both in the case of espionage and in that of 'risky war acts' the term 'war crimes' is used metaphorically. This concept should be kept for breaches of the laws and customs of war, for violations of the international law concept of *jus in bello*." B.V.A. Roling, *Supranational Criminal Law in Netherlands Theory and Practice,* 2 INT'L L. IN THE NETH. 161, 194 (1979).

¹¹ With respect to espionage and war treason, War Office, THE LAW OF WAR ON LAND ¶ 624 (Sir Hersch Lauterpacht, rev., 1958), states rather conservatively

that "the accuracy of the description of such acts as war crimes is doubtful." *See also* UNITED NATIONS WAR CRIMES COMMISSION, HISTORY OF THE UNITED NATIONS WAR CRIMES COMMISSION AND THE DEVELOPMENT OF THE LAWS OF WAR 487 (1948).

[12] Nathan Hale, Major John André, Mata Hari, Richard Sorge were not war criminals. They did not violate the laws and customs of war; each of them violated the laws relating to espionage of the enemy of the belligerent for which he or she acted — and they were punished under those laws. The United States Supreme Court erred in *Ex parte* Quirin when it stated that spies are "offenders against the law of war." 317 U.S. at 31. Similarly, Quisling, Pétain, Laval, Lord Haw Haw, Kawakita, Tokyo Rose, etc., were not war criminals. They did not violate the laws and customs of war, they were collaborationists who violated the treason laws of their own countries — and they were punished under those laws.

[13] The trials of Germans by German courts for membership in Nazi organizations determined to have been criminal in nature were mandated by the Charter of the International Military Tribunal which sat in Nuremberg and by the judgment of that Tribunal.

[14] *See* LEVIE, *supra* note 3, at 283. This case was officially known as *The Trial of Kurt Andree*. National Archives, Records Group 338, File M 1079, Rolls 1-16. It was tried by a United States military commission at Dachau, Germany, in December 1947.

[15] Archives of the Hoover Institution for War, Peace, and Revolution, U.S. Armed Forces W. Pac., File CSUZXX 191-A, Box 2; LEVIE, *supra* note 3, at 236.

[16] LEVIE, *supra* note 3, at 236.

[17] *Id.*

The Appeal of Dr. Samuel Mudd

Jeffrey F. Addicott*

I. INTRODUCTION

The Legal Forum did an outstanding job in sponsoring the moot appeal of Dr. Samuel A. Mudd. From start to finish, the logistics of the presentation were superbly handled.

Set against the backdrop of the War Between the States, the most tragic and yet defining historical event in our nation, the audience was guaranteed a production sure to capture the imagination. While the legal arguments on both sides clearly demonstrated how our system of jurisprudence has evolved since the War Between the States, in a larger sense, the moot appeal also challenged the audience to reflect back on many of the fundamental issues attendant to the war.

In weighing the appeal of Dr. Mudd, the moot court of appeals faced two primary issues — jurisdiction and sufficiency of evidence. Of these two issues, only the evidentiary question was easily and expeditiously resolved.

II. SUFFICIENCY OF EVIDENCE

Regarding the sufficiency of evidence question, even under the most favorable standard available to the government — a "more likely than not standard" — the moot court of

---

* Lieutenant Colonel, U.S. Army, Attorney at Law; Office of the Judge Advocate General, International & Operational Law Division.

appeals was certainly obliged to overturn Dr. Mudd's conviction. Indeed, a fair review of the evidence presented against Dr. Mudd revealed that there was probably not enough of a case developed to charge Dr. Mudd, let alone bring him to trial.

There can be little serious debate that the public hysteria surrounding the assassination of President Lincoln and the attempted assassination of several members of the Union's top leadership had completely prejudiced the impartiality of the fact finders.[1] Accordingly, the three member appellate panel was unanimous in finding that there was insufficient evidence presented at Dr. Mudd's trial to sustain the guilty findings of the military tribunal.

III. JURISDICTION

The jurisdictional question faced by the moot court of appeal posed a more difficult issue. Indeed, there were two theories by which the tribunal could have asserted jurisdiction: (1) under the test set out in *Ex parte Milligan*,[2] or (2) under the traditional "common law of war" standard.

In spite of the existence of these two distinct theories for establishing jurisdiction, most of the attention of the moot court was directed toward assessing the *Milligan* approach. The "common law of war" approach, which is a firm basis on which to assert jurisdiction, did not receive due consideration. Thus, on the question of whether the military tribunal had jurisdiction to try Dr. Mudd, the three member moot court split, with the majority finding that no jurisdiction existed. In my opinion, gauged by either the *Milligan* approach or the common law of war approach, this conclusion was erroneous. The military commission had jurisdiction to try Dr. Mudd.

A. *Milligan*

The test for asserting jurisdiction as set out in *Milligan* is rather straightforward. In short, the Court in *Milligan* held that a military tribunal[3] could not properly try a civilian unless "exigent circumstances" exist, e.g., unless legitimate government control is seriously challenged.

Simply put, the question is whether such exigent circumstances existed in Washington City[4] at the time that the com-

mission asserted jurisdiction over Mudd and the other conspirators. Two of the moot panel members found that no such
exigent circumstances existed, and therefore held that the
accused should have been tried in a civilian court.

The greatest obstacle in evaluating historical events rests
in the ability to accurately grasp the full range of facts surrounding the event in question. Although one might argue
that this task is not difficult, as hindsight is "20/20," many
fundamental issues relating to the War Between the States are
extremely complex and require careful study.

In this sense, it seems that the primary problem in properly gauging the exigencies related to the *Milligan* standard
turn on accurately comprehending issues related to the very
nature of the war. Unfortunately, even after 130 years, there
exists much confusion about the War Between the States. This
confusion ranges from a fair understanding of the causes,[5] to
the very name of the conflict — it was not a "civil war."[6]

The exigencies that allowed jurisdiction under *Milligan*
are fairly convincing. First and foremost, the war had not
ended when the plot was carried out, nor at the time the
military tribunal was established by President Johnson. In
addition, Washington City was still the seat of the Union war
effort. Although the Army of Northern Virginia had surrendered in April 1865, there were several major Confederate
armies still in the field.[7] The closest to Washington City after
the assassination of Lincoln was Confederate General Joe
Johnston's in North Carolina (30,000 strong). This force was
only a few days' march away. Indeed, it was not inconceivable
that Washington City might once again be attacked by a
detached portion of that army, as it had been in the Fall of 1864
when General Lee detached General Jubal Early from his
army to strike north behind enemy lines.

Second, the Confederate cabinet was still intact and operational as it traveled through Virginia and into Georgia with
the design to reach the trans-Mississippi region. President
Davis was actively engaged in gathering forces to carry on the
war and was not captured until May 10, 1865.[8]

Finally, bands of armed Confederates were still operating
in Maryland and Virginia.[9] This, coupled with a war that had
already caused over 600,000 casualties, convinced many prominent Union officers that the assassination of Lincoln was part

of a last ditch effort by the Confederacy.[10]

The majority opinion failed to properly recognize these pertinent historical facts that supplied sufficient exigent circumstances. The conclusion of the court that exigent circumstances were absent, was inaccurate and reflected a misunderstanding of the historical facts that should have been applied to the *Milligan* standard.

B. Common Law of War

Customary international law has long recognized the legality of military commissions or tribunals to try those accused of violations of the laws of nations or, to use the generic term, those accused of "war crimes." A war crime is a generic term for all illegal actions relating to the inception or conduct of warfare.[11]

A military commission derives its authority from the U.S. Constitution which provides that Congress has the power to "define and punish offenses against the law of nations."[12] In turn, Congress has traditionally turned jurisdiction over to the military to conduct military tribunals for those accused of war crimes. Armed with this authority, military tribunals have tried hundreds of individuals since the War for Independence.

During the War Between the States, the jurisdictional basis for trying war criminals was specifically authorized in Article XIII of General Orders No. 100 (issued April 24, 1863), promulgated as "Instructions for the Government of the Armies of the United States in the Field," and known as the Lieber Code.[13] "Military jurisdiction is of two kinds: first, that which is conferred and defined by statute; second, that which is derived from the common law of war." In addition, Article VIII of General Orders No. 30 (issued April 22, 1863) states: "The laws of war apply equally to all portions of our country while war exists."[14] Thus, the President had the authority to use military commissions or military tribunals to try those accused of committing war crimes.

Customary international law holds that anyone can commit a war crime, since the offense is a violation against the laws of nations. Thus, the fact that Dr. Mudd was a civilian does not exclude him from being tried in a military tribunal as a war criminal. The critical question is whether the killing of

President Lincoln by the conspirators was a war crime in violation of the laws and customs of war.

President Lincoln, as the Commander in Chief of all Union forces, was a legitimate war target. For example, had President Lincoln been shot and killed by a regular Confederate cavalry attack into Washington City, the killing would have been lawful. Under this set of facts, and because a state of hostilities existed between the Confederate States and the United States, President Lincoln would have been a legitimate military target and the Confederate soldiers would have been lawful combatants, entitled to all the protection of prisoners of war.

In the case of the Booth conspiracy, however, while Lincoln was still a legitimate military target, Booth and his conspirators were not lawful combatants. Therefore, the co-conspirators had no lawful right to kill President Lincoln, hence, the term assassination is used to describe the unlawful killing. Those who committed the killing of President Lincoln, as well as those who conspired, were guilty of a violation of the law of war under customary international law.

To address such war criminals, General Orders No. 30, Section II, specifically defined individuals who conduct activities outside of the color of legitimate authority.[15] The Booth conspirators could fall under either the definition for the "brigand," or the "guerrilla proper." The brigand is described as one who "assails the enemy without or against the authority of his own Government."[16] The guerrilla proper is defined as those who do not abide by the laws of war and do not belong "to a regular army, consisting of volunteers, perhaps self-constituted."[17] General Orders No. 30 prescribes that all who fall under either category shall "suffer death, according to the usage of nations, by sentence of a military commission."[18]

In the case of the Booth conspirators, it is certain that none were in the military service of the Confederacy, nor were they acting under any authority whatsoever from Confederate authorities, civil or military.[19] These individuals were engaged in acts of unlawful belligerency. Although they sought to hinder the Union war effort — the plot had been in the planning stage for over a year — they had no standing under the laws and customs of war to do so. Thus, they were clearly guilty of committing war crimes and subject to being tried by a military commission for their acts.

III. CONCLUSION

More than a century and a quarter after the original trial of Dr. Mudd, amid the vastly different *modus vivendi* of modern American society, the moot appeal offered a unique opportunity to visit the origins and early applications of legal principles that most citizens now take for granted.

Although the court reached the correct conclusion — that Dr. Mudd should have been released — this conclusion should have rested on the sufficiency of the evidence, rather than on a jurisdictional basis.

Notes

¹ *See* BRUCE CATTON, THE CIVIL WAR 593 (John Leekley ed., 1982). The Secretary of War, Edwin Stanton, was one of the chief parties responsible for fanning the hysteria. For example, without any basis in fact, he informed the United States "that Lincoln had been murdered by Jefferson Davis' agents, and that the whole tragedy was a direct part of the dying Confederate war effort."

² 71 U.S. (4 Wall.) 2 (1866).

³ The term military tribunal and military commission generally are treated as synonymous.

⁴ Washington, D.C., was known as Washington City in 1865.

⁵ *See* Jeffrey F. Addicott, *Values and Religion in the Confederate Armies, in* CONFEDERATE VETERAN 29-30 (Nov.-Dec. 1990). For example, the most popular revisionistic claim related to the War Between the States was that the Confederate soldier fought to perpetuate the evil of slavery. This view is misleading and historically inaccurate. While the issue of slavery was certainly a catalyst for the war, the vast majority of Confederate soldiers did not own slaves, or ever hope to own them. In general, Confederate soldiers did not view themselves as fighting for slavery. Actually, the greatest leaders in the army were strongly opposed to the institution. General Robert E. Lee owned no slaves, and he personally ensured that all of those in his wife's estate were freed by 1862. His opposition to the evil of human servitude is well documented. Before the War, he believed in a process of gradual manumission. At the conclusion of the War, having suffered total poverty from its effects, he wrote:

> So far from engaging in a war to perpetuate slavery, I am rejoiced that slavery is abolished. I believe it will be greatly for the interests of the South. So fully am I satisfied of this ... that I would cheerfully have lost all I have lost by the war and suffered all I have suffered, to have this object attained.

⁶ *See* LIEBER'S CODE AND THE LAW OF WAR 18 (Richard S. Hartigan ed., 1983) [hereinafter cited simply as LIEBER'S CODE]. Although the War Between the States is popularly called the Civil War, it was not a civil war. Francis Lieber, the author of the Union's rules regulating warfare, set forth a definition of "civil war" that clearly did not fit the facts of the conflict between the North and South. Lieber defined the term civil war as, "War between two or more portions of a country or state, each contending for the mastery of the whole, and each claiming to be the legitimate government." Clearly, the Southern Confederacy only sought legal separation from the United States, not to conquer the United States. If the War Between the States is classified as a "civil war" then the American War for Independence with Great Britain must also be termed a "civil war."

⁷ *See* THOMAS B. ALLEN, THE BLUE AND THE GRAY 309 (1992). The last

major Confederate army, commanded by General Watie, surrendered on 23 June 1865.

   [8] *See* MICHAEL B. BALLARD, A LONG SHADOW: JEFFERSON DAVIS AND THE FINAL DAYS OF THE CONFEDERACY (1986).

   [9] *But see* T. HARRY WILLIAMS, THE HISTORY OF AMERICAN WARS FROM 1745 TO 1918, at 301 (1st ed. 1981). Just before the surrender at Appomattox, Virginia, several high ranking Confederate officers suggested that the Army of Northern Virginia should scatter and "take to the hills." Lee, however, would not permit continued resistance by guerrilla methods. He replied that "this kind of warfare would bring only devastation and misery to the people the army had been defending."

   [10] *Id.* While Lincoln's assassination was not sponsored by the Confederacy, there were several "last ditch plans." One was a plan to free and arm thousands of Confederate prisoners of war at Point Lookout, Maryland, and use them to attack Washington City. This had been planned in Richmond for more than a year.

   [11] *See* John Triffterer, *Jurisdiction over States for Crimes of State*, *in* 2 A TREATISE ON INTERNATIONAL CRIMINAL LAW 86-96 (M. Cherif Bassiouni & Ved P. Nanda eds., 1973).

   [12] U.S. CONST. art. I, § 8, cl. 10.

   [13] Francis Lieber, a German international law scholar and professor at Columbia University, was asked by the Federal authorities to draft a code for the conduct of war on land. THE MILITARY LAWS OF THE UNITED STATES, War Dep't Doc. No. 64, at 779-799 (Washington, GPO, George B. Davis ed., 1897). *See also* NATIONAL SECURITY LAW 309-10 (John N. Moore et al. eds., 1990); DIETRICH SCHINDLER & JIRI TOMAN, THE LAWS OF ARMED CONFLICT: A COLLECTION OF CONVENTIONS, RESOLUTIONS, AND OTHER DOCUMENTS 3 (Dietrich Schindler & Jiri Toman eds., 3d ed. 1988). Southern forces adopted their own code of conduct for land warfare in 1861: "Articles of War, Regulations of the Army of the Confederate States." In June of 1863, James A. Seddon, the Confederate Secretary of War, pledged to abide by most of the substantive provisions of the Lieber Code.

   [14] LIEBER'S CODE, *supra* note 6, at 104.

   [15] *Id.* at 92.

   [16] *Id.* at 95.

   [17] *Id.* at 96.

   [18] *Id.*

   [19] Although numerous accusations were made to link President Davis and General Lee to the plot, it soon became clear that such machinations were totally false. Indeed, Lee's sense of humanity made such accusations totally absurd. Lee even refused to engage in legitimate reprisals, a concept well recognized in international law. This is one of the reasons he has been called the "Christian General," as reflected in his address to the troops as they marched into Pennsylvania during the Gettysburg campaign of 1863: "It must be remembered that we make war only on armed men, and that we cannot take vengeance for the wrongs our people have suffered without lowering ourselves in the eyes of ... Him to whom vengeance belongeth." THE WAR OF THE REBELLION: A COMPILATION OF THE OFFICIAL RECORDS OF THE UNION AND CONFEDERATE ARMIES, ser. I, vol. XXVII, pt. III, at 943 (Washington, GPO 1899).

The Case Against Dr. Samuel Mudd:

Why His Family's Vanity Does Not Justify Rewriting Dr. Mudd's Story

Andrew C. Carington*
with Floyd E. Risvold**

INTRODUCTION

In 1865, a nine-man military commission, presided over by Major General David Hunter,[1] convicted Dr. Samuel A. Mudd of complicity with John Wilkes Booth in the assassination of President Lincoln. The commission sentenced Dr. Mudd to life imprisonment and he was sent to Fort Jefferson, a federal prison on an island off the gulf coast of Florida. Less than four years later, on February 8, 1869, President Andrew Johnson pardoned him. By definition, a pardon reaches both the punishment prescribed for the offense and the guilt of the offender.[2]

Dr. Samuel Mudd was not satisfied with his pardon and neither is his grandson, Dr. Richard D. Mudd, an elderly resident of Saginaw, Michigan. Richard Mudd has conducted a long and highly skillful public relations and political campaign to clear his grandfather's name. Since the pardon already did this in the eyes of the law, Richard Mudd is really seeking historical vindication of his grandfather.

Pressed by Richard Mudd and several members of Congress, the Army Board for Correction of Military Records

* J.D., 1995, University of Richmond; B.A. *cum laude*, 1990, Denison University.
** Editor of Louis Weichmann's A True History of the Assassination of Abraham Lincoln and the Conspiracy of 1865 (Alfred A. Knopf ed., 1975) and author of The Minnesota Territory in Postmarks, Letters and History (1985).

agreed to review Samuel Mudd's 1865 conviction and consider expungement of the record created by the military commission.

The Board held a hearing in the Pentagon on January 22, 1992, taking testimony only from those sympathetic to Dr. Mudd. As a result of this hearing, the Board recommended to the Secretary of the Army that the conviction be set aside because the military commission lacked jurisdiction to try Dr. Mudd. Concluding that Dr. Mudd should have been tried in a civil court, the Board did not proceed to rule on his guilt or innocence. Subsequently, William D. Clark, Acting Assistant Secretary of the Army, denied the Board's recommendation for two reasons: (1) that it is not the role of the Board to settle historical disputes; and (2) that the Board had no judicial function.[3]

Later in 1992, the T.C. Williams School of Law at the University of Richmond organized a "moot appeal" from Dr. Mudd's 1865 conviction, inventing a fictional Special Court of Military Appeal for this purpose. Three highly regarded judges with military and international law backgrounds were recruited to hear the appeal. Law students were assigned to prepare briefs for Dr. Mudd's counsel and for the government's counsel. The case was argued at the law school on February 12, 1993.

Afterward, two of the judges decided that the military commission lacked jurisdiction to try Dr. Mudd. The third thought that Dr. Mudd's trial by military authorities was legal, but that the evidence presented was insufficient for conviction.

Careful review of the arguments made for Dr. Mudd in this court reveals several errors and omissions. Our intent here is to call the public's attention to the many facts ignored in the mock appeal and thus to defend the integrity of history. This article will begin by taking a look at the man who was Dr. Mudd. It will then go on to discuss procedural and evidentiary matters, demonstrating how their correct resolution by the appellate tribunal would have left a case by the prosecution sufficient to sustain Dr. Mudd's conviction. Finally, certain misleading statements made to the appellate tribunal on behalf of Dr. Mudd in the brief and oral arguments will be analyzed and corrected.

DR. SAMUEL A. MUDD

In evaluating Dr. Mudd's actions, it is proper to start with the man. Viewed by some as a simple country doctor, he was not only avowedly pro-Confederate, but also demonstrably pro-slavery. The 1860 slave census shows that Dr. Mudd's father, Henry L. Mudd, owned sixty-one slaves and that Samuel Mudd owned five himself. At the 1865 trial, two Mudd slaves, Mary Simms and her brother, Elzee Eglent, testified that Dr. Mudd shot Elzee for not obeying orders.[4] Concerning his views on slavery, Dr. Mudd did not differ from his state and his community. In the election of 1860, 92,502 votes were cast in Maryland, of which only 2,294 were for Lincoln. In Charles County where Dr. Mudd lived, 1,197 votes were cast in that election, of which only six were for Lincoln.[5] Dr. Mudd had little reason to be an admirer of Abraham Lincoln or of the Union.

On January 13, 1862, Dr. Mudd wrote a long letter to O.A. Brownson, the publisher of Brownson's Quarterly Review. In this missive, Dr. Mudd gives the full flavor of his views on slavery, "the north" and its people, and Lincoln (the "head of the government") and his administration. Dr. Mudd was not only "pro slavery," but also anti-Lincoln. He supported the Confederacy and its war aims. To take just one quote from that letter: "I confidently assert, that if there was any other man at the head of the Government of true conservative and constitutional principles, the Revolution would immediately cease so far as the South is concerned."[6]

TRIAL BY MILITARY COMMISSION

Much attention has been given to whether the Booth conspirators should have been tried by a military court. Proper analysis of this issue requires placing in military and political context President Johnson's decision to refer the case to a military commission. Because of the crisis gripping Washington at the time of the conspirators' arrests, prosecution in a military court was justified. Washington was the wartime headquarters of the armed forces of the Union. The city was ringed by some sixty forts. It had been invaded in the summer of 1864, and great battles had been fought around or near it. At the time President Lincoln was assassinated, the rebellion had not yet been extinguished. There were still substantial Confederate armies in the field, and Confederate leaders continued to express hope of ultimate success. Under conditions such as these, any attempt to assassinate the Commander in Chief by persons sympathetic to the enemy should be viewed as a furtherance of the war efforts of the enemy, and accordingly prosecuted under the laws of war.

At the time, President Johnson asked Attorney General James Speed for his opinion regarding the jurisdiction of a military commission to try the assassination conspirators. Mr. Speed's opinion confirmed the legality of this jurisdiction. In essence, the Attorney General's opinion held that, in time of war, the military could try civilians if they were "public enemies." The opinion rested in part on a constitutional provision regarding offenses against the law of nations[7] and on common rules called the "laws of war."[8] With respect to the term "public enemies," it is worth noting that a conspiracy to assassinate the heads of government, that is President Lincoln, Vice President Johnson, and Secretary of State Seward, for the purpose of affecting the course of the war, could hardly have been organized by "friends."

The whole purpose of the conspiracy, whether to capture Lincoln or to assassinate him, was to throw the Union government into confusion and disrupt its military operations. The assassination of Abraham Lincoln was a threat to the very existence of the government. There was a crisis.

DR. MUDD'S HABEAS CORPUS PETITION

It is important to remember that a question of jurisdiction is one of procedure. While resolution of procedural questions in a defendant's favor may moot any examination by a court of facts related to the underlying substantive offense, it does not magically erase those facts from existence. In this case, facts unrelated to jurisdiction prove Dr. Mudd conspired, as charged at the 1865 trial, to "advise, encourage, receive, entertain, harbor, and conceal, aid, and assist the said John Wilkes Booth."[9] Neither a subsequent presidential pardon, nor a modern-day judgment that a military commission was the wrong tribunal, can change the facts that prove Dr. Mudd's guilt.

With respect to the question of jurisdiction, Candida Steel at the "mock appeal" argued on behalf of Dr. Mudd that the

December 1866 Supreme Court decision in *Ex parte Milligan*[10] applied retroactively to the 1865 trial of Dr. Mudd and the other conspirators. Lambdin P. Milligan, a rabidly pro-Confederate Indiana man, was arrested by military authorities for clearly treasonable activities. He was brought to trial before a military commission convened in Indianapolis on October 21, 1864. He was convicted and sentenced to be hanged. The execution was delayed, and the case ultimately reached the Supreme Court by way of an appeal from a lower federal court's denial of a petition for writ of habeas corpus. In a complex decision, the Court held that circumstances in Indiana did not justify the use of a military commission because law and order had not broken down under invasion or threats, and because the civil courts were open and free to function. Four justices, led by Chief Justice Chase, dissented in part.[11]

Prompted by the decision in *Milligan*, Baltimore attorney Andrew Sterrett Ridgely filed a petition for a writ of habeas corpus for Dr. Mudd with Chief Justice Chase on December 19, 1866. Chase returned the petition on December 29th with a brief note suggesting that it be filed " ... in the District in which the prisoner is held." This was the Southern District of Florida.

In 1868, such a petition, *Ex parte Mudd et al.*, came before Judge Thomas J. Boynton of the United States District Court for the Southern District of Florida. Judge Boynton reviewed *Milligan* and held that the circumstances in Washington, where the assassination conspiracy case arose, were fundamentally different. In his September 1868 opinion, Judge Boynton concluded that *Milligan* did not apply to the military trial of the Lincoln conspirators and denied the writ. The key paragraph of his opinion reads thus:

> The President was assassinated not for private animosity nor for any other reason than a desire to impair the effectiveness of military operations and enable the rebellion to establish itself into a Government; the act was committed in a fortified city which had been invaded during the war, and to the northward as well as the southward of which battles had many times been fought, which was the headquarters of all the armies of the United States,

from which daily and hourly went military orders. The President is the Commander in Chief of the army, and the President who was killed had many times made distinct military orders under his own hand, without the formality of employing the name of the Secretary of War or Commanding-General. It was not Mr. Lincoln who was assassinated, but the Commander in Chief, for military reasons. I find no difficulty, therefore, in classing the offense as a military one, and with this opinion arrive at the necessary conclusion that the proper tribunal for the trial of those engaged in it was a military one."[12]

An appeal from Judge Boynton's decision reached the Supreme Court in late February 1869 as *Ex parte Arnold and Spangler*. Dr. Mudd's name was deleted from the title of the case because he had already been pardoned by President Johnson. The Supreme Court calendar shows that this case was argued on February 26 with P. Phillips appearing for the other two conspirators and Assistant Attorney General Ashton appearing for the government. Before the Court could reach a decision and write an opinion, President Johnson pardoned both Arnold and Spangler. Consequently, Chief Justice Chase ordered the appeal dismissed on March 19, 1869, presumably because the pardons had rendered it entirely moot. This action by Chase left Judge Boynton's decision on the propriety of military jurisdiction undisturbed and in place. His opinion that the facts of the *Milligan* and *Mudd* cases were sufficiently different so that the former decision did not control the latter has never been reversed. It seems clear from this history of Dr. Mudd's habeas petition that it cannot today be asserted that the Supreme Court's decision in *Ex parte Milligan* should dictate the outcome of a "mock appeal" in Dr. Mudd's case.

THE RIGHTS OF DR. AND MRS. MUDD TO TESTIFY
In the brief filed on behalf of Dr. Mudd in the "mock appeal," it is charged that:
1. Dr. Mudd was denied the right to offer testimony on his own behalf;[13] and
2. Mrs. Mudd should have been deemed competent to

testify.[14]

These charges plainly infer that both Dr. Mudd and his wife had a legal or Constitutional right to testify and that the military commission perversely denied them that "right." The Constitution, however, is silent on the point, and according to the common law of the time, the defendant in a criminal case was not a "competent witness." Such testimony was considered an invitation to perjury.[15] Unless there was a statute permitting a defendant to testify, the common law governed in all criminal cases, both federal and state. In 1865, only Maine by law permitted testimony by the defendant in criminal cases.[16] It was not until March 16th, 1878, that Congress enacted a similar law.[17] Therefore, no testimonial right belonging to the accused, Constitutional or otherwise, was violated by the military commission in the trial of the conspirators. Under the prevailing law, Dr. Mudd was simply not a competent witness.

Furthermore, there is nothing in the records of the 1865 trial before the military commission to show that Dr. Mudd's attorneys ever sought to call him as a witness. They certainly were not clamoring to put him on the stand. Indeed, it is doubtful that they would have taken this risky step even if it had been permitted.

With respect to Mrs. Sarah Mudd, there was no legal bar in 1865 to calling her as a defense witness. Even so, there was no record in the transcript that the defense ever attempted to call Mrs. Mudd. It is therefore disingenuous for Mudd's counsel to say in the petitioner's brief that her testimony was "not allowed" by the military commission. The question simply did not come up. Dr. Mudd's original attorneys, General Thomas Ewing and Frederick Stone, were good lawyers and probably recognized that Mrs. Mudd might have tripped on a material fact under cross-examination and wrecked the defense plans.

DID MUDD RECOGNIZE BOOTH THAT NIGHT?

At roughly four o'clock in the morning on Saturday, April 15, 1865, two men, one with a broken leg, came to the door of Dr. Mudd's country farm house. It was on that morning that Dr. Mudd set the broken leg of and otherwise assisted Lincoln's assassin.

A question long debated by Lincoln historians is whether Dr. Mudd recognized the injured man as John Wilkes Booth. The answer bears on Dr. Mudd's membership in the conspiracy. Dr. Mudd claimed that he never recognized either of the men who visited that morning. Why would he lie if not to conceal his own culpable involvement? When Dr. Mudd was questioned by Lt. Alexander Lovett, he said that the injured man had borrowed a razor to shave off his mustache. Lovett then asked Mudd if this man had any other beard. According to Lovett, Dr. Mudd replied, "'Yes, he had a long pair of whiskers.'" When asked if they might be false, Mudd was said by Lovett to have answered "he did not know."[18] Later, Dr. Mudd admitted to another Union officer that the beard may have been false. However, according to that officer, Mudd insisted that the man whose leg he set "'had his cloak thrown around his head' and that he 'did not see his face at all'" the entire time he was being treated.[19] This self-serving account of the doctor's is uncorroborated; other evidence shows that Dr. Mudd in fact knew whom he was treating. It shows that Dr. Mudd had met Booth before the assassination; indeed it establishes several meetings between the two.

The first meeting between Dr. Mudd and John Wilkes Booth took place on November 13, 1864, at St. Mary's Catholic Church in Bryantown, Maryland. Booth had come from Washington by stage the day before and spent the night as a guest of Dr. William Queen, an elderly leader of the Confederate underground apparatus in Charles County. Booth brought with him a letter of introduction to Dr. Queen. It had been given to Booth in Montreal about two weeks before by a Confederate agent, Patrick Charles Martin.[20] The purpose of Booth's visit to Bryantown was to line up clandestine assistance for a Confederate plan to capture Lincoln and carry him off to Richmond. The cover story used to explain Booth's visit was that Booth had an interest in buying land. John C. Thompson, Dr. Queen's son-in-law introduced Booth to Dr. Mudd at church that Sunday morning. There is no other satisfactory explanation of why Dr. Mudd was at St. Mary's that day; his own church, St. Peter's, was some eight miles distant and nearer to his home.

The second meeting between Dr. Mudd and Mr. Booth took place between December 17 and December 22, also in

Bryantown. Booth again came by stage from Washington and spent one night as a guest of Dr. Queen. Dr. Mudd had requested Confederate agent Thomas H. Harbin (alias Wilson) to come up from Virginia to meet Booth and discuss the plan to capture Lincoln. Dr. Mudd was present for this discussion, which was held in Booth's room at the old Bryantown tavern. Harbin agreed to participate in the plan and was active in carrying out details along the lower Potomac River right up to the time Lincoln was shot. After the war, Harbin told the famous war correspondent George Alfred Townsend about his meeting with Booth and Dr. Mudd. Townsend published an account of this meeting years later in the *Cincinnati Enquirer* for April 18, 1892.

During his second visit to Bryantown, Booth was an overnight guest in Dr. Mudd's home, probably on Sunday, December 18. The next morning the two rode over to the home of Dr. Mudd's near neighbor, George Gardiner, where Booth purchased a one-eyed horse for eighty dollars. He rode the horse back to Washington.[21] It was this horse that Lewis Payne used on the night of April 14, 1865, when he attacked Secretary of State William H. Seward and members of his household.

There was yet a third meeting between Dr. Mudd and Mr. Booth before the assassination. This occurred on December 23, 1864, when Dr. Mudd came to Washington to meet Booth by appointment. It was during this meeting that Dr. Mudd met with Confederate agent and courier John H. Surratt. Evidently, this encounter grew out of the Booth, Harbin, and Mudd conference in Bryantown a day or so before. On the evening of December 23, Dr. Mudd met Booth at the National Hotel and the two set out for the boarding house of Mrs. Mary E. Surratt with the intent of finding her son.[22] On the way, they accidentally ran into John Surratt and one of his mother's boarders, Louis J. Weichmann, on the street. After introductions, the four went to Booth's room to talk and have refreshments. At the 1865 trial, Weichmann testified that he was present at this meeting, did not hear all that was said there, and did not quite understand what he did hear. He said that the three others, Booth, Surratt, and Mudd, frequently stepped out into the hallway for private discussions.[23]

On the witness stand, Weichmann recalled the hotel meeting as having taken place on or about January 15, 1865. He went on to say that he could be more precise as to the date if he had access to the register of the Pennsylvania House where Dr. Mudd had a room that night. Thomas Ewing, Jr., Dr. Mudd's attorney, knew the correct date to be December 23, not January 15. Thus, Ewing was able to exploit Weichmann's confusion about the date by calling witnesses to show that Dr. Mudd was not in Washington on or about January 15. Ewing argued that Weichmann should not be believed on other matters as well and argued that his testimony should be disregarded. Judge Advocate John A. Bingham countered with the argument that any uncertainty about the date did not change the substance of Weichmann's testimony, and the fact of a meeting of Mudd, Surratt, and Booth remained.[24]

Ewings' arguments on this point were ultimately to no avail. Whatever the Commission may have thought about Weichmann's error, it obviously did not deter them from finding Dr. Mudd guilty. Afterward, Mudd admitted in a statement issued from his prison cell at Fort Jefferson that the meeting described by Weichmannn had, in fact, taken place, on December 23, not January 15.

At the "mock appeal," the Mudd attorneys argued that Weichmann's testimony could not be believed, because he had been "largely discredited." On the contrary, additional evidence emerged after Dr. Mudd's conviction that goes to establish the relationship between Dr. Mudd and Booth and the credibility of Weichmann. Captain George W. Dutton, who commanded the guard detail on the ship transporting Dr. Mudd to prison, signed an affidavit dated August 22, 1865 in which he stated in part:

> [Dr. Mudd] confessed that he knew Booth when he came to his house with Herold, on the morning after the assassination of the President; that he had known Booth for some time, but was afraid to tell of his having been at his house on the 15th of April, fearing that his own and the lives of his family would be endangered thereby. He also confessed that he was with Booth at the National Hotel on the evening referred to by Weichmann in his testimony; that he came to Washington on that occasion to meet Booth, by appointment, who wished to be introduced to John

Surratt; that when he and Booth were going to Mrs. Surratt's house to see John Surratt, they met, on Seventh Street, John Surratt, who was introduced to Booth."[25]

THE FALSE BEARD

These three prior meetings make it difficult to believe Dr. Mudd did not recognize Booth when the assassin called at Mudd's home on April 15, 1865. However, the mysterious false beard still persuades some that Booth could remain incognito for as long as he was in Dr. Mudd's company. The only mention by anyone of a beard or whiskers occurs in Dr. Mudd's statement to Colonel H.H. Wells at Bryantown,[26] and in the reports of interviews of Dr. Mudd and his wife by federal detectives.[27] More curious still is that, after the assassination, Booth felt comfortable sharing his identity with complete strangers, but not with Mudd, a man whom he had met three times in the past.

Eyewitness reports described Booth's sudden appearance on the stage at Ford's Theater. A well-known actor, Booth was certainly recognizable by many of those theater goers who witnessed the attack and the assassin's dramatic exit across the stage. Hundreds in the audience or backstage saw Booth; some afterwards identified him to the authorities. None spoke of a beard.

Some twenty minutes later, when Booth paused at the Navy Yard bridge, he gave his true name to the provost guard, Sergeant Silas Cobb.[28] Cobb never mentioned a beard; however, he did identify Booth from a beardless picture.

Later that night, David E. Herold, another conspirator, caught up with Booth on the road out of Washington. The two stopped briefly at the Surratt tavern in Prince Georges County, Maryland. The reason for the stop was to pick up arms and a set of field glasses. John M. Lloyd, the tavern operator, saw and talked with both men. Lloyd testified about this midnight meeting both at the conspiracy trial in 1865 and at John Surratt's trial in 1867.[29] Lloyd said he recognized Herold but not the other man. Lloyd never described the stranger as wearing a beard. In addition, Herold included no mention of a disguise in his long statement made on April 27, while a prisoner aboard the warship *Montauk*.

After Booth and Herold left the Mudd farm late in the

afternoon of April 15, they met and talked with several people as they fled to the Garrett farm in Caroline County, Virginia. Not one of those who later described meeting the two fugitives during this period ever mentioned Booth's wearing a beard, false or otherwise.

Among the people on record are Oswald Swann, Samuel Cox, Jr., Thomas A. Jones, William Bryant, Dr. Richard Stuart, William Lucas, William Rollins, John Garrett, William Garrett, and three ex-Confederates: Lt. Mortimer B. Ruggles, Pvt. A.R. Bainbridge, and Pvt. William S. Jett. Private William Jett testified at Dr. Mudd's trial that he and two other Confederate soldiers met Herold and Booth at the Rappahannock River ferry. According to Jett, Herold first sought to pass Booth and himself off as brothers, James W. and E. Boyd, but later, bragging to the three veterans that he and his companion were the "assassinators" of President Lincoln, he revealed their real names. Recounting this story to the miliary commission, Jett never mentioned that either of the fugitives made an attempt at disguise.[30]

The brief filed with the Special Court of Military Appeal on behalf of Dr. Mudd argues that the doctor should be excused for not recognizing his injured visitor because of his false whiskers disguise. Blatantly bootstrapping, the brief cites the testimony of Lt. Alexander Lovett as the basis for its claim that Booth visited Mudd incognito. As a close reading of the trial transcript shows,[31] however, Lovett was not himself asserting that the actor arrived at Mudd's farm in disguise; Lovett was merely reporting what Mudd had told him at the time of the doctor's arrest on April 21. According to Lovett, Dr. Mudd told him that Booth had "had a long pair of whiskers."

An objective look at the false beard claim leads to the conclusion that it is fiction concocted by Samuel Mudd as a desperate attempt to shore up his claim that he did not recognize Booth during his stay at the Mudd home on April 15, 1865. In effect, Samuel A. Mudd hid behind a false beard — not John Wilkes Booth.

DID DR. MUDD KNOW BOOTH HAD ASSASSINATED LINCOLN?

It ought to be clear by now that Dr. Mudd recognized

Booth when the assassin came to the doctor's home in the early morning of April 15. This leaves the important questions of how and when Dr. Mudd learned that Lincoln had been assassinated and that Booth was being sought as the assassin.

On appeal, counsel for Dr. Mudd argued that the record showed that Dr. Mudd did not even learn of the asssassination until Sunday, April 16, when he attended mass at St. Peter's Catholic Church. According to counsel, Dr. Mudd would have had no reason to suspect his two visitors of anything until after they had left his farm. Bootstrapping again from Lt. Lovett's testimony, counsel pointed to the Lieutenant's statement, "He told me that he heard, at church, that the President had been assassinated, but he did not mention by whom." Lovett was merely repeating what Dr. Mudd had told him, so only the defendant's self-serving statement made out of court supports his claim of ignorance after the early-morning arrival of Herold and Mudd at his door.

In Dr. Mudd's holographic statement given to Colonel H.H. Wells at Bryantown, Dr. Mudd stated that he first learned of Lincoln's assassination on April 15 at roughly three o'clock in the afternoon. Dr. Mudd did not indicate to Colonel Wells who had told him this, nor did he refer to Booth as the reported assassin. Twelve years later he would supply such details.

In 1877, Dr. Mudd told a friend, Samuel Cox, Jr., how and by whom he was first informed of the assassination. In the fall of 1877, the two were the Democratic candidates for the two Charles County seats in the state legislature. They traveled around together seeking votes. Cox was very interested in the Lincoln assassination. As an eighteen year-old boy, he was at the home of his adoptive father, Samuel Cox, when Oswald Swann brought Booth and Herold to their door at midnight on April 15. Therefore, the matter of Dr. Mudd's part in this was a natural subject of conversation.

As Cox subsequently recalled the discussion, Dr. Mudd said he learned of the assassination when he rode into Bryantown on the afternoon of April 15 to forward some clandestine rebel mail. He was stopped by a Union cavalry picket, who informed him that Lincoln had been assassinated by Booth.

On August 7, 1893, Samuel Cox, Jr., wrote out his recollection of this discussion on the blank pages and wide margins of his copy of a book written by a former Confederate agent.[32] Here is the pertinent portion of this entry by Cox:

> [W]hen Booth and Herold came to his [Dr. Mudd's] home the night after the assassination they told him they were just from Virginia and that Booth's horse had fallen soon after leaving the river and had broken his [Booth's] leg. That he had rendered him medical assistance while in utter ignorance of the assassination. That after he had set the broken leg, he, Dr. Mudd ... , letters he had but a short time gotten through the contraband mail for distribution, and that in going to Bryantown to mail them he was surprised to find the village surrounded by soldiers and being stopped by a sentry ... he was horrified when told the President had been shot the night before, and, upon asking who shot him the fellow had answered Booth. He then told me his first impulse was to surrender Booth, that he had imposed upon him, had twice forced himself upon him, and now the third time, had come with a lie upon his tongue and received medical assistance which would be certain to have him in serious trouble. But he determined to go back and upbraid him for his treachery which he did. And that Booth had appealed to him in the name of his mother, whom he professed to love so devotedly and that he acted and spoke so tragically that he told them [Booth and Herold] they must leave his house which they did and after getting with Oswald Swann they were piloted to Rich Hill [home of Samuel Cox].[33]

Coupled with the affidavit of Captain George W. Dutton (Dr. Mudd's previously mentioned escort aboard the vessel taking him to prison), the Cox recollections of what Dr. Mudd told him in 1877 utterly destroy any contention that Dr. Mudd did not recognize Booth when he came to the Mudd home on the morning of April 15.

The testimony of two of Dr. Mudd's neighbors, Francis R. Farrell and John F. Hardy, shows that Dr. Mudd knew Booth had assassinated Lincoln before Booth and Herold left the Mudd farm. On his way home from Bryantown on the afternoon of April 15th, Dr. Mudd stopped off at the Farrell home, where Hardy was visiting. Dr. Mudd told Farrell and Hardy that Lincoln had been assassinated. When asked by Farrell who had assassinated the President, Dr. Mudd responded: "A man by the name of Booth."[34] In Dr. Mudd's statement to Colonel Wells, Dr. Mudd stated that after leaving Bryantown on April 15, "I then went down to Mr. Hardy's, and was in conversation with him fully an hour when I returned home leisurely, and found the two men were just in the act of leaving."[35]

One can almost feel the grim reaction of the court as Farrell and Hardy testified. The members knew from circumstances and from bits and pieces of prior testimony that Booth and Herold were still at the Mudd farm at the time Dr. Mudd stopped to talk with Farrell and Hardy at about 4:00 p.m. on April 15. So here was testimony that Dr. Mudd knew that Booth was being sought as the President's assassin while the doctor was in town and the actor was back at the farm. Why did Dr. Mudd not notify the troop commander at Bryantown, Lt. David Dana, that the two men he sought were then at Mudd's house? Dr. Mudd faced a dilemma. To surrender Booth might be to reveal Dr. Mudd's prior participation in the plot to capture the President, a scheme that led directly to Lincoln's assassination. Caught on the horns of this dilemma, Dr. Mudd went to prison and almost to the gallows.

THE MISSING CONFESSION OF GEORGE A. ATZERODT

The confession of George A. Atzerodt is perhaps the most convincing evidence of Dr. Mudd's complicity in the assassination. The confession was taken between eight and ten o'clock in the evening of May 1, 1865, at the Arsenal Prison, Washington, D.C., by Maryland Provost Marshal James L. McPhail and one of his detectives, John L. Smith. Smith was Atzerodt's brother-in-law. A letter book of General John F. Hartranft, found at Gettysburg College, shows that the General admitted McPhail and Smith to the prison that night for the interrogation. This confession, by Atzerodt, never reached the War Department.

In 1867, former Assistant Secretary of War, Thomas T.

Eckert, was asked about this confession while testifying before the Judiciary Committee of the House of Representatives during the Johnson impeachment investigation. Eckert admitted knowledge of it and said it had been taken by one of McPhail's men named Smith. Eckert supposed the confession might be found in War Department files. At the 1865 trial, McPhail testified

> that a brother-in law of Atzerodt is on my force, and for a time a brother of the prisoner was on it, and they repeatedly told me that Atzerodt desired to see me. After consulting with the Secretary of War, a pass was given me, and I saw the prisoner. I saw him first on the gun-boat, and afterward in his cell. There was no threat, or promise, or inducement of any kind made.[36]

There was no move to produce this confession for the commission trying the conspirators.[37] At one point in the confession, Atzerodt made the following statement about Dr. Mudd and his relationship with Booth, "I am certain that Dr. Mudd knew all about it, as Booth sent (as he told me) liquor & provisions for the trip with the President to Richmond, about two weeks before the murder to Dr. Mudd."[38] This shows that Dr. Mudd was cooperating with Booth in late March, when Booth still planned to capture Lincoln and ransom him for Confederate prisoners of War.

Atzerodt's statement on this point is not without support. In early December 1881, F.A. Burr, a crack reporter for the Philadelphia Press, located John Matthews, an actor friend of Booth. Matthews had been in the cast at Ford's Theater on the night Lincoln was shot. Matthews told Burr that, in March 1865, Booth had asked him to take a trunk to Baltimore to be routed on to another destination. The trunk was filled with provisions to feed a captive Lincoln on the way to Richmond. Matthews refused to give Burr the names of those involved because some were still living.[39]

WHAT MUDD'S LAWYER THOUGHT OF MUDD'S GUILT AS AN ACCESSORY

In June of 1883, the reporter George Alfred Townsend made a swing through the lower counties of Maryland and interviewed several people who had knowledge of the Lincoln assassination. He called on Frederick Stone and, among other things, discussed Dr. Mudd. Townsend (who also made public the Confederate agent Harbin's account of the conspiracy) published this interview, under the heading, Broadway Note Book, in the New York Tribune for June 17, 1883. In pertinent part, Townsend quoted Stone as saying:

> The court very nearly hanged Dr. Mudd. His prevarications were painful; he had given his whole case away by not trusting even his counsel, neighbors, or kin. It was a terrible thing to extricate him from the coils he had woven about himself. He denied knowing Booth when he knew him well. He was undoubtedly accessory to the abduction plot, though he may have supposed it would never come to anything, when this was preposterous. He had been even intimate with Booth.

Frederick Stone here spoke of Dr. Mudd's prevarications. Consider, for example, the doctor's sworn statement to Colonel Wells. In this statement, Dr. Mudd told of going with Booth to the nearby home of George Gardiner, where Booth purchased a one-eyed horse for eighty dollars. This was on Monday, December 19, 1864. Dr. Mudd went on to tell Colonel Wells that "I have never seen Booth since that time to my knowledge until last Saturday night [April 15]."[40] Dr. Mudd was obviously concealing from the Union authorities his conference with Booth at the National Hotel on December 23, 1864. Surely, this is one of the prevarications that Stone had in mind.

CONCLUSION

A simple country farmer, Dr. Mudd was not. Well-documented confessions and testimony taken near the time of the trial, coupled with common sense establish this fact, and it has been ratified by accounts coming to light only long afterward. Although it might be convenient to believe that a false beard could disguise an acquaintance with whom Dr. Mudd had met recently more than once, that argument has already been made, and properly been rejected. Dr. Mudd may have gotten his pardon, but he doesn't deserve to have his record expunged. To do so would be to rewrite history as fiction, a result that threatens the meaning of our past, and serves to dictate our future.

Notes

[1] This military commission has also been referred to as the Hunter Commission.

[2] *See Ex parte* Garland, 71 U.S. 333, 380 (1866).

[3] *In re* Mudd, ABCMR No. AC91-05511 (January 22, 1992). On behalf of the Secretary, William D. Clark, Acting Assistant Secretary of the Army for Manpower and Reserve Affairs, rejected the Board's recommendation saying:

> It is not the role of the ABCMR to attempt to settle historical disputes. Neither is the ABCMR an appellate court. The precise issue which the ABCMR proposes to decide, the jurisdiction of the military commission over Dr. Mudd, was specifically addressed at the time in two separate habeas corpus proceedings, one before the Chief Justice of the Supreme Court, the other before the U.S. District Court. There was also an opinion by the Attorney General of the United States.
>
> The effect of the action recommended by the ABCMR would be to overrule all those determinations. Even if the issue might be decided differently today, it is inappropriate for a nonjudicial body, such as the ABCMR, to declare that the law 127 years ago was contrary to what was determined contemporarily by prominent legal authorities.

See Appendix C *infra* pp. 273-75.

[4] BENN PITMAN, THE ASSASSINATION OF PRESIDENT LINCOLN AND THE TRIAL OF THE CONSPIRATORS 170-71 (1865) (Testimony of Elzee Eglent).

[5] *The Presidential Election, Official Vote of Maryland*, BALTIMORE SUN, Nov. 24, 1860, at 1.

[6] Letter from Samuel A. Mudd to O. A. Brownson (January 13, 1862) *in* THE LIFE OF DR. SAMUEL A. MUDD (Nettie Mudd ed., 1906) (privately published by Richard D. Mudd, Saginaw 1962) (Original letter is in the O.A. Brownson Collection at the University of Notre Dame, South Bend, Ind.)

[7] U.S. CONST. art I, § 8, cl. 10.

[8] 11 Op. Att'y Gen. 297 (1865); PITMAN, *supra* note 4, at 403-09.

[9] PITMAN, *supra* note 4, at 18-21 (Charge and Specification Against Conspirators), *microformed on* National Archives M-599, Reel 16, Frame 0357.

[10] 71 U.S. (4 Wall.) 2 (1866).

[11] *Id.* Prompted by the decision in *Milligan*, Baltimore attorney Andrew S. Ridgely filed a petition for a writ of habeas corpus for Dr. Mudd with Chief Justice Chief Justice Chase on December 19, 1866. The petitioner is listed as Jeremiah Dyer, who was Dr. Mudd's brother-in-law. Justice Chase denied the petition on December 29th and suggested that it be filed in the district in which Mudd was imprisoned.

[12] Ex parte Mudd, 17 F. Cas. 954 (S.D. Fla. 1868) (No. 9,899). The opinion was published in the National Intelligencer on Oct. 5, 1868, *see* Appendix A *infra* pp. 253-57.

[13] Brief for Petitioner at 33-34; *see* Brief on Behalf of Samuel A. Mudd *supra* pp. 3-31.

[14] Brief for Petitioner at 36-37.

[15] *See* Marjorie L. Rifkin, *The Criminal Defendant's Right to Testify: The Right to Be Seen But Not Heard*, 21 COLUM. HUM. RTS. L. REV. 253, 257 (1989).

[16] Robert Popper, *History and Development of the Accused's Right to Testify*, WASH. U. L.Q. 454, 463 (1962).

[17] Act of Mar. 16, 1878 (codified as amended at 18 U.S.C. § 3481) (1948).

[18] PITMAN, *supra* note 4, at 87-90 (Testimony of Lt. Alexander Lovett), *microformed on* National Archives M-599, Reel 9, Frames 790-801.

[19] Statement of Dr. Samuel Mudd to Col. H.H. Wells (April 21, 1865), *microformed on* National Archives M-599, Reel 5, Frames 0212-25 [hereinafter cited simply as Statement of Dr. Samuel Mudd].

[20] PITMAN, *supra* note 4, at 178 (Testimony of John C. Thompson), *microformed on* National Archives M-599, Reel 11, Frames 2221-35.

[21] Statement of Dr. Samuel Mudd, *supra* note 19.

[22] PITMAN, *supra* note 4, at 421 (Dutton Affidavit).

[23] *Id.* at 113-20 (Testimony of Louis J. Weichmann).

[24] *Id.*

[25] *Id.* at 421 (Dutton Affidavit).

[26] Statement of Dr. Samuel Mudd, *supra* note 19.

[27] PITMAN, *supra* note 4, at 87-88 (Testimony of Lt. Alexander Lovett).

[28] *Id.* at 84 (Testimony of Silas T. Cobb).

[29] *Id.* at 87-90 (Testimony of John M. Lloyd), *microformed on* National Archives M-599, Reel 8, Frames 0396-0458.

[30] Others who later described meeting Booth and Herold somewhere between Mudd's farm and Garrett's farm include Oswald Swann, Samuel Cox Jr., Thomas A. Jones, William Bryant, Dr. Richard Stuart, William Lucas, William Rollins, Mortimer B. Ruggles and A.R. Bainbridge. None mentioned a disguise in general or a beard in particular. *See* WILLIAM BRYAN, THE GREAT AMERICAN MYTH 253-58 (1940) (describing his experience); THEODORE ROSCOE, THE WEB OF CONSPIRACY 361, 364-65 (1965); OSBORN H. OLDROYD, ASSASSINATION OF ABRAHAM LINCOLN 100-10, 290 (1901) (describing the experience of Thomas Jones); LOUIS J. WEICHMANN, A TRUE HISTORY OF THE ASSASSINATION OF ABRAHAM LINCOLN AND THE CONSPIRACY OF 1865, at 198-202 (Floyd E. Risvold ed., 1975); Prentiss Ingraham, *Pursuit and Death of John Wilkes Booth*, 39 CENTURY MAG. 443, 444 (1890) (describing experience of Mortimer Ruggles and A. R. Bainbridge); Statement of Willie S. Jett (May 6, 1865), National Archives, M-599, Reel 4, Frames 0086-0099; Statement of William Lucas (May 6, 1865), National Archives, War Department Record, File S, *reprinted in* THEODORE ROSCOE, THE WEB OF CONSPIRACY 363-64 (1959); Statement of Oswald Swann (n.d.), *microformed on* National Archives M-599, Reel 6, Frames 0014, 0227. *See also infra* notes 32, 33.

[31] *See supra* note 18.

[32] THOMAS A. JONES, J. WILKES BOOTH (Chicago, Laird & Lee 1893).

[33] Cox's copy of the Jones book with his manuscript notes is now in the

possession of the Maryland Historical Society. So far as known, Cox made no public disclosure of this Mudd revelation until he was visited by the famous Lincoln collector, Osborn Oldroyd. During a 1901 walking tour of the Booth escape route, Oldroyd called on Cox at Rich Hill in Charles County, Maryland. Cox gave him essentially the same account that he had entered on the blank pages and wide margins of the Jones book. Oldroyd published all this in his 1901 book entitled ASSASSINATION OF ABRAHAM LINCOLN.

[34] PITMAN, *supra* note 4, at 218 (Testimony of Francis R. Farrell), *microformed on* National Archives M-599, Reel 13 Frames 3799-3812; Testimony of John F. Hardy (June 8, 1865), National Archives M-599, Reel 13 Frames 3832-48.

[35] Statement of Dr. Samuel Mudd, *supra* note 19.

[36] PITMAN, *supra* note 4, at 148 (Testimony of Marshal James L. McPhail), *microformed on* National Archives M-599, Reel 9, Frames 1169-1177.

[37] Atzerodt's confession finally turned up in 1977 in the hands of descendants of Major William E. Doster, who defended Atzerodt before the commission. The original was purchased from the Doster heirs and is now in the Risvold collection.

[38] *Id.*

[39] *Also a True History*, PHILA. PRESS, December 4, 1881, at 114.

[40] PITMAN, *supra* note 4, at 168-69 (Testimony of Col. H.H. Wells); Statement of Dr. Samuel Mudd, *supra* note 19.

Colonel Wells interviewed Dr. Mudd several times at the old tavern in Bryantown where Wells had set up headquarters. In his testimony at the 1865 conspiracy trial, Col. Wells expressed some exasperation at the way these interviews went:

> Dr. Mudd's manner was so very extraordinary, that I scarcely know how to describe it. He did not seem unwilling to answer a direct question; he seemed embarrassed, and at the third interview alarmed, and I found that, unless I asked direct questions, important facts were omitted .... It was at the last interview that I told him he seemed to be concealing the facts of the case, which would be considered the strongest evidence of his guilt, and might endanger his safety.

PITMAN, *supra* note 4, at 168-69 (Testimony of Col. H.H. Wells).

Incidently, the Brief for Petitioner quotes only the emphasized portion of this testimony and astonishingly construes this to be proof that "Dr. Mudd was eager to cooperate with investigators," and that such cooperation showed that "Dr. Mudd was not guilty of any crime." The full testimony of Wells, on this point, does not support such sweeping conclusions. On the contrary, Wells thought that Mudd was evasive and was concealing the facts of the case.

Appendix A:
The Decision Denying Dr. Mudd a Writ of Habeas Corpus

This is an application for a writ of habeas corpus to release from imprisonment SAMUEL A. MUDD, SAMUEL ARNOLD AND EDWARD SPANGLER, who were sentenced by a military commission sitting in the City of Washington, in the Spring of 1865, to military confinement at Fort Jefferson, within this judicial district.

It is usual rather than otherwise for judges or courts to grant the writ of habeas corpus on application, and await the return and response of the person to whom the writ is addressed, before deciding the main question, whether the petitioner ought to be discharged from custody (3 Peters, 193; 4 Wallace, 100), but where the petition states the facts fully, and the return can throw no new light on the matter, or where the petition contains insufficient allegations on which to base a demand of discharge, the provision of the Constitution, relating to this subject, is as fully answered by a determination of the question, whether there ought to be a discharge from imprisonment, in the first instance, on the application, as by the granting of the writ and its determination afterward. And the propriety of this course has been fully remarked upon by the Supreme Court in the case of *Ex parte Milligan*, the principal case relied upon in this application, so that I need not further occupy attention with my reasons for pursuing that course in this case. The facts here are a part of the history of the country: the return of the officer who has charge of the prisoners would add nothing to the date on which a decision ought to be based.

Let us proceed, therefore, at once to the question, whether the prisoners ought to be discharged. Two points are relied upon in support of the affirmative of this question: First, that the military commission had at the time and the place at which it was held no jurisdiction to try and sentence for the offense these persons were charged with. Second, if they were rightfully imprisoned up to the 4th of July last past, they were pardoned by the proclamation of the President of that date, and ought now to be set at liberty.

I think there are clear, definite and solid reasons which necessitate the overruling of both these points, and the consequent refusal of the application. The reported case principally relied upon in support of the first position, is that of *Ex parte Milligan* (4 Wallace, Sup. C.R., 110), in which the Supreme Court decided that the trial and conviction of a resident of Indiana by a military commission during the war were invalid, and generally that miliary tribunals have no authority to try civil offences in districts where the regularly organized civil courts of the country are in undisturbed possession of all their powers. There was a minority opinion by four members of the Court in this case, in which it was maintained that the Congress may, if it chooses, in time of war, establish military tribunals in parts of the country undisturbed by war operations to exercise the functions ordinarily exercised by the civil courts of the country. The decisions of the Supreme Court are binding on the inferior courts; and no decision was every more willingly followed than would be the decision and the reasoning of the majority of the Supreme Court in Milligan's case by this court in any case where that decision was in point. I believe that the further we recede from troublous times the more will the public judgment, from calm reflection, settle down on the opinion that the power to detain evil-disposed or suspected persons until the public peril has ceased, is all the power the Government can ever need in time of war for purposes of national security, or can ever exercise with safety to private rights. If the Supreme Court had been equally divided in opinion on this point, I should find it impossible to follow any other reasoning in any case presenting that point, than such as would lead to the conclusion arrived at by the majority of the Court. But I do not think that *Ex parte Milligan* is a case in point here. There is nothing in the opinion of the Court in that case, nor in the third article of the Constitution, nor in the Habeas Corpus Act of 1863, to lead to the conclusion that if an army had been encamped in the state of Indiana, (whether in the immediate presence of the enemy or not), and any person, a resident of Indiana or any other state (enlisted Soldier or not) had, not from any private animosity, but from public reasons, made his way within the Army lines and assassinated the Commanding General, such a person could not have been legally tried for his military offense by a military tribunal and legally convicted and sentenced.

The President was assassinated not from private animosity nor any other reason than a desire to impair the effectiveness of military operations and enable the rebellion to reestablish itself into a Government; the act was committed in a fortified city, which had been invaded during the war, and to the northward as well as the southward of which battles had many times been fought, which was the headquarters of all the armies of the United States, from which daily and hourly went military orders. The President is the Commander-in-Chief of the Army, and the President who was killed had many times made distinct military orders under his own hand, without the formality of employing the Secretary of War or commanding general. It was not Mr. Lincoln who was assassinated but the Commander-in-Chief of the army, for military reasons. I find no difficulty, therefore, in classing the offense as a military one and with this opinion arrive at the necessary conclusion that the proper tribunal for the trial of those engaged in it was a military one.

I understood the counsel who last addressed the Court in support of the application to admit at least a doubt whether the original trial was illegal; but he contended that the President's proclamation of amnesty and pardon of July 4, 1868 embraces these persons, and that they ought therefore to be discharged. But that proclamation plainly excludes all persons standing in the position of these petitioners, whether they have been convicted or not. It pardons the crime of treason; that is, it pardons persons who have levied war against the United States, or given aid and comfort to their enemies, within the laws and usages of war; but it pardons no person who has transgressed the laws of war, no spy, no assassin, no person who has been guilty of barbarous treatment of prisoners. Let us bring out the point by a supposed case. Two soldiers or officers fight side by side in the same battle; their forces remain masters in the field. After the battle, one conducts himself in an unimportant manner, and the other sabres the wounded or prisoners. They are both guilty of treason, but one is guilty of treason with an important plus sign added. It is the opinion of the Court that the proclamation of the President reaches one of these cases and not the other. Can it be supposed that if England and France were at war, and a party of men (soldiers or not) should, for the purpose of affecting military operations, enter the military lines of one of the armies of one nation and assassinate the commanding general, that a subsequent peace, with provisions for the rendition of ordinary prisoners of war, would necessitate the delivery of those persons? I think not. Such a provision would refer to those prisoners who had made open and honorable war, and not transgressed the fearfully wide rules which war allows to be legal.

The proclamation of May 25, 1865, the principal proclamation of pardon anterior to the one here recited, pardons "all persons who have, directly or indirectly, participated in the existing rebellion," on certain conditions, and with fourteen excepted classes. If the present proclamation had employed the same language and not excepted these persons or persons in their position, I should have doubted whether they ought longer to be imprisoned. But the proclamation grants "to all and every person who participated, directly or indirectly in the late rebellion (with certain exceptions) full pardon and amnesty for the crime of treason against the United States or the adhesion to their enemies during the late civil war."

I think it is clear that the President, wishing no longer to make other than necessary exceptions, and to pardon all who were only guilty of participating in the rebellion, purposely chose this language to effect his purpose, and no other one. I do not see that under it a person who transgressed the laws of war, who was guilty not only of treason but of additional military crimes, may not still be tried for additional crimes.

It is not improper to add a word upon a point not necessary to be alluded to for the purpose in this decision. It is a matter of public notoriety that some persons, more or less acquainted with the evidence on which these convictions were based, doubt the fair sufficiency of that evidence to necessitate beyond reasonable doubt the conclusion arrived at. but this is a question with which I have nothing to do. For the purposes of this application the prisoners are guilty of the charge on which they were convicted — of a conspiracy to commit the military crime which one of their number did commit, and some of them of more or less participation. The question which I have to decide is whether the military tribunal had jurisdiction to try and sentence, and whether the proclamation of the President reaches their case. It is my opinion, for the reasons which I have stated, that the military commission not only had jurisdiction, but was the proper tribunal for the purpose; and that the President's proclamation does not embrace the situation occupied by these petitioners.

Appendix B:
The Report of the Board for Correction of Military Records

DEPARTMENT OF THE ARMY
Board for Correction of Military Records
1941 Jefferson Davis Highway, 2nd Floor
Arlington, VA 22202-4508

PROCEEDINGS:

IN THE CASE OF: MUDD, SAMUEL A., M.D. (Deceased)
BOARD DATE: 22 JANUARY 1992
DOCKET NUMBER: AC91-05511

I certify that hereinafter is recorded the true and complete record of the proceedings of the Army Board for Correction of Military Records in the case of the above-named individual. The following members, a quorum, were present.

Mr. Charles A. Chase   Chairperson
Mr. James C. Hise   Member
Mr. John Lee   Member
Mr. James T. Lucas   Member
Mr. Eugene P. Visco   Member
Mr. David R. Kinneer   Executive Secretary
Mr. Richard H. Allen   Examiner

The applicant, who is the grandson of Dr. Mudd, appeared before the Board and was represented by counsel.

The applicant requests correction of military records as stated in the application to the Board and as restated herein.

The Board considered the following evidence:

Exhibit A: Application for correction of military records.
Exhibit B: Summary of Archival Records (including advisory opinions).
Exhibit C: Case Summary.
Exhibit D: Transcript of Hearing.

FINDINGS:

1.   The applicant has exhausted all administrative remedies afforded by existing law or regulations.

2.   The applicant requests, in effect, that his grandfather, Dr. Samuel A. Mudd, now deceased, who was tried and convicted by a "military commission" in June 1865 of conspiracy to assassinate President Lincoln, be declared innocent.

3.   The applicant states that his grandfather's trial was illegal because the civilian courts were open and functioning. Further, that his grandfather's only act was to medically treat and harbor a disguised John Wilkes Booth while not then knowing that President Lincoln had been assassinated.

4.   The applicant submits a copy of Dr. Mudd's defense counsel's argument to the military commission in May 1865, questioning whether the commission was even a court and whether it had jurisdiction over his client and the other seven individuals with whom he was jointly tried, or over the crimes with which they were charged. A copy of the defense counsel's argument on the pertinent law and the evidence in Dr. Mudd's case is also submitted. Two independent reports to contemporary Presidents are also submitted, one by the applicant, the second by a Lincoln scholar, which attempt to prove Dr. Mudd's innocence. He also submits correspondence from several members of Congress who support the granting of the requested relief, and he states that a number of state legislatures have gone on record supporting relief. Finally, he

submits information intended to show why Dr. Mudd did not know about the plans of John Wilkes Booth to kidnap President Lincoln, and a map which he contends shows that the route most likely to have been used to move the kidnapped President to the Confederate lines was not even close to his grandfather's home.

5. The applicant has made two prior applications to this Board. Until now, the Department's position had been that while this Board might have jurisdiction to review the case, the Secretary of the Army did not have the authority to set aside the conviction. The applicant had also previously been advised by the Office of the President that no Presidential relief, other than the pardon issued by President Andrew Johnson, could be granted by that office.

6. Then, on 7 December 1990 and 24 June 1991, in connection with the applicant's current submission, the offices of the Judge Advocate General and the Army General Counsel, opined that not only may it review the case, but that this Board, under certain circumstances, may recommend to the Secretary that he set aside the conviction. In expansion of their opinions, each stated, in essence, that the Board may review the record of conviction, but only to determine whether the Commission lacked jurisdiction over Dr. Mudd, or over the offense (that is, whether he was convicted of an offense for which he was not charged, or not arraigned, or which was not a crime at all) or that Dr. Mudd was denied due process to such an extreme extent that it amounted to fundamental unfairness. The General Counsel also opined that since clemency has already been granted in the form of the pardon by President Johnson, the only meaningful relief that could be granted by the Secretary would be to set aside the conviction.

7. History records that Dr. Mudd was born on 20 December 1833, in Charles County, Maryland. He was educated at several institutions of higher learning and was certified as a physician in 1856. He then returned to his home in Charles County, where he set up a medical practice and farmed tobacco. He married and fathered nine children. He never served in the military, and during the Civil War continued to practice medicine and to farm. On 21 April 1865, he was arrested by Federal authorities on suspicion of being involved in the plot to assassinate President Lincoln. He was subse-

quently tried and convicted of conspiracy to assassinate the President and then spent four years of a "life" sentence in a military confinement. After his pardon in 1869, he returned to his home in Maryland and resumed his medical practice and farming. He died in January 1883 at the age of 49 from pneumonia.

8. On 3 March 1863, because of the Civil War existing between the various states, Congress passed "An Act Relating to Habeas Corpus and Regulating Judicial Proceedings in certain Cases." In effect, this law authorized the President to suspend the right to request a writ of habeas corpus from a civilian court in any part of the United States, whenever it was deemed necessary to ensure the public safety. This empowered the military to establish martial law in any given area of the United States and to arrest violators, either military or civilian. Under this law, not only were military personnel to be tried by courts-martial for violations of military rules and regulations, but civilians who violated any laws, military rules or regulations, or the laws of war, were also subjected to immediate arrest by military authorities. Theoretically, these civilians could then be tried by a military commission comprised of military officers, and if convicted, fined, imprisoned, or even put to death. A military commission was, therefore, akin to a military court-martial and operated under the same general principles.

9. As is generally accepted by historians, John Wilkes Booth, a fairly famous actor in 1865, entered the Presidential Box at Ford's Theater on Friday evening, 14 April 1865, at approximately 22:15 hours, and shot President Lincoln in the head while he was watching a play at the theater. Booth then jumped from the box to the stage, injuring his left ankle/leg, but escaped on horseback. At about the same time, an unsuccessful attempt was made by Lewis Paine (alias Powell) elsewhere in Washington to assassinate Secretary of State William Seward. Early the next morning, Booth and a companion, David E. Herold, knocked on the door of Dr. Mudd's home and requested medical assistance. The story ostensibly given was that Booth's horse had fallen on his leg and ankle. Dr. Mudd examined the leg and found that it was broken just above the ankle. After cutting off his boot, Dr. Mudd placed a homemade cast on Booth's leg and fashioned some crude

crutches. Supposedly, he was paid $25.00 for this treatment. Later in the morning of the same day, Dr. Mudd and Herold attempted to rent a carriage in the area for movement of Booth, but were unsuccessful. While the two men were still at his home, Dr. Mudd is said to have gone into the nearest town where he learned of the assassination of President Lincoln. Federal troops were already in the area looking for the assassin. Booth and Herold supposedly left Dr. Mudd's home on horseback, at about the time he returned in the late afternoon, having asked for directions to a minister's house, which was across a large swamp near Dr. Mudd's farm.

10. On the next day, after attending Easter Sunday church services, Dr. Mudd, expressing no sense of urgency, asked his cousin, a respected local citizen and also a physician, to report the details of the visit of the two "strangers" to his home to the military authorities in the nearby town. His cousin informed the local military authorities on Monday; however, the local military authorities did not visit Dr. Mudd until Tuesday, and then asked only a few questions before leaving. On Friday, 21 April 1865, Dr. Mudd was arrested. At that time Booth's boot, which had been left behind, was produced by the family. Two written statements were also obtained from Dr. Mudd that day. In both statements he maintained that he had not recognized Booth, claiming the injured man had been wearing false whiskers. These disclaimers were made despite the fact that Dr. Mudd supposedly knew Booth, having met him on one or more previous occasions. He was then taken to Washington and held in a military prison, along with the other alleged conspirators, and witnesses in the case. There is no evidence that he was ever charged with any offense during the investigative phase of the case.

11. Booth was subsequently killed on 26 April 1865, in a tobacco barn on the Garrett farm, near Bowling Green, Virginia. Herold was taken prisoner at that time and was also taken to Washington to await trial.

12. On 1 May 1865, President Andrew Johnson ordered the establishment of a military commission by the Department of War to try the persons implicated in the assassination of President Lincoln and the attempt on the life of the Secretary of State. This order was supported by a one-line opinion from the Attorney General that the military had jurisdiction

in the case.

13. Accordingly, on 9 May 1865, a military commission was convened at the Old Penitentiary Building located at the Washington Arsenal, now known as Fort McNair. The nine-member Commission, chaired by Major General David Hunter, consisted of six more general grade officers, a colonel and a lieutenant colonel. The chief prosecutor was Brigadier General Joseph Holt, Judge Advocate General of the Army. He was assisted by a special prosecutor, the Honorable John A. Bingham, a former Congressman, and Brevet Colonel H. H. Burnett.

14. Eight persons, including Dr. Mudd, were arraigned and charged, on 9 May 1865, with conspiring to kill the President and other government and military officials. Dr. Mudd was also specifically charged with conspiring with the named conspirators to aid and assist in their escape from justice after the assassination.

15. The commission's rules were established at the first session. The eight defendants, all of whom were handcuffed and some of whom were also in foot chains, were to be tried jointly. The defendants were entitled to defense counsels (but were unable to obtain them until after the initial session on 9 May. The actual trial process began on 10 May.) The commission overruled all requests for a change in venue to the civilian courts in the District of Columbia, which were open and functioning. Several requests by some of the defendants to separate the trials were also denied. The defense attorneys were to present evidence only on matters raised by the prosecution or the commission. Dr. Mudd and the other defendants were not permitted to testify in their own behalf. The trial lasted from 10 May to 30 June 1865.

16. Dr. Mudd had two defense counsels, Mr. Thomas Ewing, Jr., formerly a brigadier general and military lawyer, and Mr. Frederick Stone, a well-known local attorney. Twenty-four witnesses were presented by the government against Dr. Mudd. Seventy-four witnesses appeared on his behalf.

17. All eight of the conspirators were found guilty of the charge and specification. Four were sentenced to be hanged and were hanged after review of their sentences by the President. Dr. Mudd and two other conspirators were sentenced to life imprisonment, initially at Albany, New York. The place

of confinement was later changed to Fort Jefferson, Dry Tortugas, Florida (a military prison on an island approximately 70 miles by water from Key West). The eighth conspirator was sentenced to six years in prison.

18. In the summer of 1867, a very serious yellow fever epidemic struck Fort Jefferson. After the regularly assigned military medical officer died early in the epidemic, Dr. Mudd served for a time as the prison physician. He was credited with saving many lives, both prisoners and military troops assigned to guard the prison. He, himself, contracted the disease, but survived.

19. On 9 February 1869, President Andrew Johnson issued a pardon directing that Dr. Mudd be released from Fort Jefferson. In the pardon, the President stated that Dr. Mudd's direct involvement in the assassination was only after the fact, that it was within the obligations of professional duty, and that there was uncertainty as to the true measure and nature of his complicity in the escape of the assassins. The President then cited Dr. Mudd's dedicated efforts during the yellow fever epidemic.

20. After the war had ended, John Surratt, a named conspirator who had escaped to Canada before the trial, and the son of Mary Surratt, the lone woman conspirator who was hanged, was found in Europe and brought back for trial. He was tried by a civil court in Washington in the summer of 1867. The jury, however, was unable to reach a unanimous verdict; therefore, it was dismissed, and the government chose not to prosecute the case further.

21. In July 1865 the Attorney General issued a written opinion expanding his earlier guidance to the President in May 1865, in which he had stated that a military commission had jurisdiction to try the eight conspirators for the assassination of the President. His assessment was that the Civil War was still going on; Washington was a city under "siege" and was surrounded by fortifications; the President was the Commander-in-Chief of the armed forces; and the laws of war were in existence at the time of the conspiracy and assassination. Referencing the Constitution, which speaks of "law of nations" and the "laws of war," he opined that since the offenses were essentially against the President and the military, and the acts were a violation of the laws of war, the

offenses should be tried by the military authorities, under such rules and regulations that were in effect at the time. The Attorney General went on to state that if the offenses had been civilian in nature, then the matters could have been settled in the civil courts, which he acknowledged were open and in operation.

22. On 3 April 1866, the United States Supreme Court decided by a vote of five to four in *Ex Parte Milligan*, that the military authorities in Indiana had not had jurisdiction to try a citizen of the United States for such offenses as conspiracy against the government in the time of war or for inciting insurrection. In the opinion of the Court, as written by Justice Davis, it was noted that the 3 March 1863 Act of Congress authorizing the President to suspend the right of a citizen to request a writ of habeas corpus, required that if the military had arrested a civilian, that fact and the particulars of the case must be reported to a civilian judge of the nearest district or circuit court within 20 days of the arrest. Further, it was noted the law required that if a grand jury then met and did not indict or present the case for trial, the individual should be released from military confinement and discharged. In reviewing the *Milligan* case, the Court observed that he was a United States citizen of a non-secessionist state; that he was not held as a prisoner of war; and that he had never served in the military or naval service. The Court also noted that his arrest by the military had never been reported to a Federal court as required by the Act.

23. The Supreme Court's opinion went on to note that the Constitution guarantees the right of trial by jury in all cases involving a crime, except impeachment. Further, the Fifth Amendment to the Constitution states "that no person shall be called to answer for a capital or otherwise infamous crime unless on presentment by a grand jury, except in cases arising in the land or naval forces, or in the militia, when in actual service in time of public danger, nor be deprived of life, liberty, or property without due process of law." The opinion next noted that, "The Constitution of the United States is a law for rulers and people, equally in war and in peace, and covers with the shield of its protection all classes of men, at all times, under all circum-stances." The Court then questioned the judicial power of the commission which tried Milligan and his

companions stating that the commission was not a court ordained or established by Congress; rather, it had been created at the mandate of the President, who is charged with the execution of the law, not to make laws. The Court noted there is "no unwritten criminal code to which resort can be had as a source of jurisdiction." Therefore, the rights of Milligan were infringed upon because he and his companions were tried by a court not ordained and established by Congress, and not composed of judges appointed "during good behavior."

24. The Court emphasized that martial law could not be imposed solely by a military commander because of a "threatened" invasion; it must be an actual invasion, with closure of the courts and loss of civil administration. That had not been the case in Indiana in 1864 and 1865. The civilian courts had been open and operating. The Court also noted that the imposition of martial law should only be temporary, until the return of civilian law and the civilian courts were again in operation; any further imposition of martial law beyond that point would be a "gross usurpation of power."

25. The minority opinion in that case, which was written by Chief Justice Chase, while concurring in the granting of the writ of habeas corpus in the Milligan case, stated that Congress could, in fact, legislate the imposition of martial law, even if the civilian courts were open and operating during the time of war.

26. Dr. Mudd's case was appealed to the Supreme Court early in 1867, and to a district court in the state of Florida later in 1867, citing the decision in *Ex Parte Milligan*. However, the appeals were denied.

27. In the processing of this case, the staff of the Board has reviewed the Articles of War, 1806 (Chapter XX, Statute I, Ninth Congress, session 1) and the Articles of War, 1874 (Title XIV, United States Code, chapter 5), as well as various treatises written between 1841 and 1943 on the subject of military courts-martial and military commission rules of operation, including "The Practice of Courts Martial" by Major General Alexander Macomb, 1841; "Observations on Military Law, and the Constitution and Practice of Courts Martial" by Captain William C. De Hart, 1846 and 1859; "A Treatise on Military Law and the Practice of Courts-Martial" by Brevet

Lieutenant Colonel S.V. Benet, 1866 and 1868; "An Abridgment of Military Law by Lieutenant Colonel W. Winthrop, 1892 and 1893; "A Treatise on the Military Law of the United States: by Major General George B. Davis, 1898, 1913 and 1915; and "The Law of Martial Rule" by Lieutenant Colonel Charles Fairman, 1930 and 1943. There appears to be a general consensus that an accused should be presented (arraigned on) the charges on a timely basis, that the trial should be held within a short period of time (the term of 8 days is sometimes quoted) and that the accused had the right to a defense counsel. It appears that in the mid-1800s, the accused was expected to conduct his own defense, with the assistance of counsel; however, the counsel usually was not permitted to verbally present any matters to the court. One more recent authority (*ibid.*, Fairman) noted that military commissions, while generally following the procedural methods of a court-martial, could make deviations which would not entitle the accused to an acquittal.

28. The official record of the proceedings before the Hunter Commission is not maintained by the Department of the Army. That record, entitled: "Investigation and Trial Papers Relating to the Assassination of President Lincoln," consisting of more than 4400 handwritten pages, all of which were reviewed by the staff of this Board, is maintained by the Archivist of the United States, under Record Group 153, Office of the Judge Advocate, War Department. It is also available on microfilm, National Archives Microcopy No 599. In addition, several other references were reviewed by the staff of the Board, to include the Pitman and Poore versions of the testimony before the commission, the book "Come Retribution" by William A. Tidwell, with James O. Hall and David Winfred Gaddy, 1988, and "The Milligan Case" by Samuel Klaus, 1929.

29. During the formal hearing before this Board, the 90-year old applicant appeared with counsel, two of them being descendants of Dr. Mudd, the third being a descendant of Mr. Ewing, Dr. Mudd's primary defense counsel in 1865. Several expert witnesses were called. Much of the testimony centered on the lack of proof of direct involvement of Dr. Mudd in any conspiracy to assassinate or kidnap the President. Another witness testified as to the professional requirement for Dr.

Mudd to provide medical treatment for the injured Booth, irrespective of whether he knew him. One witness, a recognized expert on the constitutional aspects of civilian versus military law, concentrated on the jurisdiction of the commission to try Dr. Mudd for the alleged offenses, noting that the civilian courts were open in the District of Columbia and that no state of war existed in the area. He further noted that Dr. Mudd was a citizen of Maryland, a Northern state which did not secede from the Union. He stated that the principles cited by the Court in the *Milligan* case also applied in Dr. Mudd's case. He then went on to compare the criteria for martial law and trial by military commissions. He observed that in several more recent decisions by the Supreme Court and by lower Federal courts during World War II, it was ruled that United States citizens are entitled to trial by civilian courts, even if the offenses were military in nature and had occurred in a military theater of operation. In conclusion, he stated that in his expert opinion, Dr. Mudd had been denied his right to due process under the Constitution.

30. Title 10, United States Code, section 1552, provides, in pertinent part, that the secretary of a military department, acting through boards of civilians, may correct any military record of that department when he considers it necessary to correct an error or remove an injustice. The statute further provides that except when procured by fraud, a correction under this authority is final and conclusive on all officers of the United States.

CONCLUSIONS:

1. The record of Dr. Mudd's conviction is a military record over which this Board has jurisdiction under Title 10, United States Code, section 1552.

2. Under that authority and within the guidelines set forth in the recent opinions of The Judge Advocate General and the Army General Counsel, this Board has carefully reviewed the available records to determine if the Military Commission had jurisdiction over Dr. Mudd and, if so, whether he was denied due process to such an extent that it amounted to fundamental unfairness. Those guidelines do not authorize the Board to consider the innocence or guilt of Dr. Mudd.

3. In its analysis of the case, the Board has had the advantage of hindsight and, therefore, has looked at the facts and circumstances of the case with more calmness, deliberation, and detachment than was possible in the emotionally charged atmosphere that existed after the Civil War.

4. Another advantage the Board has had is the availability of the Supreme Court's decision in *Ex Parte Milligan*, which was decided after Dr. Mudd's trial, but which the Board finds so analogous to Dr. Mudd's case that it should not be ignored.

5. Borrowing from the rationale in that case, the Board concludes that the evidence submitted by the applicant and the information uncovered during the Board's research clearly show that the civilian courts were fully open and operating in the District of Columbia in the spring of 1865; that at the time President Lincoln was assassinated, Dr. Mudd was a civilian and a citizen of Maryland, a nonsecessionist state; and that he had never served in the military or naval service. Notwithstanding the Attorney General's opinion in 1865, the crimes he is alleged to have committed were not uniquely military in nature, and none of the individuals with whom he was alleged to have conspired were members of, or closely involved with, the military.

6. Furthermore, the Board notes that General Robert E. Lee had surrendered at Appomattox on 9 April 1865, a month before the trial began. There is no evidence that the capital was "under siege" or that any Confederate forces had invaded or were likely to invade the District of Columbia in the spring of 1865.

7. Under these circumstances, the Board finds no good reason why Dr. Mudd should not have been tried by a civilian court. It, therefore, unanimously concludes that the military commission did not have jurisdiction to try him, and that in so doing denied him his due process rights, particularly his right to trial by a jury of his peers. This denial constituted such a gross infringement of his Constitutionally protected rights, that his conviction should be set aside. To fail to do so would be unjust.

RECOMMENDATION:

That the Archivist of the United States, the custodian of

the Hunter Commission's report of the conviction of Dr. Samuel A. Mudd for his complicity in the assassination of President Abraham Lincoln, a Department of Army record, correct the records in his possession by showing that Dr. Mudd's conviction was set aside pursuant to action taken under Title 10, United States Code, section 1552.

/s/ Charles A. Chase
Charles A. Chase
Chairperson

Appendix C:
The Decision of the Assistant Secretary of the Army

DEPARTMENT OF THE ARMY
OFFICE OF THE ASSISTANT SECRETARY
Washington, D.C. 20310-1813

22 July 1992

MEMORANDUM FOR EXECUTIVE SECRETARY, ARMY
BOARD FOR CORRECTION OF MILITARY RECORDS

SUBJECT: Dr. Samuel A. Mudd

I have carefully considered the records in this case, including the findings, conclusions and recommendation of the Army Board for Correction of Military Records (ABCMR), as set forth in its Report of Proceedings dated 22 January 1992. I have ultimately concluded that the ABCMR's recommendation should be denied.

This application is founded upon actions which took place more than 127 years ago. The applicants, descendants of Dr. Samuel A. Mudd, have asked the Board to review the historical facts and declare Dr. Mudd innocent in the conspiracy to assassinate President Lincoln.

I note at the outset that the ABCMR did not consider the guilt or innocence of Dr. Mudd, and that its recommendation does not speak to the question of his guilt or innocence.

The ABCMR concluded that the military commission which tried Dr. Mudd did not have jurisdiction over civilians and recommended that Dr. Mudd's conviction be set aside on that basis.

Accordingly, my denial of that recommendation should not be taken as a determination of either the guilt or the innocence of Dr. Mudd. It is not the role of the ABCMR to attempt to settle historical disputes. Neither is the ABCMR an appellate court. The precise issue which the ABCMR proposes to decide, the jurisdiction of the military commission over Dr. Mudd, was specifically addressed at the time in two separate habeas corpus proceedings, one before the Chief Justice of the Supreme Court, the other before a U.S. District Court. There also was an opinion by the Attorney General of the United States.

The effect of the action recommended by the ABCMR would be to overrule all those determinations. Even if the issue might be decided differently today, it is inappropriate for a nonjudicial body, such as the ABCMR, to declare that the law 127 years ago was contrary to what was determined contemporarily by prominent legal authorities.

Accordingly, I have rejected the ABCMR's recommendation and have denied the application for relief. A memorandum for the Commander, U.S. Army Reserve Personnel Center, indicating that the application has been denied, is attached.

> /s/ William D. Clark
> William D. Clark
> Acting Assistant Secretary of the Army
> (Manpower and Reserve Affairs)

Attachment

DEPARTMENT OF THE ARMY
OFFICE OF THE ASSISTANT SECRETARY
Washington, D.C. 20310-1813

22 July 1992

MEMORANDUM FOR COMMANDER, ARMY RESERVE
PERSONNEL COMMAND

ATTN: DARP-PAS
SUBJECT: ABCMR application Regarding Dr. Samuel A.
           Mudd

Having considered the findings, conclusions and recommendations of the Army Board for Correction of Military Records, and under the provisions of 10 U.S.C. 1552, it is directed:

That in the case of Dr. Samuel A. Mudd, the application for correction of military records be, and hereby is, denied.

/s/ William D. Clark
William D. Clark
Acting Assistant Secretary of the Army
(Manpower and Reserve Affairs)

Index